THE BLACK MAN'S CHANGING ROLE ON THE AMERICAN SCREEN

THE CINEMA OF SIDNEY POITIER

LESTER J. KEYSER / ANDRE H. RUSZKOWSKI

THE BLACK MAN'S CHANGING ROLE ON THE AMERICAN SCREEN

THE CINEMA OF SIDNEY POITIER

LESTER J. KEYSER / ANDRÉ H. RUSZKOWSKI

SAN DIEGO • NEW YORK
A. S. BARNES & COMPANY, INC.
IN LONDON:
THE TANTIVY PRESS

The Tantivy Press
Magdalen House
136-148 Tooley Street
London, SE1 2TT, England

First Edition
Manufactured in the United States of America
For information write to A. S. Barnes and Company, Inc.,
P.O. Box 3051, San Diego, CA 93038

Library of Congress Cataloging in Publication Data

Keyser, Lester J   1943-
The cinema of Sidney Poitier.

Filmography: p.
Bibliography: p.
Includes index.
1. Poitier, Sidney. I. Ruszkowski, André,
joint author. II. Title.

PN2287.P57K4   791.43′028′0924

ISBN 0-498-02511-X

1 2 3 4 5 6 7 8   84 83 82 81 80

PRINTED IN THE UNITED STATES OF AMERICA

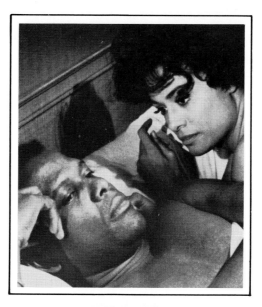

CONTENTS

ACKNOWLEDGMENTS

George C. Vietheer, when he was vice president of the Motion Picture Producers Association, Inc., first suggested the value of a study of the career of Sidney Poitier, and, without Mr. Vietheer's suggestion, this book would probably never have been started. Thus, it is first to him that we direct our sincere gratitude.

Some of the research for this text was made possible by a grant from the Committee of International Exchange of Persons, the Fulbright Committee, which also established many contacts for research throughout the United States. Mrs. John D. Leary of the committee took care of many arrangements for travel and programming. She deserves a very special thanks. Part of this research was also done under the aegis and with the support of the Department of Sociology, Loyola University, Chicago.

The film industry provided most generous cooperation. Motion Picture Producers Association officers in New York, Washington, and Los Angeles, as well as the Academy of Motion Picture Arts and Sciences in Hollywood, opened their files, arranged meetings, and granted personal interviews. One name in particular must be mentioned: Jack Vizzard, who, as Assistant Director of the Production Code Administration, went out of his way to make research in Hollywood possible. The individual studios and companies for which Poitier worked were also most helpful, and we must mention here the particularly efficient cooperation received from Miss Hortense Schorr, Coordinator of Publicity for Columbia Pictures in New York. Many prominent members of the profession kindly agreed to be interviewed about the experience of working with Sidney Poitier. Among them were Martin Baum, Pandro Berman, Richard Brooks, James Clavell, Ivan Dixon, Stanley Kramer, Ralph Nelson, Frederick O'Neal, Brock Peters, George Stevens, and Max F. Youngstein.

A number of black community leaders have also shown interest in the project and contributed materials. It is impossible to name them all, but to all we are most grateful.

Our project also profited from fine research libraries in both Canada and the United States. In Canada, we received efficient help from the Office des Communications Sociales in Montreal, both for screening films and for using reference material. In the United States, the Motion Picture Department of the Library of Congress in Washington, D.C., put at our disposal their film collection and documentation. The Film Study Center at the Museum of Modern Art in New York and the Theatre Research Division of the Lincoln Center Library of the Performing Arts, a branch of the New York Public Library, provided indispensable resources. The staff at both the Museum of Modern Art and Lincoln Center Library are especially to be thanked for their diligence and good humor.

The distinguished film scholar Gene D. Phillips also contributed substantially to the completion of this study, and we want to thank him for his friendship and encouragement. His dedication, thoroughness, and insight provide a model for scholarly research in cinema.

This acknowledgment would, of course, be incomplete if we did not express our gratitude to Sidney Poitier himself, who granted three interviews in Hollywood during the filming of *In the Heat of the Night* and a later interview in New York when he was shooting *For Love of Ivy*.

To all these individuals and institutions, we are deeply grateful. The best features of the text which follow were developed with their help. The errors in fact, judgment, analysis, and evaluation are all our own, however, in this unauthorized and completely independent assessment of Poitier's cinema.

Lester J. Keyser
André H. Ruszkowski
New York and Ottawa

INTRODUCTION

For the love of Ivy . . . was Bryant's favorite; it made him cry but it also made him
laugh a lot, and it was his favorite. Soon he had surrendered to it, seeing in the
Poitier of that film a version of himself that no one — really no one, and that was
the terrible part — would ever get to know: the man who had died within the body
Bryant carried, shown in that film in all his truth, the man Bryant knew to be
himself, without the edginess and the anger and the pretend ugliness, the laughing
man, the tender joker. Watching the film, he began to grieve for what
was denied him. . . . He began to sob; and other people were sobbing with him.

— V. S. Naipul, *Guerillas*

"Out There Wailing for Us All"—The Unique Position of America's Black Superstar

Every performer has some responsibilities to his fans, but none is so haunted by his audience and his people as Sidney Poitier, black America's ambassador-at-large, for Poitier is the only black box-office champion, the one black star to shine on the white screen. Poitier is the avatar, the standard-bearer, and the archetypal figure, yet he is not altogether comfortable in these roles. Early in his career, Poitier outlined his ambivalence clearly: "I am sure that there are those among Negroes who would see in me a certain extension of themselves in terms of what their hopes and dreams are. As I see myself, I'm an average Joe Blow Negro. But, as the cats say in my areas, I'm out there wailing for us all." Poitier's "wailing" has brought him numerous awards, including an Oscar, and it has had a significant effect on race relations in this country. Poitier's "wailing" involves artistry and propaganda, entertainment and enrichment, and makes his career one of the most interesting and provocative in the history of cinema.

Poitier has played in over three dozen films over the last three decades, and he is the only Negro superstar in the United States, the only minority member to outgross white performers at the neighborhood box office. And what makes this achievement more remarkable is that Poitier's success

The most imperfect but authentic amateur film showing President Kennedy's assassination can have more significance than the most artistically elaborate reconstruction of this event by a creative film-maker. Only a small minority can really appreciate the formal beauty and careful structuring of Cousteau's films, but everyone feels enriched by the personal discovery of the deep water scenery.

The very humanity of a performer, his personality, his physical presence, indeed his character traits, frequently overwhelm or transcend a role. Audiences still clamor for Chaplin or W. C. Fields or Mae West movies, just to be with the star a little longer in intimate human contact. Similarly, Sidney Poitier is always there as Sidney Poitier in his films. And he, Sidney Poitier the successful movie actor, has his own impact upon each viewer; Poitier engages each viewer in a deep personal relationship and elicits a separate response quite apart from the reaction motivated by the actor's role in the film. Like Gable, Garbo, and Harlow, Sidney Poitier is a star, and demands attention as a human being, as a person, as well as a persona.

Like John Wayne or Cary Grant, Poitier has a particular gift of piercing the screen and giving the audience an impression of personal presence. Without actually knowing Poitier, millions of people consider him a friend. This special relationship must be considered carefully in any study of the impact movies can have on race relations. Prejudice has its roots in emotionalism and ignorance, and movies can attack both these elements. Sidney Poitier overcomes innate hostility by destroying emotional barriers and revealing the human qualities of a racial group. For this reason, at a dinner of the Southern Christian Leadership Conference, Dr. Martin Luther King, Jr. saluted Poitier for carving "an imperishable niche in the annals of our nation's history"; activist Reverend Andrew Young amplified these remarks when he observed that "in a society that denies all dignity and worth to black men, Poitier has made us proud to be black and taught us that black was beautiful and it's beautiful to be black" through "his sermons in cinematography."

came during America's most traumatic period in race relations. Poitier was on screen wailing during the marches and riots, before and after the assassinations; he was the major black presence in cinema for both the Sixties and Seventies, outlasting both Selma and "benign neglect," Stepin Fetchit and Superfly. A survey of Poitier's career is, to a large degree, a perplexing examination of social attitudes.

Critical questions haunt any consideration of Poitier. Would Sidney Poitier have become a star if massive changes had not occurred in society during the last thirty years? And to what degree can it be said that without Poitier and his films the changes would have taken place?

In spite of the numerous theoretical studies of the relationship between movies and society, little concrete is really known, for there are so many aspects and variables, including the psychological, aesthetic, ideological, and commercial. Recent film studies have frequently emphasized the artistic values of cinema and underplayed its importance as a carrier of information. Many film critics, impressed by Andre Bazin's statement that nothing can be said in a movie without giving it a form, seem to forget that form, though indispensable, may be transcended by the information it carries.

The Early Years—A Biography of the Young Poitier

Sidney Poitier's life history is a perfect Cinderella story. Were this still the nineteenth century, Poitier would surely be lionized as the greatest of primitive talents, the noblest of savages. This Academy Award

winner is the child of an underdeveloped nation, born in poverty and ignorance, the offspring of farmers; yet he is also a sojourner in urban ghettos, a victim of contemporary racism, and a refugee from the slag heap of modern society. If Poitier's naiveté and boyish charm is a sparkling reminder of his rural youth, the scar on his leg from a policeman's bullet is a grim memento of race riots in Harlem. Poitier's films have successfully run the full gamut of black experience because he himself has seen it all in his life. Poitier has been there; he's been a dreamer locked in a primitive life style, an innocent bruised by virulent racism, a fighter caught up in the tides of history.

Sidney Poitier was born 24 February 1927 in Miami, Florida, literally a transient; for his parents, Reginald and Evelyn, had come to the United States to sell tomatoes from their farm on Cat Island in the Bahamas. What was to have been a short business trip was complicated by a pregnancy, and Sidney Poitier, by a simple twist of fate, became an American citizen. Three months later, the Poitiers returned to Cat Island, where the forty-year-old Reginald labored hard to support his large family. Life on the island was primitive, to say the least. In a seminar at Fordham University, Poitier noted that his first home was really a hut without running water, and that life on Cat Island was pre-industrial: he had

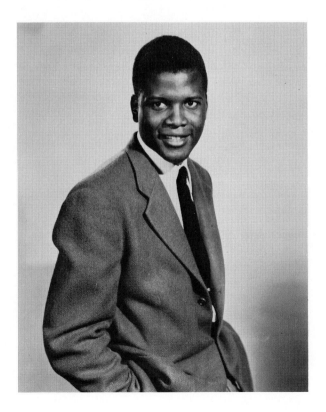

never even seen a car. The Poitier family was not a very close-knit one, and Sidney frequently found himself alone, lost in his dreams. He would, he told Normand Poirier, frequently roam the island only to end up at the shore where he would "conjure up the kind of worlds that were on the other side and what I'd do in them."[1] These daydreams were Poitier's defense mechanism against an incredibly harsh and mean life of hand-me-downs and hunger. Farming was not easy on Cat Island; the soil was rocky and had to be replenished with earth carted from caves. As Poitier saw it, he and his family "were so poor we didn't even own dirt."

Yet things were to get worse. A widening economic depression scourged the Bahamas and all small farms were wiped out. The Poitiers lost their property and joined a mass immigration of the dispossessed into the cities. Sidney Poitier and his mother took the first long boat ride to Nassau on New Providence Island; the family followed them later. The eleven-year-old Sidney was literally overwhelmed by his first contact with modern civilization. Cars seemed large insects to him, and the hustle and bustle of the city almost put him in shock.

Within a year, however, the demands of a modern age were molding Sidney in an all-too-familiar way. He gave up school, after only eighteen months of formal education, to work with pick and shovel as a common laborer. His friends and he quickly got into mischief; they spent most of their free time drinking, gambling, and going to the movies. They would steal empty bottles and then sell them to go to the movies, an art form the young Poitier much enjoyed. Films gave him the education which had been denied by circumstance: "Films taught me about other people, how to dial a telephone, geography, names of places, things I never knew before." Interestingly, however, the films he saw did not feed his need for role models; in the films of his youth, Poitier later complained, "[I] very rarely saw a Negro man when I was looking for myself."

These movies in Nassau did give Poitier, however, invaluable training in acting. Many of his friends and several people in his family could not afford the luxury of a movie ticket. For them, Sidney Poitier gave command performances; after each screening, he would come back and act out the whole film. He enjoyed this, he told Normand Poirier, "more than I enjoyed seeing the movie." The child dreamer was becoming the entertainer who would deliver new dreams for the impoverished masses.

But the road to stardom was still a long and arduous one. Several of Poitier's friends were enmeshed in troubles with the police, and his father thought Sidney was getting out of control. To

avoid any further trouble, Reginald Poitier asked Sidney's brother Cyril, who lived in Miami, to take Sidney into his home and to supervise his behavior. Cyril agreed to be a guardian for Sidney, and, at the age of fifteen, Sidney returned to the city of his birth. The homecoming was most inauspicious; for the first time in his life, Sidney Poitier was the victim of racial prejudice. Miami was quite different from the Bahamas, where 80 percent of the population is black. If the physical life on Cat Island and New Providence Island was difficult, the psychic torment of being black in the deep South was almost too much for Sidney. Racism was, he later declared, "all over the place like barbed wire, and I kept running into it and lacerating myself." For example, Frederick Morton details Poitier's reactions to an incident when Sidney was hitchhiking without knowing it was illegal and just happened to be picked up by a car with six southern policemen. As Poitier recalled it:

> Oh, they had fun with me, I want to tell you, *they haad fuuuun.* They put a pistol right to my forehead and felt around with the shooting end of it, and they kept saying little things like 'Now, where shall we shoot our blackie, in the left eye or the right eye, huh?' And then they just talked about the weather for ten minutes. But, man, that pistol remained right there against my head. And then they let me out and said 'Walk. But don't look back.' I walked and—*dig now*—they kept riding and laughing alongside me for half an hour. I looked at the reflection of the car in the store windows, since I couldn't turn my head. I probably was afraid. But I don't remember being afraid. I remember being angry.

There were many other such incidents. There was a woman who slammed the door in his face because he, a delivery boy, called at the front door of her house. She later had four male friends trace his address to "club a bit of etiquette into the Negro boy." And there was a navy officer at a recruitment station who greeted Poitier by shouting, "Boy, take off that cap." These incidents, and the omnipresent "white" and "colored" signs, propelled Sidney Poitier to the North. When Cyril Poitier gave his brother Sidney an ultimatum to settle down or return home, Sidney Poitier created his own escape. He began a three-month odyssey to the Mecca of the displaced, New York City.

As usual, New York was waiting with open arms for this illiterate immigrant. Within an hour, all of Sidney Poiter's meager belongings had been stolen and he was left with his capital, $1.50. Poitier quickly found work as a per diem dishwasher, then as a chicken plucker, busboy, and porter. He lived in the public bathrooms at the Port Authority Bus Terminal, sleeping in the lavatory booths or on rooftops overlooking Broadway.

After a year of this catch-as-catch-can existence, Sidney Poitier decided to enlist in the Army; at least it provided room and board. He was assigned to a psychiatric hospital at Northport, Long Island, but he just couldn't adjust. He was so disoriented and overwhelmed that the Army discharged him in a year for "Utter Bewilderment": as Poitier explains it, "The world was just too big for me. I was a kid and I was lost and they decided I wanted to go home."

But there was no home for Poitier to return to. He surely didn't belong in Nassau, or in Miami, so it was back to New York City and back to dishwashing, an occupation which at least assured Poitier of his meals and of enough money to scrape by. For a while, he worked as a transient dishwasher, but then he decided to look for a permanent job in one restaurant. This turned out to be a fateful decision, for, as he looked through the *Amsterdam* (N.Y.) *News* in 1945, he saw an announcement by the American Negro Theater, opposite the want ad page, which said "Actors wanted." Poitier decided to audition as an actor despite his total lack of experience.

His first audition was an abysmal failure. He was rudely dismissed because of his West Indian accent. The curtness and indelicacy of the rejection angered Poitier, and he resolved to show everyone at the American Negro Theater that Sidney Poitier was a man to be reckoned with. For the next few months, Poitier listened to the radio, and then imitated what he heard. He also studied books and magazines to improve his English. Then he auditioned again. He was still terrible, but a piece of luck saved him. The American Negro Theater frequently found more qualified women than men, and had, in Poitier's words, "to pad the male side." Thus, he was invited to study with the group for three months. Again he failed, and, after three months, they asked him to leave. Poitier was still determined to be an actor, however, and negotiated a deal whereby he could continue his lessons in exchange for being a janitor for the theater group.

Poitier made many friends among the students at the American Negro Theater, but his best friend was Harry Belafonte. Poitier knew that Belafonte's obligation to his family frequently kept him from attending rehearsals, so Poitier conspired to be his understudy. One night, when Poitier was subbing for Belafonte, he was noticed by director James Light, who gave him a very short part in *Lysistrata*, which was opening on Broadway. The play was short-lived, but it marked Poitier's breakthrough. Soon he was signed as an understudy in *Anna Luscasta,* and he toured with the play from 1946 to 1948, playing different roles, learning his trade, and getting necessary exposure.

The time was ripe for Poitier's appearance on the screen. In 1949, he faced the camera for the first time in an Army Signal Corps documentary called *From Whom Cometh My Help*. Soon thereafter, he was approached by a Broadway producer who offered him $75 a week to be in *Lost in the Stars*, the Kurt Weill and Maxwell Anderson play. Simultaneously, Darryl Zanuck offered him $750 a week for a Hollywood film directed by Joseph L. Mankiewicz, *No Way Out*. Poitier chose Hollywood, and vowed he "would never ever work in a film that was not cause for members of the Negro audiences to set up straight in their seats."

Poitier kept his vow, as a look at his films will show. He brought all his past with him to the screen, the hard times and the humiliations, the folk wisdom and the anger. Out of poverty and rejection, he created strength and dignity. He so transformed the screen by the power of his presence that a recent American Film Institute study sees Poitier's entrance into film in 1950 as the date which "conveniently marks a turning point in the fortune of blacks on the screen and in Hollywood." The poor farmer's son from the Bahamas was to transform the American film industry. No longer would black people be without an image on screen; Sidney Poitier became the personification of the black experience, the measure and mirror of the black role in society. He and his people were unalterably wedded on the screen. Poitier became more than a movie star; he became the only black movie star.

Notes to Introduction

1. In 1978, during a one-year sabbatical from the screen, Sidney Poitier announced he was preparing his autobiography, a process he described as a "very painful experience." The publisher has yet to be announced. There are two early biographies: William Hoffman, *Sidney* and Carolyn Ewers, *Sidney Poitier: The Long Journey*. Poitier's own comments on his life are scattered in the numerous articles on his career. Poitier suggested that the most accurate biographical material written about him was in Frederic Morton's article "The Audacity of Sidney Poitier," in the June 1962 *Holiday Magazine*. Other useful sources include the articles by James Baldwin, Helen Dudar, Normand Poirier, and Sidney Poitier mentioned in the selected bibliography.

THE ROAD TO STARDOM

(1950-1957)

Black artists of the postwar generation, principally writers and musicians, knew quite well that the largest psychological and indeed physical fault in the state of California divided the ghettos of Watts from the sound stages of Hollywood. Beverly Hills was a white man's land, its films a white man's entertainment, which reinforced the racism not only of this affluent enclave but of the whole nation. Eastern novelists like Ralph Ellison might speak with reticence and declare that "in the struggle against Negro freedom motion pictures have been one of the strongest instruments for justifying some white Americans' anti-Negro attitudes and practices,"[1] but West Coast novelists and writers, closer to the fray, would be more inclined to agree with activist novelist John Oliver Killens' explosive charge: "I accuse Hollywood of being the most anti-Negro influence in this nation in the twentieth century." More than the Klan, more than vitriolic public officials and race-baiters,

more than lynch mobs and pamphleteers, the movies, Killens felt, formed the American image of the Negro. They created "the lying, stealing, childish, eyeball-rolling, feet-shuffling, sex-obsessed, teeth-showing, dice-shooting black male, and told the world this was the real Negro in the U.S.A."[2]

From *Birth of a Nation* on, Hollywood had been content with stereotypes, with a reductionist view of the Negro that denied his humanity and his individuality. Some modern film histories like Donald Bogle's *Toms, Coons, Mulattoes, Mammies, and Bucks* offer comprehensive catalogs of the minor variations on this prejudiced theme, but few improve on a work done by Lawrence Reddick in 1944.[3] Reddick, the curator of the renowned Schomburg Collection of Negro Literature in the New York Public Library, analyzed one hundred important films which featured blacks in substantial roles. He found seventy-five of these one hundred important films were markedly anti-black, thirteen neutral, and only twelve presented a positive image. A full three-quarters of the films reflected, Reddick observed, the "principal stereotypes of the Negro in the American mind," which he outlined as "the savage African, the happy slave, the devoted servant, the corrupt politician, the irresponsible citizen, the petty thief, the social delinquent, the vicious criminal, the sexual superman, the superior athlete, the unhappy nonwhite, the natural born cook, the natural born musician, the perfect entertainer, the superstitious churchgoer, the chicken and watermelon eater, the razor and knife toter, the uninhibited expressionist, and the mental inferior." These stereotypes were especially pernicious, Reddick demonstrates, because they represent a "ceiling" for black achievement in film, a barrier that few individuals could ever surmount. Hollywood films were, in effect, teaching both blacks and whites their roles in society. To be white, Anglo-Saxon, and Protestant was to be free. To be black was to be subordinate. Reddick is very explicit on this point; films like the majority of those he analyzed, he argues, are tools of the oppressors which "operate to thwart the advancement of the Negro, to humiliate him, to weaken his drive for equality, and to spread indifference, contempt, and hatred for him and his cause."

Drives for Negro equality had made little headway by 1945 in Hollywood itself. Despite the numerous letters of agreement between producers and black groups generated during the war years, by the end of World War II, there were still more black custodial workers on the Warner Brothers lot than black extras registered at central casting; and, while a black could be named head of custodial services, it was unthinkable to suggest a black might be named head of a studio. On some of the backlots, there were still a few "For Whites Only" signs over studio water fountains. On screen and off, the black was still getting the same message; as William Thomas Smith observed in his "Hollywood Report" for 1945, "Hollywood's attitude toward the Negro actor, the Negro worker, and the Negro race remains unchanged; the democracy it preaches is, as usual, 'For Whites Only.'"[4]

World War II, however, had made a deep impression on the American conscience and consciousness. It was hard for even the most bitter racist to shout patriotic slogans and denounce racist policies in Germany without sensing to some small degree the irony of maintaining racism at home. Roy Wilkins posed the problem most poetically when he spoke of the inconsistencies of going to war against a "Jude" sign in Europe when at home there were still "For Colored Only" signs. Similarly, by the end of the war, many white soldiers had made contact with blacks fighting in Europe. Battlefield emergencies made total segregation of the races in the armed services difficult at times, and a heightened sense of the black's part in American life was an inevitable result. On the home front, the labor shortages of the postwar period opened jobs for Negroes, luring them from rural communities into the cities, from the South to the North, from farms onto assembly lines and into factories.

Hollywood films soon found it impossible to ignore these massive social pressures. Blacks were not only moving from one geographical area to another, they were also demanding social mobility. The inevitable clashes between races, between stereotypes and expectations, between dreams and realities, generated a new cycle of films, the so-called problem films. Problem films flourished from around 1946 until 1950 and were, as Donald Bogle suggests, one way the studios catered to "audience expectations and demands, their quirks, their insecurities, and their guilt feelings."[5] The Democratic Convention of 1948, it might be remembered, had been bitterly divided over the civil rights plank; race was on America's mind.

Hollywood's commitment to problem films was not, however, a spontaneous manifestation of blind altruism and civic service. Movies were in trouble in the late forties because of the new kid in town, television. And, while studio heads were relatively slow to understand the challenge free entertainment in suburban homes posed to expensive entertainment at downtown theaters, they did see that problem films treated topics too mature and too serious to be handled on the boob tube. So, as weekly attendance dropped from eighty-two million in 1946 to only thirty-six million in 1950, studios struggled to use these weighty materials to regain their share of the entertainment dollar, which had declined by 50 percent between the war and 1950.

Thus, when movie mogul Darryl Zanuck sent for Sidney Poitier after seeing him perform in *Anna Lucasta*, Zanuck had already selected the perfect vehicle for a new young Negro actor, a problem film entitled *No Way Out*. Ironically, this first professional screen appearance by Poitier was to mark what most critics consider the end of the whole cycle of problem films. *No Way Out* was to do badly at the box office, and the dearth of paid admissions to this highly controversial melodrama spelled doom for the idea of using serious dramas

Poitier and director Joseph Mankiewicz prepare a scene in *No Way Out*.

concerning race relations to lure television addicts from their sets.

Poitier's personal decision to come to Hollywood was not an easy one, for two offers had come at once, one a hundred-dollar-a-week role on Broadway in *Lost in the Stars*, and the other, Zanuck's offer of a role in *No Way Out* for a $7,500 flat fee for ten weeks' work. Poitier was tiring, however, of the New York Scene, where he felt, as he told a *New York Times* interviewer, that he had been "knocking my head against the wall ever since coming."[6] Hollywood might, he thought, be better and there was also the money. Like most Americans, Poitier was eager for material success; his biographer, Carolyn Ewers, quotes the young actor as making success his real goddess in this period: "I became an actor not for self expression, but for success. To have money. When I thought of what I wanted to do, I wanted to rest for three months on a boat fishing in the Bahamas, just kind of lallygaggin' around. . . . Without success, that would be impossible."[7]

The spur of his desire for success gave Poitier many anxious moments in Hollywood, and may account, to some degree, for the suppressed energy many critics note in his performances. Poitier wanted to make good, and his early films all reveal the intensity of his commitment. Like all novices, Poitier felt a little lost in the labyrinthine offices of the studio and was overawed by their solemnity. When he first visited Zanuck's office, Poitier was afraid even to audition for *No Way Out*: "I went there and sat hoping to kind of slip in. There were many others with their agents, and there seemed little hope for me. A secretary asked me to come back at a more suitable time. I did. I was auditioned and made it."[8] Poitier couldn't know it then, but there was no more propitious time for him to arrive on the Hollywood scene. If the forties could create problem films, the fifties would provide the first real black star, Sidney Poitier himself. Yet, as Dennis Hall so astutely notes, if Poitier had come ten years earlier, "his immense talent as an actor would have been overlooked by Hollywood producers because he was a Negro."[9]

No one could possibly overlook Poitier's talent or his race after his performance as Dr. Luther Brooks in *No Way Out*. Brooks is a young intern in a major metropolitan hospital whose treatment of a wounded white prisoner raises questions about the Negro doctor's competence and about society's ability to accept black professionals. Brooks is the pivotal figure in a heated interracial conflict, abused and attacked by psychotic bigots, interrogated and evaluated by his white colleagues, and supported and championed by his family and the black community. The role is a juicy one, and Poitier even lied about his age to make sure he wouldn't lose it. Poitier felt such a "neurotic fear of failure" before *No Way Out*, he told Martin Levine, that, when he calculated the intern had to be at least twenty-seven or twenty-eight years old, Poitier changed his own age on employment applications and records: "Well, I was 22. So, instead of saying I was born in 1927, I said I was born in 1924—presupposing that if they found out how old I really was, they'd fire me because I couldn't be old enough to play the character."[10] This switch in ages made Poitier one of the few prematurely aged actors in film; most performers lie to fit roles considerably younger than their years, as Poitier himself would when he later starred in *Blackboard Jungle*, playing a teenage boy.

Even at twenty-seven or twenty-eight, Dr. Luther Brooks is a young doctor, just completing his state board exams, and much of the focus in *No Way Out* is on his competency as a professional.

Poitier as Dr. Luther Brooks in *No Way Out*.

The psychopathic villain in the film, Ray Biddle, played to the hilt by Richard Widmark, rants and raves that no Negro doctor can treat him or his brother, quickly tying the issues of race and competency together. Brooks is nervous and somewhat unsteady in his treatment of Ray's wounded brother, Johnny, for what seems to be a routine gunshot wound. During Brooks' ministrations, Johnny dies; obviously perplexed and shaken, Brooks calls the chief medical resident, Dr. Daniel Wharton, played by Stephen McNally.

Dr. Wharton attempts to dismiss the whole episode, advising Brooks to sign a death certificate, but Brooks insists that Wharton examine Johnny himself. Brooks worries about both his diagnosis of brain tumor and Ray Biddle's wild threats. Wharton assures Brooks his diagnosis is one viable possibility, but notes that only an autopsy could confirm the real cause of death, and the family of the deceased must give permission for an autopsy.

When Ray Biddle refuses permission for an autopsy, the problem in *No Way Out* is fully developed: what is to be done about a white patient's death when he was under the care of a black physician? The hospital administration is torn between the desire to support Brooks, the fear of publicity, and a deeper fear that maybe Brooks was wrong. Racists like the Biddles are left to scheme a proper retaliation, and blacks like Brooks, his family, and his ghetto community are under intense pressure to defend themselves.

As the diverse elements of the plot develop, the racial conflict escalates to seemingly inevitable confrontation; there seems to be, literally, "no way out." As Brooks, Poitier finds his only emotional support coming from his wife, Cora, and his family. He is progressively more isolated by the hospital, which refuses to renew his contract. The white plot to punish Brooks and ravage the entire black community spurs black hospital personnel, led by the elevator operator, Lefty, to launch a preemptive strike against the whites of Beaver Canal. The ensuing race riot, eerily lighted by flares and photographed in documentary style, is a victory for the blacks, who easily rout the whites, filling the hospital with new victims.

Brooks's final victory is less dramatic. After more abuse at the hospital from white patients, including a mother who screams "Keep your black hands off my boy," Brooks risks his life and career by having himself arrested for Johnny Biddle's murder. Now an autopsy is required, and Brooks is vindicated. Ray Biddle remains unconvinced and makes one more attempt on Luther's life, killing his dead brother's wife in the process and suffering a wound himself. The film ends on Dr. Brooks' rather ironic promise to Ray: "Don't cry, white boy. You're going to live." Ray will live because Brooks is there to treat him.

No Way Out lives as a film, too, largely because Sidney Poitier is there in the title role. All problem films suffered somewhat from melodramatic plotting, rather too intense concern with theme, and thin characterizations, but *No Way Out* transcends all these weaknesses to create a believable human document about the black middle class in the North. In an era when whites had followed the Pied Piper of modernity to Levittown, leaving the city in droves for the joys of suburbia, *No Way Out* gives Poitier a marvelous chance to explore racism not as it existed in the Confederate South, but as it haunted the Northern cities of the fifties. Poitier has often said that his acting depends on his ability to relate his role to his life. As Luther Brooks, Poitier has many chances to re-create the immense hurt he felt when he was ensnared in racism he found everywhere in America. Poitier's role as a doctor further allows him a subtle exploration of the psychological torment of the black bourgeoisie. The role provides a complex outlet for the agony of the dispossessed; Poitier skillfully limns a man who wants desperately to belong, to achieve in the world of medicine, a largely white world, but who still hears the world "nigger" ringing in his ears, and who must still depend on an all-black community to nurture him and fight for him. The vitality of *No Way Out* does not derive from the restless narrative, but emanates from the subtext of Poitier's performance. More than any black actor before, Poitier suggests in his understated gestures, his precise diction, and his changing posture the immense rage within. Many contemporary reviewers comment on Poitier's fine sensitivity to his role in *No Way Out*, including the *New York Times* reviewer whose description of Poitier's "quiet dignity" comes closest to highlighting the real contribution Poitier brings to a sometimes too frenetic film. There could be no doubt after seeing Poitier as Luther Brooks that the *Hollywood Reporter* was correct in its trade-oriented assessment: "Sidney Poitier is a young and talented Negro actor whose quiet dignity and persuasive style mark him for an important future."[11]

The future of problem films was somewhat more questionable. *No Way Out* received rather favorable press: the New York *Herald Tribune* praised it as "the most grimly compelling and honest statement of an unanswered question that has yet reached the screen"; *Look* hailed it as "a film the entire film industry can be proud of"; and *Life* declared the film "makes all the previous efforts look like pussyfooting."[12] There could be no doubt of the seriousness of the creators nor their good intentions. Director Joseph Mankiewicz was the most revered talent in Hollywood; his *All About Eve*, which was also released in 1950, merited him the Oscars for best direction and screenplay, duplicating his similar coup a year earlier when he won the same Oscars for his *A Letter to Three Wives*.

Poitier confronts Richard Widmark in *No Way Out*.

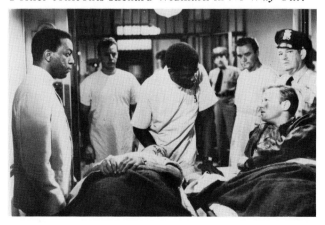

No Way Out and *All About Eve* were, Mankiewicz felt, two central works in his continuing series of features designed to provide a "continuing comment on the manners and mores of our contemporary society in general, and the male-female relationship in particular."[13] His co-scenarist, Lesser Samuels, the creator of the original story, had been prompted to write *No Way Out* by an experience involving his daughter. She had married a doctor, and among her friends was a Negro intern in a public hospital. After meeting that intern, Samuels planned a meditation on the plight of black professionals, who lived, he told interviewers, "in an economic and social no man's land from which, at the moment, there seems no way out and our story points to none." In all his comments at the time of the film's opening, Samuels emphasized the humanistic theme of the melodrama: "My sole object was to tell a dramatic story of the corrosive effect of hatred, especially as it pertains to the bitter, unreasoning animosity of the ignorant white man for his black brother living in a world that has been made impossible for him. If that drama makes audiences indignant at social injustices, good."[14] Unfortunately, neither Mankiewicz nor Samuels was to see his good intentions rewarded. *No Way Out* won no Oscars and offended few audiences. Black doctors and race riots proved poison at the box office, and *No Way Out* disappeared into commercial oblivion.

Like many of Poitier's early films, however, *No Way Out* spawned controversy far out of proportion to its appeal at the box office. Blacks in film might not be hot stuff at the turnstile, but in 1950 they generated untold heat for producers, censors, and exhibitors. Poitier's career, the importance of his cinema, can only be understood in the context of these bitter contretemps. Poitier was constantly in a peculiar double jeopardy. His career depended on the flow of dollars to studio coffers, but still other responsibilities haunted him as a black man in America. Poitier's race was always on the line. His films were constantly subject to venomous attack from white racists, potent criticism from black activists, and to the most scrupulous analyses of both aesthetes and sociologists.

Harsh criticism was plentiful around Hollywood in 1950, for, as Dalton Trumbo so eloquently put it, this was "the time of the toad." Political discussion found a new nadir pinpointing "un-American activities" in the universities and on screen. Richard Nixon and his henchmen were seeking reds in every pumpkin patch. In this atmosphere, problem films like *No Way Out* drew special ire as red-inspired propaganda. No excess seemed beyond the self-appointed guardians of Newthink; as James Baldwin notes, "Not even the most vindictive hatred could have imagined the slimy depths to which the bulk of white Americans allowed themselves to sink: noisily, gracelessly, flatulent and foul with patriotism."[15] The irrepressibly stupid head of the notorious Cinema Education Guild, Myron C. Fagan, who had discovered, he proclaimed, hundreds of movie performers who had "enabled Moscow to get control of our screen," used *No Way Out* as principal text for his lecture "Hollywood Reds Still at It!" piously charging that "Darryl Zanuch [*sic*] was a producer who was responsible for *Gentleman's Agreement, Pinky* and other films which so effectively advance Red ideology" and declaring *No Way Out* equally Communist in orientation.[16] Fagan's remarks are important because they suggest an attitude few others would publicly declare, but which influenced studio heads during the early fifties: anything but the rosiest picture of American life was regarded as anti-American propaganda. Problem pictures were not only unpopular; they were unpatriotic as well. And, since it was hard to incorporate blacks in a blissful image of America, black roles became scarce. Poitier found himself competing mostly for parts in small, independent productions outside the studio structure. And, when the new roles took him out of the States to the emerging nations in Africa, where three of his fifties films were shot, the constant danger was an identification with a worldwide conspiracy. Nothing Poitier could do, no role he took, could escape criticism; his was always a special case.

Poitier's race generated ticklish problems in dealing with state censorship boards, which dotted

The aftermath of the race riot in *No Way Out*.

the country and controlled access to the most lucrative markets. If nudity didn't go on screen, neither did the wrong sort of social interactions; race relations, most boards determined, must be carefully exposed to vulnerable, innocent audiences. Thus, censors in Pennsylvania deleted most of Ray Biddle's most inflammatory lines, including his dramatically essential definitions of the problem as his twisted mind perceived it: "I'm supposed to forget my brother couldn't have a white doctor—forget he'd be alive if he did. Edie, I want to ask you something. If you had a kid, would you send him to a nigger doctor? Would you like one putting his dirty black hands on you?" Pennsylvania also ordered considerable reduction of the riot scenes, including the white Rocky's invitation to another girl to join the fight: "Take that, you black crud. How do you like that, black boy? You want to try it, baby? You want to hit a nigger?" Boards in Ohio, Maryland, and elsewhere ordered even more deletions. In Chicago, the film was just banned outright with the chief police-censor declaring "the picture put it on heavy. . . . It might stir up trouble among a more abnormal faction."[17]

In the South, *No Way Out* was anathema. An earlier survey of censorship boards indicated just what studios must avoid: among the "most objectionable" material were films in which Negroes were shown "acting, or talking, or dressing like white folks . . . acting smart-alecky and talking back to white folks . . . shooting or striking white folks . . . or in any manner committing any breach of the code which would be implication or otherwise create an equality between the races . . . ."[18] Distributors didn't even try to bring *No Way Out* to Atlanta, for, as Gerald Weales reported in 1952, "No theater or other booking outlet in Georgia has been willing to take the picture."[19] There was no need for Georgia's censorship board to ban *No Way Out*; exhibitor timidity had already sealed its fate.

In the North, the attacks on *No Way Out* were equally fatal, if rather more intellectually substantive. In a most provocative article published in the Jewish intellectual journal *Commentary*, Nathan Leites and Martha Wolfenstein convincingly demonstrated that during in-depth analysis of the film, "certain negative elements begin to appear that might well counteract, *on a deeper level*, the good intentions of the movie makers."[20] The argument they present is a subtle and detailed one, pointing to images in the film which are indeed discordant: Poitier does appear to the untrained eye to be behaving strangely in treating a leg wound, the race riots are shockingly violent, the

Mildred Joanne Smith and Sidney Poitier in *No Way Out*.

idea of autopsy is bloody and mysterious, it is burdensome to have to defend a black colleague, and Edie does betray her former lover to help Poitier. As Leites and Wolfenstein suggest, all these elements might affect a viewer's reactions; the whole film could be misinterpreted, or one negative image could undo the whole pattern. Similarly valid criticism came from other quarters. By making all the racists sociopaths, for example, some charge, the real universal prevalence of racial prejudice is disguised. And by making Luther Brooks so saintly, the film may indeed have precipitated what Maya Angelou has called the "age of the noble savage." Poitier's role may have been too good to be true, merely another stereotype. When a white woman spits on him as he treats her son, one might wish for more of a reaction than disengagement.

For all this criticism, however Poitier's achievement in *No Way Out* should not be underestimated. Without denying the enormous importance of the thematic content in a movie, it is also desirable to remember a new and important element is present in cinema which cannot be found in the script: the human performer, the actor. His performance "transcends" the role created by the writer for the purpose of the film. Poitier's physical presence, his voice, gestures, and mannerisms are all working their charm on the audience. This black man on screen is having his impact on the viewer, who engages in a personal emotional reaction, quite different, frequently, from the reaction motivated by the actor's part in the movie. The film industry knows this so well that it developed a whole era based on a "star" system. The uproar at Valentino's death and after James Dean's fatal accident are just two of many incidents which indicate that audiences finally react to human beings and not only to characters in the film.

Some performers have a particular gift of "piercing" the screen and giving the audience an impression of personal presence. Poitier demonstrated this power in *No Way Out*; all of his career was to depend on this magic, as he well recognized: "There are some actors, whose skills are not necessarily gargantuan, who have what some people call 'force,' others call 'presence' or whatever. So there are some actors with a certain energy, conspiring with other externals, that helps to produce a certain longevity. I think that's what happened in my case."[21]

Poitier's personal dynamism was to bring a black man to the center of the American screen. Poitier recognized that many of his roles were not perfect vehicles, that frequently good intentions overwhelmed both art and realism. In an interview with Gordon Gow concerning problem films in a comprehensive review of *Hollywood in the Fifties*, Poitier's understatement was an eloquent testimonial to his understanding:

> Now, to filmmakers, the Negro is not an oddity. He's not a rarity. They see him every day. . . . They feel they have in their hands the authority and the ability to determine what a film will do. So they say, "Well, now, I'm going to make a wonderful humane statement with the presence of this Negro person who has lived under great handicaps and great denial all of his life." So they make a statement. And the statement finally is, "You should be nice to your colored friends. They too are human beings." Well, this is messy, you know.[22]

Messy or not, Poitier's presence on screen, the energy and charisma his graceful performance generated, all remind one constantly of James Baldwin's observation about movie stars: "One does not go to see them act: one goes to watch them *be*."[23] Poitier's screen appearance in *No Way Out* was an overpowering reaffirmation of black reality on a white screen; as Baldwin later observed in his moving tribute to Sidney Poitier, "The presence of Sidney, the precedent set, is of tremendous importance for people coming afterward. And perhaps that's what it's really all about—just that."[24]

Among the many people who were impressed by Sidney Poitier's screen debut was Zoltan Korda, a British director who had worked with another great black talent, Paul Robeson, on the film *Sanders of the River*, and who was garnering his own reputation as a director with a flair for location shooting in films like *The Four Feathers, Sahara,* and *The Macomber Affair*. Korda's next project was to be filmed in South Africa, and Korda invited Poitier to consider a role in his adaptation of Alan Paton's *Cry, The Beloved Country*. Little could Korda know that Poitier had turned down a Broadway role in the musical adaptation of Paton's novel, *Lost in the Stars,* to appear in *No Way Out*.

Poitier almost missed out on *Cry, the Beloved Country* again. As Poitier explained it to Fred Hift of the *New York Times* in April 1951, when Korda first saw Poitier, he took only one look and asked him: "Do you want a job?" Poitier was taken back by the rapidity of the offer and overslept the appointment Korda arranged at the airport the next day. Poitier then "forgot about the whole thing" until Korda sent him a letter six weeks later inviting him to London for a screen test.[25]

This was only the beginning of Poitier's troubles, however. Poitier could only enter South Africa as Korda's indentured servant; to have the role, he literally had to sign away his freedom. For all Korda's protestations that it was only a formality, Poitier knew the truth. It was a serious insult, a grievous humiliation. Poitier decided, however, despite vocal opposition from other blacks, that only by taking the role could he speak to the issues. William Hoffman, an early biographer of Poitier, quotes the actor at length on this important question: "*Cry, the Beloved Country* gave me the chance to say some things about apartheid that needed saying. There are few roles that I've prepared harder for. I wanted to project what it was like to be black and under the iron heel of a vicious, racist, white minority. I think how I felt came across in the film. Sure, it was a humiliation to have to indenture myself, but sometimes you have to take a punch to land a harder one."[26]

On location, Poitier was to take quite a few more punches. The shooting took place in and around Johannesburg and in a village near Durban; Negroes in the cast weren't allowed to sleep in the cities and were sheltered on small farms. Everywhere he went, Poitier told Fred Hift, he found poverty and oppression: "Around us we saw colored people living in incredible misery. Their

Canada Lee, Sidney Poitier, and Scott Harrold in *Cry, the Beloved Country*.

houses consisted of nothing more than corrugated boxes. . . no electricity, no sewers, no sanitary facilities of any kind. Often there was no water. It was pitiful.'' Poitier's reaction was to throw himself more and more into his craft, to retreat to a movie truck and read or study the script. The blacks on location couldn't go anywhere; there was no night life; even liquor was forbidden. The only thing there was in abundance, Poitier declared, was fear: "Everyone there is living in fear."[27] The blacks feared the wrath of the whites, just as the whites feared uprisings by the blacks. Poitier was living *Cry, the Beloved Country* as a black, not just acting in it.

Poitier's experiences in South Africa shaped his racial consciousness for years to come. Looking back on the whole episode, he told Helen Dudar, who prepared a feature on him for the *New York Post* in March and April 1959, that he "came back pondering the validity of fighting fire with fire, hate with hate. I finally resolved it by deciding that not only was hate alien to my nature, but evil.''

Poitier was surely not insensitive to prejudice nor docile about oppression, but the fear he encountered in South Africa taught him, he felt, a critical lesson: ". . . hate and prejudice are destructive and prevent any man from fully living his life. It can do nothing but eat away at your values and build a barrier against living a full life.''[28]

Much of both the novel and the film of *Cry, the Beloved Country* depends on a similar insight into the debilitating effects of racial prejudice. The tragedy of black and white relations is embodied in two principal characters, Stephen Kumalo, played by Canada Lee, and James Jarvis, played by Charles Colson. Kumalo, an old fashioned *umfundisi* living in the hills around Natal, leaves home in response to a letter from Reverend Msimangu (Sidney Poitier). His journey to Johannesburg in an attempt to aid his sister, find his son, and visit his brother immerses Kumalo immediately in all the grief of modern Africa. Gertrude, his sister, has become a prostitute, his brother an embittered political activist, and his son a renegade who murders a prominent white, coincidentally the son of Kumalo's rich white neighbor, James Jarvis. Jarvis and Kumalo meet in Johannesburg during the boy's trial for murder, and each comes to appreciate the other's difficult position. So, although Absalom Kumalo's appeal is denied and the boy is executed, Stephen Kumalo and Jarvis form a new friendship and begin a new cooperation between white and black based on their mutual losses and their hopes for a better future.

For all its tortured coincidences, heavy-handed symbols, and strained ironies, *Cry, the Beloved Country* is a powerfully moving story sensitively filmed by Zoltan Korda and intelligently played by a largely amateur cast. Korda's commitment to location really pays off. South Africa was hoping to develop a film industry to bolster its economy, so every effort was made to facilitate expeditious shooting. The desire to accomodate meant that South African authorities allowed Korda's camera crews to roam as they pleased; the resulting footage exposes the very worst aspects of racial oppression. Korda was also allowed to interview thousands of natives to find just the people he wanted. Like many of his contemporaries, including critic James Agee, Korda felt a real person filmed in his native environment could reveal more of the essence of human situations than the most skillfully trained actor. While the results of this commitment to amateurs are uneven in the eyes of most critics, Korda was quite pleased his minor roles could all be given to black South Africans.

Among the professional actors Korda did bring to Africa for major roles, Poitier had a role second in importance only to those of the two principals. As interpreted by Poitier, Reverend Msimangu typifies the enlightened new native clergy in Africa, religious leaders committed to social change as well as conversions. Msimangu can be charming and considerate to old priests like Kumalo, excusing their naiveté, comforting them in their doubts, and consoling them during their trials, but he is also a relentless seeker after truth. In the film, Msimangu forces all the discoveries, exposes all the horrors, and denounces the injustices. Perhaps Poitier's most masterful scene in the film comes after the trial of Kumalo's son, Absalom, who is found guilty partly because he lacked the guile of the attorney who defended his compatriots. When Kumalo's own brother, whose son was also on trial, declares "Justice has been done," Poitier cannot suitably express his contempt in words. This is a man whose hand he has just shaken, now revealed as an enemy of truth. Poitier asks sharply,

"Where can I wash my hand?" Looking furiously around, he finally cleans his hands on his cassock. Commenting on this scene, James Baldwin, who didn't like the film, still remembered and praised Poitier's "moving miracle of indignation."[29]

Poitier's personal triumph in the film involves his stunning ability to give bite to Paton's theme. If it is Jarvis and Kumalo who live out Paton's moral lesson, it's Poitier who drives it home to the audience. His critical intelligence and nagging righteousness highlight the preposterousness of racial oppression. Behind that moustache and smile, beneath that cassock, Poitier's determination and energy remind the audience how much Africans have lost at the hands of whites. Paton clearly defined the issues his book raised: "Africans saw and envied the white man's world—his wealth, his comfort and his alien ways; meanwhile their own ancient tribal controls had been weakening. Their young men went astray; their old men were troubled and puzzled. Crime increased; the racial character deteriorated in the wretched hovels where the black man huddled in the slums of the white man's cities. This is the central theme of my novel, *Cry, the Beloved Country*."[30]

Poitier deserves much of the credit for bringing that theme so powerfully to the screen in what historian Gary Null has declared "one of the best black movies ever made."[31] Critic Bosley Crowther of the *New York Times* was so impressed by the film in his feature review for 27 January 1952 that he was moved to question "why our American filmmakers have not yet risen to the eloquent height of *Cry, the Beloved Country* in expounding the subject of race—why have they not exposed the problem in terms stronger than wrath or sentiment?"[32] *Cry, the Beloved Country* was so clearly superior to American racial dramas of its day that the Museum of Modern Art awarded it the Golden Laurel Award of 1952, a prize given to the film that "made the greatest contribution to mutual understanding and good will between the peoples of the free and democratic world."

Cry, the Beloved Country also contributed a great deal to black Americans' understanding of their place in the free world. As the first of Poitier's many African films, this serious consideration of intercultural confrontation highlighted the black's African heritage. The destruction of African tribes in *Cry, the Beloved Country* graphically reminded American blacks of the destruction of their own roots. As Edward Margolies has demonstrated, the destruction of all interpersonal and intercultural contacts among slaves had "an unimaginably destructive impact on the African's

Edric Connor, Canada Lee, and Sidney Poitier in *Cry, the Beloved Country*.

personality and the deleterious results of this de-individualization—extended and aggravated by three hundred years of slavery and oppression—remain today as a burning scar on the personality formation of most Negro Americans."[33] *Cry, the Beloved Country*, by isolating the continuing de-individualization of blacks in contemporary Africa, could only heighten awareness of the importance of race and nation for American blacks. Stokely Carmichael, who could joke to assuage his horror about his youthful discovery that the natives he called out to Tarzan to kill were really his ancestors and psychologically parts of his own identity, found the essence of black power to be closely related to a rediscovery of Africa: "To the extent to which black Americans can and do trace their roots to Africa, to that extent will they be able to be more effective on the political scene."[34] Poitier's physical journey to South Africa and his indenture forced many American blacks to relive their psychic journey from Africa.

Like many of Poitier's early films, *Cry, the Beloved Country* was not for all audiences. Korda's location shooting and amateur acting didn't provide the normal gloss, neat plotting, nor star billings seemingly so important to American filmgoers. *Variety* quickly noted its limited mass appeal and consigned it commercially to "specialized and art houses," while Gilbert Seldes mused in the *Saturday Review* that all these departures from the norm seemed to "have cut it off from the largest part of the movie audience."[35] One striking indication of the small faith exhibitors had in the film comes in the story of its Richmond release, as reported in *Saturday Review*, 29 August 1953. Two Richmond women had seen the film in Canada and asked their local theater to book it. The manager refused, declaring that such films, religious pictures with social themes, never proved successful. The women were determined, gathered their friends, and underwrote a showing for $600 with profits to go to the missions. The theater was swamped and continued the film for three more days under this arrangement. The manager then booked the film himself for its exclusive Richmond screening, where 14,999 citizens eventually saw it. Unfortunately, most cities lacked such determined citizens, and *Cry, the Beloved Country*'s appeal to exhibitors sank so low that a new ploy was tried, and the film was re-released under a rather more sensational title, *African Fury*.

Sidney Poitier was also forced to look for more commercial properties; his dreams of success and leisure in the Bahamas demanded that he find more popular vehicles. Budd Boetticher's routine war adventure, *Red Ball Express*, released in 1952, gave Poitier a small role at a time he desperately needed both money and exposure. Coming as it did during the escalation of the Korean Conflict and amidst all the ambiguities of the cold war, *Red Ball Express* was an unabashed tribute to the Army Transportation Corps and their heroics in World War II as they supplied Patton's advancing troops. Though the film obfuscates the issue considerably, the "Red Ball Express," named after the slang for top priority freight on railroad lines, was a major operation by black troops. Seventy-three percent of all the truck companies in the European theater were black units, and a full sixty-seven percent of the drivers at the peak of the operation, even after whites had been transferred to this vital project, were blacks. Between 25 August and 13 November 1944, the "Red Ball Express" hauled over 400,000 tons of materials from the beaches to the front lines, averaging round trips of 500 miles and more. Boetticher's film constantly emphasizes the fact that Patton was "rewriting military history," taking his tanks, his men, and "a dash of his private courage," heading "right up the middle to Paris"; and, in a sequence which borders on unmitigated didacticism, General Gordon lectures his tank crews on the importance of logistics to their daring maneuvers: "If it weren't for the Red Ball Express . . . we might never be able to keep attacking . . . whenever they hand you a gallon of gas or a bullet, be grateful because it might be the one that saves your life or the life of your country."[36]

War stories demand heroes, of course, and *Red Ball Express* chronicles Lieutenant Chick Campbell's dramatic demonstration of supernatural courage, forbearance, and humility. Most of the film focuses on his fight to shape clerks and griping subordinates into a cohesive unit. All this is complicated by a previous history of tension between the lieutenant, played by Jeff Chandler,

and Sergeant Kallek, played by Alex Nicol. Chandler surmounts racial tension, personal animosities, and impossible odds, however, and *Red Ball Express* ends with a unified chorus of "Lift that load / One for Hitler / One for the road."

Despite its trite, chummy ending, *Red Ball Express* manages to raise several significant questions about race relations during World War II. These questions are all the more fascinating in the context of Truman's desegregation order for the military services in 1948, and the gradual integration of the armed forces slowly taking place in Korea. As Ulysses Lee notes in his study of "The Draft and the Negro," the tremendous manpower needs of the Korean War "rendered battlefield segregation, if not discrimination, both inefficient and dangerous. Likewise, the pressures to mobilize rapidly made segregated training and transport undesirable. . . . Having started with a segregated army, the Korean War came to a halt with the most fully integrated society America had ever known—the armed forces."[37] Most World War II melodramas had a token black or two, but Boetticher's *Red Ball Express* not only glorified a black unit, it actually pictured significant numbers of black soldiers risking their lives in the war effort.

The spokesman for the grievances of these black heroes is Corporal Andrew Robertson, angrily portrayed by Sidney Poitier. Poitier's racial consciousness bristles from his very first appearance on the screen, just in time to hear a white soldier's racist crack that this outfit is like "a minstrel show." Poitier retaliates so sharply, "Then why don't you tell a joke?" that other black soldiers intervene to discount the episode. Later, on board his truck, riding with Jeff Chandler, Poitier tries to strike up a conversation, only to be rebuffed by another reference to color. Poitier snarls, "I get it" and will speak no more, hiding his feelings behind a forced smile.

Real fireworks erupt down the road at a rest stop. Some Red Cross workers are serving coffee, and Poitier orders some coffee and doughnuts only to have a southern soldier start a fight: "Black boy, you don't give orders to nobody. You take them." Poitier's rejoinder is swift and aggressive: "I'm not taking any orders from you." A fight ensues, but is quickly broken up by Jeff Chandler. For blacks, this exchange marks a memorable moment in screen history. Donald Bogle cites this scene as one of the first militant depictions of an emerging black consciousness: "Young black audiences loved him for it. Here at long last was a sane black man, free and strong enough to shout back at whitey."[38]

Hollywood convention demanded, of course, that Poitier finally learn that at least one white man was worthy of respect, good old heroic Jeff Chandler, but that respect comes quite grudgingly and only after Poitier gets in quite a few more licks about racism. In an emotional exchange with Chandler after this incident, Poitier requests a transfer. As they discuss the problem of racism, Poitier makes a dramatic point, "Punches I can handle, sir," not altogether buried by Chandler's declaration that it "was never my intention to treat you differently from anyone else in this company." Even with his black comrades, Poitier constantly has all the most powerful lines, warning them about Chandler, because "he outranks us the way we've been outranked all our lives." Poitier constantly demands that whites prove themselves to him. At the beginning of the film, all he can see is their inadequacy: "All I ever hear them do is argue and complain, feel sorry for themselves, and try to take their misery out on someone else." His colleagues assure him that all the whites have to do is get "their spirits moving" and "You're gonna see an outfit grow right up in front of you, one you'll be proud of." *Red Ball Express* chronicles the development of that fighting unit and Poitier's gradual assimilation; Poitier sees many valiant acts by both blacks and whites, and witnesses Chandler's moving demand that he finish a funeral service for a black soldier before they move on, even if that delay means a court martial. When Chandler later offers Poitier a chance to transfer as he requested, Poitier meekly asks the matter be forgotten. The Red Ball Express is now his outfit. This total commitment to the group reaches symbolic fruition when blacks and whites choose to drink and celebrate together on their short liberties, and Poitier calls out to white private Ronald Partridge, just returned from a romantic interlude, "We'll all be in the bar, partner. You can join us there."

In real life, Poitier made other important commitments in 1952. As he told Murray Shumach in a touchingly personal interview, acting was becoming a central part of his identity, not just another job: "I have always thought of survival in terms of my internal self. That is more important than the external self. I wanted to be, in my own terms, worthwhile. I wanted to be acceptable to myself. And I felt that way in acting." Unfortunately, just as he found his vocation, Poitier also discovered a curious shortage of roles available.

Hollywood wouldn't consider him, he told Shumach, for anything but "Negro roles and that sure had a lot to do with the scarcity of my jobs during those three years. Yet there were lots of nondescript parts that could have been played by any good actor, regardless of race or color. I don't say it was all conscious prejudice. You might call it institutionalized omissions."[39] Speaking to Fred Hift, also of the *New York Times*, in 1951, Poitier was very specific about the "Negro roles" available to him: "Hollywood as a rule still doesn't want to portray us as anything but butlers, chauffeurs, gardeners, or maids. They just don't want to make us part of contemporary American life." Poitier wasn't looking for any special concessions, he told Hift: "As an actor, if I have the ability, all I ask is the opportunity. When it's denied to me because of my color then I can't help feeling resentful."[40]

Poitier's desire for work didn't blind him to his special responsibilities as a black artist, a conflict felt by other black artists before Poitier. In *Here I Stand*, Paul Robeson described his own initial willingness to take any role and his growing awareness that he must select roles that allowed him dignity and pride. Poitier was always selective about his roles, as agent Martin Baum would discover. Interviewed in Hollywood in 1966, Baum recalled that he knew producers Daniel Bishop and Richard Kiley were looking for a black actor for their project *Phenix City Story*. Baum suggested Poitier to them, even though Poitier was an independent performer, not bound to any agent. As Baum recalls it, the offer was made, a good offer of $1,000 a week for a four-week minimum guarantee. Poitier seemed happy to get the call, especially in view of the approaching Christmas holidays, took the script, and went home. The next day, Poitier came back, and, as Baum describes it, rejected the part saying, "It is a wonderful script and an excellent part, but I can't play it. It's the role of a men's room attendant, and I believe some day the Negro performer should be given other parts than the traditional waiters, cooks, and Pullman car attendants." Baum was impressed by Poitier's integrity and became his agent and close personal friend. Although Poitier's career would have a couple more shaky years, Baum's influence and advice would later be quite important elements aiding Poitier in winning his Oscar.

Poitier's own account of the *Phenix City Story* affair, which appears in an interview with Frank Daley of the *Ottawa Journal* under the provocative headline "The Black Man's Burden," actually downplays the racial aspects of his decision and stresses his desire for professional growth. The money for this film, Poitier recalls, could "have paid hospital bills and bailed me out," but "I never chose simply to work." In *Phenix City Story*, Poitier felt the role "was not what you would ordinarily term a derogatory role. It was a fairly decent part, but it was not a part that distinguished me from any other actor. It was a part that was unbecoming in terms of what my aspirations were." Amplifying these remarks somewhat, Poitier stressed that exercising real choice in his roles gave him power over his career: "I turned it [*Phenix City Story*] down. I said I didn't want to do it. So what I did do was I went and hocked the furniture and I borrowed some money and I paid for the baby and I got my family through. But I didn't do it because I just couldn't do it. Not because it was derogatory to black people; it just had no real substance. Okay. Doing that at that stage in my career told me that I would always be able to make that choice and I did throughout my career."[41]

One of the images which recurred years later in Poitier's lengthy psychoanalysis was that of a jungle with many animals fighting but only one animal in control precisely because he had the power to choose. Even in this bleak period in the early fifties, Poitier knew he must take charge of his professional life; he had to make the key decisions. This self-confidence and sense of artistic mission is all the more remarkable when one recalls, as historian Daniel Leab does in his text *From Sambo to Superspade*, that "prestigious films like *No Way Out* and programmers like *Red Ball Express* brought him little money or opportunity. In 1954, at the age of twenty-seven, Poitier seemed to have reached a dead end."[42]

In 1954, Poitier made his first screen appearance in over two years in a low-budget entertainment, *Go, Man, Go!*, a feature obviously designed to exploit black audiences who previously frequented the defunct independent black film circuit. *Go, Man Go!*, an understated, amiable film, traces the humble origins of the Harlem Globetrotters in Chicago, detailing in documentary footage their grueling climb to the top of professional basketball, and chronicling basketball promoter Abe Saperstein's many schemes to surmount an odious color barrier that limited the Globetrotters' access to major arenas. Much of the black and white footage is game footage, interspersed with dramatic re-creations of the havoc an over-ambitious schedule played with lives and bodies. As Inman Jackson, Sidney Poitier travels with the team and serves as a lightning rod for many grievances. His attempts to salvage a romantic interest with Ruby Dee also provide some comic relief from the tense game footage. Fortuitously, the Globetrotters discover they can build up big point leads in their games and then rest for a while by clowning on court. The fans love it and the Harlem Globetrotters' inimitable style is born. However, the team must win that one last tournament, and they do it in dramatic, come-from-behind Hollywood style, convincing white entrepreneur James Willoughby (Bram Nossen) of the wisdom of booking black teams in his arenas.

Interestingly enough, the director of *Go, Man, Go!* is an ex-athlete, a boxer turned cameraman named James Wong Howe, who came to Hollywood from Kwantung, China, to become one of the most distinguished cinematographers of all time, numbering an incredible array of masterpieces among his credits, including *They Made Me a Criminal*, *The Strawberry Blonde*, and one of the finest sports films of all time, *Body and Soul*. *Go, Man, Go!* Howe's only directorial effort, occupies a fond spot in his heart, for as he explained to Charles Higham, the tight budget and twenty-day shooting schedule really taxed everyone's ingenuity: "That's what is so good about low-budget pictures; you have to use your ingenuity, your imagination. The whole thing cost $130,000 dollars. It cost that much just to put in power lines and telephones for *The Molly Maguires*." The austerity on the set of *Go, Man, Go!* is well illustrated by Howe's comments on the problem the crew faced with the numerous shots of the Globetrotters travelling in their jalopy: "We couldn't afford process shots. We took the wheels off the touring car and set the car on a trailer

Patricia Breslin, Edmon Ryan, Dane Clark, Sidney Poitier, and Anatol Winogradoff in *Go, Man, Go!*

chassis, so there was room to put the camera on as well, then we drove around. But we had a problem because the trailer's diesel made a shattering sound and drowned out the dialogue. So we'd go to the tops of hills and let the trailer chassis go without the engine, and off the whole thing would go to the foot of the hills. So the Globetrotters were always going downhill in the picture!''[43]

Sidney Poitier might well have thought his career was going all downhill in *Go, Man Go!* for, as Dennis Hall notes, the film provided him with "some of the worst dialogue he ever had to contend with.''[44] Inman Jackson, a small, forgettable performance, gave little indication of how far Poitier would go in Hollywood, just as the film *Go, Man Go!* barely suggested how the Globetrotters would grow into what Red Smith has called "the most popular medium of sports entertainment in history,'' a team that would play in more than 144 different nations to untold millions of fans. Both Poitier and the Harlem Globetrotters were destined for bigger things.

His next assignment, as Gregory W. Miller in Richard Brooks's topical film of Evan Hunter's best-selling novel, *The Blackboard Jungle*, offered Sidney Poitier a giant step toward popularity and stardom. In the mid-fifties, America was obsessed by juvenile delinquency. The *Saturday Evening Post* declared street gangs "the Shame of America''' as sociologists churned out endless tomes on what seemed to be America's biggest headache. Hunter's novel skillfully caught the mood of the times in its desperate picture of a bewildered young teacher facing an incorrigible class whose pranks quickly escalated to crimes, including a vicious physical assault, slanderous letters to his nervous pregnant wife, and, finally, attempted murder right in the classroom. If this made for torrid prose, Brooks transformed the novel into a film so sensational that even the studio heads at MGM thought it was too hot to handle. Mr. Mayer himself told Brooks: "You don't make MGM movies''; instead, Mayer charged, Brooks's films were "always with dirty fingerprints on the wall. I hate the stuff." Only when *Blackboard Jungle* smashed all box office records was Brooks welcomed back to the fold.[45]

Brooks's principal inspiration for *Blackboard Jungle* was a song he heard on a black radio station, "Rock Around the Clock," and Brooks wrote his screenplay to the record and used the music not only on the soundtrack, but "all through the making of the film."[46] Brooks had intuited the link between soul music, rock and roll, rhythm and blues, and the generation gap which America was

Sidney Poitier as Gregory Miller in *Blackboard Jungle*.

to experience for the next decade. In Hunter's novel, the musical tension is between jazz and such pop talents as Julius La Rosa and Joni James. Richard Brooks knew where the real action was; his picture of hot rods and switchblades rocks relentlessly to the dramatic, driving rhythms of Bill Haley. Brooks heard the existential beat of angel-headed hipsters and added to Hunter's original characterizations an anarchic, totally dropped-out consciousness of America. Consider the almost prophetic anti-war, anti-establishment lines in the last confrontation between the sociopathic Artie West and the teacher he will later try to kill, Richard Dadier:

Richard: You know what happens when those kids are caught?

West: What's that, Teach?

Richard: Reform school—year in jail—maybe more.

West: Oh, you know, a year from now, the army comes by and they say 'Okay, Artie West, you get into uniform and you save the world and you get your lousy head blowed right off.' Well, maybe—maybe I'll get a year in jail and maybe—when I come out the army they don't want Artie West to be a soldier no more. Maybe what I get is—is—is out.

Brooks's ear proved unerringly attuned to the rhetoric of the Bomb generation, a downbeat message to which the college professors and the detectives of *Blackboard Jungle* have no response.

In this dark universe, Sidney Poitier's characterization of Gregory Miller serves as the scale on which the earnest intentions and pious declarations of Glenn Ford as Mr. Dadier are weighed against the animal energy and street wisdom of his disillusioned classmates. As the natural leader in the class, Miller challenges Dadier's abilities; Dadier must woo Miller from rebellion to cooperation if the teacher is to survive.

Director Richard Brooks's cognizance of Miller's importance to *Blackboard Jungle* manifested itself in the long series of screen tests he conducted with black actors before selecting Sidney Poitier. Discussing the film in a private interview, Brooks called attention to the importance of Poitier's role and pointed to the scene on the school steps, where Dadier falsely accuses Miller and insults him, as central to understanding both the film and the nature of prejudice:

> In my mind, the role played by Poitier in this picture is an extremely vital one. It served to show that even an open-minded teacher, who is entirely in favor of integration, could not get free from a certain prejudice. He supposes that it is the Negro boy who leads the pupils' opposition against him. . . . In the decisive scene when they meet on the staircase, the boy has a natural reaction to such a violent and unfounded treatment, and provokes Glenn Ford's strong reply: "You black . . . " It is only when the teacher catches himself that he realizes how wrong his subconscious feeling was.[47]

Brooks added one interesting anecdote about this scene that reveals a great deal about what Sidney

Poitier confronts Glenn Ford in *Blackboard Jungle*.

Poitier's presence on the set could do. Poitier touched his colleagues just as he reached audiences through his screen presence. According to Brooks, Glenn Ford could not force himself to say this line, in spite of several tries. Finally, deciding that Poitier was the only person who could talk to Ford about it, Brooks asked him to help. Poitier then persuaded the reluctant Ford he should not hesitate on these words and the scene was recorded with no further problems.

Like so many of Poitier's films, *Blackboard Jungle* ran into innumerable problems after its release. Lloyd Binford, the chief censor in Memphis, who had never banned an MGM film before, declared it "the vilest film I've seen in 26 years as a censor. The teenagers start off bad. I thought they would reform and we would have to pass it but they are just as bad at the end." Needless to say, the ninety-year-old Mr. Binford broke his clean record with MGM and banned *Blackboard Jungle*.[48] The film was also banned in Georgia for the simple reason that it showed blacks and whites in the same classroom, a blasphemy local censors could not allow; as a result of this decision, the Atlanta *Constitution* filed suit and took the case all the way to the Supreme Court in an attempt to lift the ban.

Blackboard Jungle not only troubled the courts in 1955; it also embarrassed the foreign service. America's ambassador to Italy, Clare Booth Luce, created a censorship brouhaha when she barred the film from the Venice Film Festival as an official United States entry. Interestingly enough, normally liberal *Time* magazine echoed Luce's objections when it argued that "culturally distorted novels and movies far more than Communist propaganda" were responsible for the repulsive picture of American life prevalent in foreign countries.[49] The studios responded to these charges in the person of Sam Goldwyn, who reminded the zealots of patriotism that "when a country chooses only to show nice things about itself and not the other aspects, then it [the film] becomes propaganda. Life in no country is only beautiful and, therefore, should be shown as it is."[50]

Life "as it is" seemed to involve few black Americans for major studios, however, and Sidney Poitier found himself again seeking suitable roles. In 1956, his only film appearance was in a family film, a juvenile boy-and-dog opus entitled *Goodbye, My Lady*, which was sensitively directed by veteran Hollywood director William A. Wellman. Wellman kept this trite tale from wallowing in sentimentality and pious platitudes,

Poitier and the other students eye Margaret Hayes in *Blackboard Jungle*.

and managed to mold fine location shooting in Georgia into an uncluttered disquisition on the training of a Basenji hound, a rare African dog.

The plot of *Goodbye, My Lady* is pure *Bildungsroman*. Young Skeeter (Brandon de Wilde) lives with his uncle and guardian Jesse Jackson (Walter Brennan) in a small cabin deep in Mississippi's Pascagoula Swamp. Skeeter and Jesse discover a strange dog with a peculiar laugh and almost human tears. Skeeter adopts his ''lady,'' and spends long hours training the dog according to the precepts he's learned from Gates, a neighbor and good friend, played by Sidney Poitier. Just as Lady and Skeeter form a compatible hunting team, an advertisement for a lost dog appears from the real owner of this rare and expensive Basenji. All the adults know the right course of action for Skeeter, but they leave it to him to make this sad decision; giving up Lady will be his avenue to responsible adulthood. Skeeter opts for honesty and, as he loses Lady, Uncle Jesse and Cash, an influential store owner and community leader, invite him to

share a cup of ''black'' coffee. Skeeter has become a man.

Despite the relative brevity of Poitier's role in *Goodbye, My Lady*, his character, Gates, presents an engaging image of black farmers in the South. Unlike the illiterate whites around him, Gates has a college diploma. He alone recognizes the African Basenji and teaches Skeeter how to train it. As a mentor, Gates displays considerable wisdom and humanity. Both he and his mother, played by Louise Beavers, love Skeeter without reservation. She tries to mother the boy, and Poitier is every bit as wise a father figure as Uncle Jesse. Poitier sees the ad for the lost dog, and, though he could really use the money offered in reward, he allows Skeeter to face the decision himself. As Skeeter's teacher and friend, Gates recognizes the overwhelming importance of experience in growth. So, while Gates may not be a role guaranteed to advance a career, it provided Poitier with one more positive image for a black man on screen, an image of education and compassion.

The bloody climax to *Blackboard Jungle* which shocked Ambassador Luce.

Poitier's next role, a major one as Tommy Tyler in Martin Ritt's *Edge of the City*, also exuded humanity and compassion, so much so that many critics denounced Tyler's characterization as too saintly for his own good, a sacrificial black dying for mixed-up white folks. Agent Martin Baum had arranged the Tommy Tyler role for Poitier as a televised appearance in Robert Alan Aurthur's original script "A Man Is Ten Feet Tall," broadcast as part of the prestigious Philco Playhouse. This daring casting generated, social scientist Royal Colle observed, an interesting case history in how anti-black attitudes influenced the mass media; when Poitier became the first black to have a major role in a television drama, the racist elements in the country quickly responded. As Colle reported, "Newspaper editorials, petitions, name-calling, threats from consumers never to buy a Philco product, and cancellation of distributorships by Philco franchise holders stood out as a reminder to

other advertisers who might tread into this delicate area."[51] Advertiser timidity could not blind critics to the merits of the teleplay; and the project, like so many other highly lauded television dramas, including *Marty*, was transferred to the larger screen and given a new title.

Basically, *Edge of the City* expands the characterizations in "A Man Is Ten Feet Tall," maintaining its basic narrative with all its echoes of *On the Waterfront* and other neo-realistic stories popularized by television writers like Paddy Chayevsky and Rod Sterling. Axel North (John Cassavetes), an obviously disturbed army deserter fleeing his family, the police, and a guilty conscience, signs on as a stevedore in New York City despite the kickbacks he must make to a sadistic foreman, Charlie (Jack Warden). Black coworker Tommy Tyler (Sidney Poitier) befriends Axel, protects him, and restores his self-confidence; Tyler even introduces Axel to a schoolteacher, Ellen (Kathleen Maguire), with whom he finds love and some security. All this harmony infuriates Charlie, who baits Axel so mercilessly that Tommy intervenes on his behalf. After a pitched battle with baling hooks, in which Tommy spares Charlie's life, Charlie stabs Tommy in the back. Axel begins to flee, but the dramatic reminder from Tommy's widow, Lucy (Ruby Dee), that "You were supposed to be his friend" prompts a now obviously more mature Axel to call the police and to avenge Tommy's death in a fight with Charlie. On the television screen, the one-hour episode was heavy on murder and mayhem; on film, the humanity of Tommy Tyler, the value of the black-white friendship, and the growth in Axel's personality are more important.

Sidney Poitier recognized the intense pressure he was under to dig more deeply into the psyche of Tommy Tyler. On television in general, he told interviewers, "you do a great deal of shooting or stabbing or stealing or murder, and sometimes all of them together all in an hour, and you do nothing in the way of understanding people anyhow." For that reason, Poitier felt television generally was not for him: "There's no real characterization on television. There's no dimension. It's not my scene. I can't make it. I don't dig it."[52] It was on film, where he had the most room to stretch his artistic muscles, that Poitier would work most comfortably, transforming Tommy Tyler into what film historians and contemporary critics would hail as "one of the more human portrayals of the Negro every encountered in films."[53]

Edge of the City offered Poitier a rare chance to work with a promising young production crew and cast, whose enormous talents were to transform the whole film industry. The credits for *Edge of the City* read like the honor roll for the "New York School" of independent film-makers. This is, for example, the first film project for producer David Susskind, who would later back Poitier again in *Raisin in the Sun* and do another famous television-to-film project, *Requiem for a Heavyweight*. *Edge of the City* also marked Martin Ritt's directorial debut; he would work again with Poitier on *Paris Blues*, as well as create other distinguished black projects such as the Broadway-to-screen adaptation *The Great White Hope* and the film *Sounder*. Writer Robert Alan Aurthur, also a newcomer to the screen, would become Poitier's frequent collaborator and good friend; like the protagonists of *Edge of the City*, white writer Aurthur and black actor Poitier developed an almost color-blind bond that results in some of Poitier's most personal films. Aurthur seems uniquely able to synthesize Poitier's vision and his own in a script.

Writer Aurthur described the youthful enthusiasm and incredibly hard work, as well as the comraderie which distinguished *Edge of the City*, in an exclusive article for the *New York Herald Tribune*. *Edge of the City* was a New York project from start to finish, he notes; unlike *Blackboard Jungle*, the shooting was done right in the city and involved many only-in-New York City type anecdotes, including bad weather, intrusive background noises, and angry hot-dog vendors. The basic script was, in fact, conceived on the backstretch of Belmont Park racetrack, where Martin Ritt held court amidst the regal company of "Al the Brain" and "Louie the Genius." During the shooting, Ritt assuredly spent as many dollars at the track as Sidney Poitier, another inveterate gambler, contributed to Philip Rose's notorious high stakes poker game.

Long hours of difficult location shooting created their own tensions, of course. Shooting some of the fight footage at a railroad yard near the Hudson River generated a live audience for one of the most explosive moments in the film, a duel to the death between a lovable black man and a detestable white

Sidney Poitier as Tommy Tyler in *Edge of the City*.

John Cassavetes and Sidney Poitier as coworkers and friends in _Edge of the City_.

man. Everyone's nerves were on edge for that take, according to Robert Alan Aurthur:

> The scene was planned with care and a whole day was set aside for the sequence. Poitier and Warden worked out their moves almost as ballet dancers, because real, unblunted baling hooks were to be used and a mistake might mean serious injury. A doctor was called to the set to stand by. When we were ready to shoot, the word had gone out all over the yards . . . and dozens of workmen hurried to the scene.
> For almost five minutes Sidney and Jack fought. . . . Somewhere, after the first minute, the planned moves seemed to be forgotten and we were watching a real fight, a fight of such violence that one could only hold his breath to keep from crying out in protest.

When Martin Ritt finally called "Cut!" Aurthur remembers, a "concerted gasp arose from the spectators, then a spontaneous burst of applause." Director Ritt wanted even more, however, and demanded a retake.[54]

The murderous confrontation between Tommy and Charlie in _Edge of the City_ seems especially devastating because so much of the film assumes that blacks and whites can interact as equals, without tension, racial consciousness, or self-consciousness. _Edge of the City_ envisions an integration and social interaction between races far different from the tempestuous confrontation marking the many roads from Little Rock to Selma and Birmingham. Aurthur and his colleagues in Jonathan Productions gambled on possible profits where art paralleled headlines, pledging their financial resources to a low-budget film despite "opposition somewhere to what it might say." The revolutionary aspects of the film were well recognized by Archer Winsten of _The New York Post_, who dedicated one of his most insightful reviews to a compelling argument that the understated nature of the human relationship between Poitier and Ruby Dee, the black characters, and John Cassavetes and Kathleen Maguire, the white characters, marked a new milestone for adult film fare: "There is none of that pious 'look, Ma, I'm crossing a barrier—I'm a pioneer' attitude which has marked and marred so many of the few films attempting this sort of thing. . . . The lack of brilliance, the ordinary quality of the happenings and dialogue, are what makes these sequences so memorable."[55]

Edge of the City does bedazzle in its quiet moments. In an age when integration and revolution were closely linked, when a cold drink at the soda fountain was an act of civil disobedience, and when a film like *Edge of the City* could fail in Detroit, because, as David Susskind later noted, whites stopped coming when black patrons appeared at the theater, Poitier managed to appear both liberated and comfortable, playing his bongo drums, joking with his wife and friends, dancing, and enjoying his cigars and brandy. Poitier is so clearly the finest character in the film that many wondered what he was doing on the waterfront messing around with all the poor white trash. Poitier, one of the few blacks pictured as a stevedore, is a boss, and the brightest, most complete human being in the whole film. Poitier's performance in *Edge of the City* also marked him as a singular talent, a uniquely qualified actor. *Edge of the City* reinforced his standing among professionals and critics alike. There were even rumors of an Oscar nomination for the role of Tommy Tyler.

All this fine publicity inspired director Richard Brooks, who earlier had trusted Sidney Poitier with the critical role in *Blackboard Jungle*, to turn to him again for a major role in Pandro S. Berman's

Jack Warden and Sidney Poitier fight with baling hooks in *Edge of the City*.

production of Robert C. Ruark's blockbuster African novel *Something of Value*, a searing account of the Mau Mau uprisings in Kenya. The studio paid over a quarter of a million dollars for the screen rights to *Something of Value* and budgeted over two million dollars for the project, yet up-and-coming screen personality Poitier was, in fact, the first actor signed to a role; he would later be joined by box office magnet Rock Hudson, pretty Dana Wynter, and established character actors like Juano Hernandez and Wendy Hiller.

Scenarist Brooks actually used only small parts of Ruark's sprawling tale for his film. As originally written, *Something of Value* contained three mammoth sections, treating the "home life" of white settler Peter McKenzie and of Kikuyu warrior Kimani, their separate careers as "young warriors," and their inevitable murderous clash during the "Mau Mau" terrorism. Ruark weaves a complex tale of broken taboos, bloody rituals, ruptured marriages, and psychological torment as two parallel lives unfold. Peter, the great white hunter, finds himself propelled to kill the best friend he ever had, and Kimani's heightened political and cultural consciousness leads him to war against all whites. The root of the conflict, Ruark indicates, can be found in the old Basunto proverb which provides the title for his novel: "If a man does away with his traditional way of living and throws away his good customs he had better first make certain that he has something of value to replace them." This theme, so reminiscent of the major motif in *Cry, the Beloved Country*, dots every page of Ruark's text. Receiving its fullest statement in the words of the white patriarch Henry McKenzie, a man who understands both settlers and natives alike: "You tell the natives to quit killing the Masai and not to dance the big dance and don't circumcise the women. You teach 'em to read and write and don't give 'em anything to use it on. . . . You take away all the old stuff and you don't give them anything to replace it with."[56] This same message is promulgated by Mau Mau organizers, who themselves echo the sentiments of the imprisoned Jomo Kenyatta: "First the white man stole away the land and then he stole away our customs and finally he stole our God. One day he will fall upon us in force and kill us all" (*Something of Value*, p. 267).

Ruark's novel emphasizes the horror of both Mau Mau terror and the white man's widespread torture and bloody retaliation. Page after page catalogs brutal killings, savage dismemberments, and cruel sexual perversions. The Mau Mau force a widow to squat on the severed penis of her

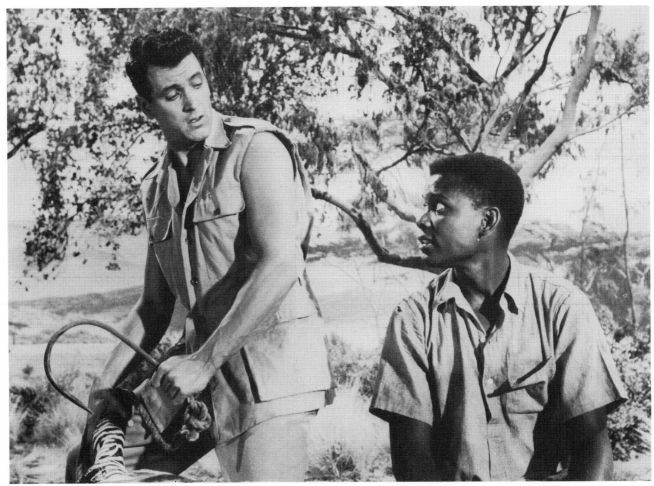

Rock Hudson as Peter McKenzie and Sidney Poitier as Kimani in *Something of Value*.

husband; whites scare a spread-eagled African prisoner to death with a snake near her vagina. *Something of Value* shocked its contemporary readers and had a rather sensational reputation by the time Richard Brooks began to adapt it for the scene. It was obvious that he was going to have to make some changes, if only to tone down the torture and mutilations.

Brooks was well aware of the problems, and described his preparation for the task in an interview in Hollywood in 1966: "After reading Ruark's book, I wanted to visit Africa and see for myself what parts of it are actually motivated. After my arrival in Kenya, I was immediately approached by the late Ambassador to the United Nations, Mboya, who told me that many things described in the book were untrue. When I answered him, 'I am here to find out,' he went through our first script and found it was better, but still needed to be improved." Mboya introduced Brooks to Professor Louis Leakey, the distin-guished anthropologist, curator of Kenya's Museum, and brother of a Mau Mau victim. When Brooks described his purpose to Leakey as "not so much a commercial one, but rather an interest in finding out about the Mau Mau in view of deter-mining what is the future for Africans, both Negroes and whites," Leakey chatted at length with Brooks on the project and put him in touch with Major Henderson, another white who spoke the Kikuyu language. Brooks found Henderson "a marvelous young man" and was quite impressed by Henderson's comment that "unless the white men become partners with the black, it won't be long before they will have to leave Africa." As a result of these contacts, Brooks admits: "I rewrote the whole script, and decided to develop it around the following point: There is a young African Negro and his friend, a white 'European,' born in Africa in the same environment. They grow up in the same household, but eventually are split apart by the situation created by the Mau Mau war. This originated the tragedy, whose meaning was the crisis of the traditional white-Negro relationship."

By the time he finished, Brooks had transformed Ruark's scathing indictment of both sides into a fraternal plea for mutual understanding. All the horrors and killings become mere episodes preparing the audience for Rock Hudson's and Sidney Poitier's noble and ill-fated attempts to find an honorable peace and a new basis for cooperation. Ruark was reported to be less than pleased with the adaptation; rumor had him mocking the new script's earnestness with biting irony: "These kids struck out in the humor department and the come-to-Jesus ending is just plain bad."

One clear indication of the vast chasm between Brooks's vision of a future solution and the grim reality of the present African scene can be found in the accommodations problem Brooks faced in housing Sidney Poitier on location. As Brooks recalls the situation, Poitier had to be declared a non-black before he could stay at the hotel: "It was not quite so easy to bring Sidney Poitier to Kenya. The manager of the Nairobi Hotel did not want to house him with us. He offered him a cottage. We refused, and asked him to bring the matter to the owners. After a week, a question came: 'How much is Mr. Poitier paid for his work?' 'Thirty thousand dollars,' was the answer. 'Oh, that is about ten thousand pounds?' 'Yes.' 'Well, then he is not a Negro and there is no problem in accommodating him in our hotel.' " Similar problems occurred whenever the cast wanted to go out to eat. Brooks once arranged a picnic lunch to avoid the embarrassment of all-white restaurants, but Brooks well knew that Sidney Poitier understood.

Sidney Poitier also understood that, to play a Mau Mau, he had to speak to some Mau Mau leaders. Major Henderson arranged a meeting, and Brooks, Hudson, Poitier, and Henderson drove deep into the back country in a Land Rover for a clandestine rendezvous. During this rather nervous meeting near Mount Kenya, the film artist made some rather remarkable discoveries about the global village of media. Brooks described the exchange between artists and Mau Mau warriors with no small degree of surprise and irony: "When we finally arrived at a small hut and sat down to talk, they told us that they recognized us from far away by the smell of soap around us. There was a pregnant woman among the warriors, who had killed several people. When we introduced Sidney as the one who would play the part of their leader, they smiled, and told us he came from America.

They knew it by the way he walks, and eats, and by the structure of his body and bones. Without any paper or radio (the only one—shortwave military type), they knew very well what was happening in the world. They asked us questions about Little Rock." If Poitier had come to Africa to discover his roots and the truth of black and white relationships, he also learned of the affinity warring Africans felt for black unrest in America. As so many commentators were noting, the Third World and the American ghettos all resembled colonies under white rule.

Sidney Poitier no doubt had much of this on his mind when he again suffered the humiliation of an African odyssey so he could play a militant black. Poitier has almost every exciting line in the script. A clear indication of the tone of the best scenes in the film comes in a dramatic conversation between Kimani (Poitier) and his imprisoned father:

Karanja: You have much to look forward to my son. You will become head man as I was.

Kimani: Is that to be my life? Head man for a white boss? 'Yes, Bwana. No, Bwana. Yes, Bwana.' This land can serve me, too. I want my own land.

Karanja: Then you must earn it.

Kimani: I will, Father.

In many episodes, Kimani espouses an "Africa for Africans" philosophy that, by extension, advocates real black power everywhere. Only when Hudson appeals to Poitier's friendship and his concern for the future, and talks as well of the promise of substantive change, does Kimani attempt a reconciliation. Betrayed by the white, Kimani is killed; in a mirror of their childhood Hudson then takes the infant son of Poitier to raise with his own boy. This time, Peter McKenzie vows, things will be different, better, "if it's not too late." In case any viewer missed the symbolic import of all this, the film ends with a quotation on screen from Sir Winston Churchill: "The problems of East Africa are the problems of the world."

Something of Value obviously posited that racial problems all over the world could be solved by the courageous actions of individuals. Sidney Poitier in 1957 shared much of the widespread enthusiasm for individual acts of conscience as an antidote for, indeed a weapon against, racism; so, when he read the script, he fell in love with the film. He believed in material, he told the editors of *Newsweek*, that "has texture, quality, something good to say about life. When I read my part in *Something of Value*, I felt good, you know." Poitier felt so good that he immediately began the arduous preparation that always precedes his seemingly casual and spontaneous film performances; he described that process for this film quite explicitly: "The first day I got the script I went over it eight times. Each day after that I double it. On the fourth day, after reading it sixty-four times, I put it away and begin to work on the motivations, not the words. Kimani's experiences in the picture come before he is prepared to make an adjustment to life. It's a hell of a part."[57] Kimani was indeed a hell of a role. As *Variety* saw it, *Something of Value* is "Ruark's story, and it is Poitier's film."[58] Kimani may die in the end, but his bold claim to dignity left a massive impression wherever audiences got a chance to see the film.

In 1966, Richard Brooks estimated that *Something of Value* was still banned in almost three-quarters of the world. In the Orient and in Africa it could not be shown; even in France, most notably at the Cannes Festival, its exhibition was banned because of provocative parallels to the Algerian situtation. In 1957 and for many years thereafter, audiences did not recognize the lack of

realism that scholars John Nottingham and Carl G. Rosberg exposed in their 1969 study *The Myth of Mau Mau: Nationalism in Kenya*. In 1957, in America and around the world, the clearest ramifications of the film involved the forceful demand for civil rights Kimani makes to Peter in the jungle:

Peter: Then you know the war goes badly for you.

Kimani: It is possible to lose a battle and still win a war.

Peter: Must Africa always stink of death? Can we not live together as friends?

Kimani: Friends have equal rights.

Peter: They will come.

Kimani: Only when we take them.

Peter: I think we're ready to give them.

As Kimani, Poitier waged his own war for civil rights on screen before people reluctant to yield them to blacks.

In one of the ironic reversals that checker Poitier's unique career, the Venice Film Festival, which had previously dropped *Blackboard Jungle* under protest, cited Poitier as best actor for his performance in *Something of Value*. Poitier's star was rising, and the *Hollywood Reporter* again raised the possibility of an Oscar. On 25 April 1957, it reported that *Something of Value* was "sure to get Sidney Poitier an Academy Award nomination." Actually the Academy still wasn't ready for Poitier, but *Something of Value* did establish him as a permanent fixture on the Hollywood scene.

Sidney Poitier's next screen appearance found him costarring with Hollywood's number one leading man, Clark Gable, in Raoul Walsh's adaptation of Robert Penn Warren's civil war novel *Band of Angels*. Robert Penn Warren, a luminary in Southern literary circles, attempted in *Band of Angles* a complex exploration of the theme of black and white identity. Told in the first person by the protagonist, Amantha Starr, who is raised as a Southern lady but discovers she is, in fact, a black and is sold into slavery, *Band of Angels* chronicles her perplexing quest for an answer to the question "Who am I?" Along the way, virtually every character she meets has a similar split-personality. Her owner and eventual lover, Hamish Bond, now an almost too beneficent master, reveals himself as the former Mr. Hicks, a notoriously cruel slave trader. His favorite slave, Rau-Ru, is transformed by circumstances into Union

Black nationalist Poitier and white-colonial Hudson war in Something of Value.

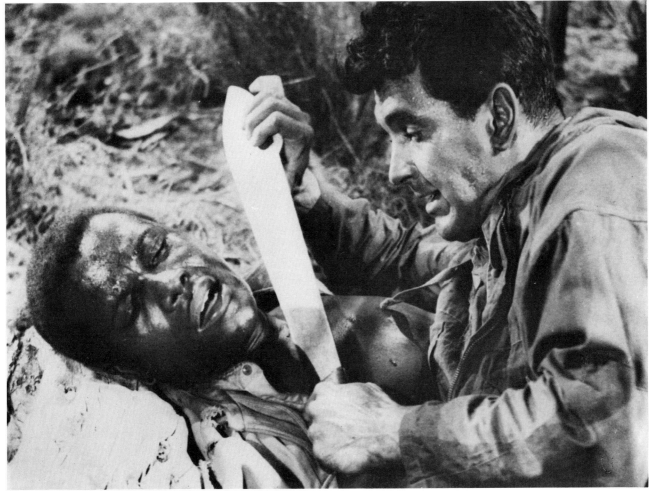

Sidney Poitier and Rock Hudson in *Something of Value*.

officer Lieutenant Oliver Cromwell Jones, a major leader in the Civil War battle to free his people. Amantha's pious college acquaintances finally emerge as lecherous bigots; even her seemingly faithful husband betrays her in a scandalous adultery. Nothing, Warren suggests, perplexes more than reality, and, as Amantha finally muses, the real question of identity involves a puzzling paradox: "Was life only that, a perpetual re-enactment of what you thought you could not bear, but which was, somehow, the very essence of what your self was?"[59]

Literary critics vary in their assessment of Warren's novel. Most laud *Band of Angels*, but some mavericks like Leslie Fiedler view it as an unusual novel of miscegenation because it transforms the genre "from the masculine murder mystery to the feminine bosom book, the erotic historical romance, creating a hybrid form whose strange pedigree would read: out of Margaret Mitchell by Mark Twain."[60] The pedigree for

Raoul Walsh's film adaptation is even more bizarre and bastardized: *Band of Angels* comes from Warren through *Gone with the Wind* by way of Rhett Butler. Virtually no film critic or reviewer could take Walsh's film seriously for one minute. Even Rene Jordan, who wrote a lavish book on Clark Gable, admits that in *Band of Angels* "the deification of the star" exceeds the bounds of good taste and "the awesome symbolism was getting a little out of hand."[61] To take but one example, in the novel Hamish Bond commits suicide; in the film, Clark Gable sails off into the sunset with Amantha. The tone of this idyllic conclusion is best suggested by the notes Page Cook prepared for the soundtrack record album of Max Steiner's lush melodies; in the "Finale," as they set sail, Cook notes, "A bit of the sea chanty 'Blow the Man Down' is tinted during the exciting conclusion as the musical pattern is tightened and becomes a surging and turbulent river of seething cross-sections of brass punctuation and dynamic tempi.

Sidney Poitier as Rau-Ru and Carolle Drake as Michelle in *Band of Angels*.

A beautiful *cor anglais* is heard above the music in a grand sentence that binds together the running motif beneath. The timpani attempt to take over the triplet theme from the trumpets (mute) but a superbly shaded movement ultimately attaches the love theme's return to the scoring and an expressive and exquisite orchestration attains the music's rhapsodic nature with a final statement of physical triumph."[62]

Sidney Poitier recognized quite well that his Rau-Ru was not a triumphant characterization. While Rau-Ru does have some powerful scenes defending Amantha Starr's honor against a would-be rapist who is white, and does slap her soundly because she's ashamed of her race and too abject in her love for the white master, Hamish Bond, even Poitier declares: "Period films haven't worked for me."[63] Rau-Ru's militancy fades in the face of Hamish Bond's blandishments, just as Poitier's role is eclipsed by the attention lavished on Clark Gable. *Band of Angels* was so intent on the vision of a poor man's Rhett Butler that it frankly didn't give a damn about anything else. Sophisticated audiences probably shared novelist John O. Killens' comic recognition of the absurd juxtaposition which could be made between current events and the hackneyed emotions the film plays upon. Killens especially noted one scene when "all of his [Hamish Bond's] happy faithful slaves were gathered there singing a song of welcome to old massa." As Killens described the audience reaction around him, "White people in the theatre were weeping, some slyly, some unashamedly, at the touching scene, when suddenly my friend and I erupted with laughter, because we thought that surely, in the time of Montgomery and Little Rock, this must have been put into the film for comic relief."[64]

A touch of humor might have helped, and surely couldn't have hurt, the next film project Poitier was involved with, an insignificant sermonette, *Mark of the Hawk*, filmed under the auspices of the Board of Foreign Missions of the Presbyterian Church, financed in post production by the Methodist Church of America, and finally edited by Universal International for a short and unsuccessful theatrical distribution only to be sold to television in an even more truncated version. No amount of reshaping could disguise the heavy-handed allegory, preachy style, and stilted diction of this well-intentioned plea for a return to brotherhood and religion. The message hadn't been one part of the artistic endeavor; the message was the film in this case.

Filmed in Nigeria, though no specific African

Sidney Poitier defends the honor of Yvonne DeCarlo against the attack of Patric Knowles in *Band of Angels*.

Sidney Poitier's final showdown with Clark Gable in *Band of Angels*.

nation is mentioned in this simple parable, *Mark of the Hawk* casts Poitier as Obam, the first Negro elected member of the legislative council, an honest patriot swayed by both the militant rhetoric of his terrorist brother, Kanga (Clifton Macklin), and the sweet gentle appeals of his wife, Renee (Eartha Kitt), a woman of mixed blood who would be glad to identify more and more with white people. Renee, whom Kanga accuses of being "not quite African," keeps house in the tradition of the English cottager, dresses in high heels and fancy gowns, and, in the only truly commercial sequence of the film, pines for Poitier in a stylized torch song. Most of the other characters in *Mark of the Hawk* are cardboard parodies of colonial life in Africa, who confront Obam at cocktail parties or political gatherings to debate the issues with him. There are, for example, the governor general (Gerard Heinz), who, although he's convinced the end of foreign rule is near, intends to maintain its laws as firmly as possible, and the white missionary, Craig (John McIntire), who converts Poitier to Christianity with a prolonged sermon on the need for Jesus in every revolution. And, of course, there's the aggressive white planter, Gregory (Patrick Allen), who wants to eradicate all dissident natives, and the meek and scholarly black Christian minister, Amugu (Juano Herdandez), whose quest for peace and interracial harmony demands nonviolent tactics.

As the sounding board for all this rhetoric, Sidney Poitier as Obam does manage some mighty speeches himself. Dramatically clad in African attire, which accents his handsome features and powerful personal presence, Poitier demands freedom from the legislative council in stirring words: "It is not that my people want to be treated freely or to move freely. My people want to *be* free. The history of their captivity, whatever its incidental benefits, burns deeply. Only name a date for freedom. Give us a timetable for independence. Set a date, any date at all, and we will work together toward the day when this country shall again be free." When the legislative council refuses even his first three demands, a broadened franchise, elected council, and an end to the curfew, Poitier storms out angrily to speak directly to his labor constituency. In the most powerful sequences of the film, Poitier then addresses the black miners in words, images, indeed in the rhythmic cadences of a traditional preacher: "They have taken your wealth and what have they given you in return? Do you have more land? Those of you who once plowed your own fields now work the land of the white planter. For what? For a white man's salary? Do you have more wealth? Those of you who work in a white man's mine, what is your wealth? Is it the few coins you receive at the end of a week's hard labor? Is this your wealth? If you are Africans, listen to me. If this is your country, listen to me. If this is your land, listen to me."

Minister Amugu interrupts Poitier's rally,

Sidney Poitier as Obam in *The Mark of the Hawk*.

however, to present "another side," and it is his doctrine of love and charity which dominates the rest of the film. Amugu reminds the miners that, though much of what Obam cites is true, and while "some would deny freedom to us," other white men have "given us the word of God that we may be freed from the jungle swamps of fear and sin." Speaking privately with Obam later, Amugu counsels the angry militant that "we must not become the men we condemn. How do we justify ourselves if, hated only because we are not white, we return that hatred simply because others are not black? We are working for a better tomorrow than that." Amugu's argument parallels in many respects the classic religious position on non-violence so eloquently developed by the spokesman of the Southern Christian Leadership Council, Dr. Martin Luther King, in his classic 1963 "Letter from Birmingham Jail": ". . . nonviolence demands that the means we use must be as pure as the ends we seek. I have tried to make clear that it is wrong to use immoral means to attain moral ends." Obam listens to Amugu, and to Craig's lengthy dissertation and exemplum glorifying the revolutionary nature of Christianity, a faith which assures, Craig stresses, that "you are not alone" and that all Christians are "more than conquerors." Craig adds the final touch to what is becoming the longest moral in the history of film: "The greatest gift one man can give another is Christ, but the giving is not enough. The Chinese Christian, the African Church, must know Christ is theirs. The gift is their very own to hold and give again."

Obam's newly acquired faith is quickly put to the test as white settlers discover a native plot led by Kanda and ambush the natives. Craig intervenes, as does Poitier, but the missionary is killed and the born-again African is hauled before a tribunal. Again, Poitier gets a chance to orate; this time, it's on God's behalf. Striding confidently to the bar, Poitier confesses his personal guilt and proclaims his new faith: "I am guilty because I yielded to hatred. . . . I wanted freedom; I gave only the desire to destroy. . . . I have failed the company of Christians. . . . I will now work with them toward our country's freedom and love and understanding. . . . I am no longer alone." As the music swells, Renee joins Obam, and the hawk, his symbol, ascends into the heavens.

Religious audiences no doubt found all this uplifting, but Poitier himself knew his career depended on finding more commercial material that still met his standards regarding humanistic content. Discussing this period in his career with

Sidney Poitier's final speech at the formal hearing in *The Mark of the Hawk*.

Frank Daley of the *Ottawa Journal*, Poitier recalled: "I did only those parts that I wanted to do. However, there was not a variety of parts offered to me. Even though I exercised free choice, I was exercising free choice over a fairly one-dimensional set of material. I didn't really have a wide range of offers."[65] If films like *Blackboard Jungle* and *Something of Value* made Poitier a major prospect for stardom and leading roles, he was still a star in search of a vehicle.

Notes to Chapter 1

1. Ralph Ellison, *Shadow and Act*, p. 275.
2. John Oliver Killens, "Hollywood in Black and White," in *White Racism*, ed. Barry Schwartz and Robert Disch (New York: Dell, 1970), p. 401.
3. Lawrence Reddick, "Educational Programs for the Improvement of Race Relations: of Motion Pictures, Radio, the Press, and Libraries," *Journal of Negro Education* 13 (1944): 368-69. This influential article is reprinted in Lindsay Patterson, ed., *Black Films and Film-makers* (New York: Dodd, Mead, 1975), an excellent anthology on black film distinguished by the high quality of its selections and the lucidity of its arrangement. Among the many recently published histories of blacks in films listed in the bibliography, the works of James Baldwin, Donald Bogle, Thomas Cripps, and Gary Null deserve special attention.
4. William Thomas Smith, "Hollywood Report—1945," *Phylon* (1945). Reprinted in Patterson, ed. *Black Films*, p. 134.
5. Donald Bogle, *Toms, Coons, Mulattoes, Mammies, and Bucks*, p. 202.
6. Fred Hift, "Negro Actor's Impressions of South Africa," sec. 2, p. 5, col. 5.
7. Carolyn Ewers, *Sidney Poitier: the Long Journey* p. 59.
8. These remarks are part of a seminar for educators Sidney Poitier conducted at Fordham University in the summer of 1967. A tape of that seminar was made available to us by Professor John

Culkin who presented the original program at Fordham. Most of the material on the tape was reprinted in the Los Angeles magazine *Pace*, under the title "Sidney Poitier Tells How He Got into Motion Pictures." An undated contemporary clipping of the *Pace* article can be found in the Sidney Poitier file maintained in the Film Study Center at the Museum of Modern Art.

9. Dennis John Hall, "Pride Without Prejudice: Sidney Poitier's Career," p. 40.

10. Martin Levine, "Poitier Sees His Film Role as Historic," *Record*, 26 July 1974, p. 20.

11. *Hollywood Reporter*, 2 August 1950; *New York Times*, 17 August 1950.

12. *New York Herald Tribune*, 17 August 1950; *Look*, 12 September 1950; *Life*, 4 September 1950.

13. Joseph L Mankiewicz, *More About All About Eve* (New York: Random House, 1972), p. 29.

14. Interviews with Lesser Samuels from unidentified sources form part of the *No Way Out* clippings file at the Lincoln Center Research Library, a part of the New York City Public Library system.

15. James Baldwin, *The Devil Finds Work*, p. 83.

16. Most of Fagan's writings have fallen into justified obscurity. This material is quoted in Andrew Dowdy, *The Films of the Fifties* (New York: William Morrow and Company, Inc., 1973), pp. 23-24.

17. Detailed records of censorship actions, containing voluminous correspondence and some vicious audience reactions, including hate mail of the most obscene sort, are part of the private files of the Motion Picture Association of America. The Chicago censor is quoted in *Life*, 4 September 1950.

18. This survey is cited by Smith, "Hollywood Report—1945" without further identification. Reprinted in Patterson, ed., *Black Films*, pp. 137-38.

19. Gerald Weales, "Pro-Negro Films in Atlanta," *Films in Review*, November 1952. Reprinted in Patterson, p. 47.

20. Nathan Leites and Martha Wolfenstein, "Two Social Scientists View *No Way Out*," pp. 338-91.

21. Sidney Poitier, "Dialogue on Film," p. 38.

22. Gordon Gow, *Hollywood in the Fifties* (South Brunswick and New York: A. S. Barnes, 1971), p. 98.

23. Baldwin, *Devil Finds Work*, p. 29.

24. James Baldwin, "Sidney Poitier," p. 58.

25. Hift, p. 5.

26. William Hoffman, *Sidney*, p. 86.

27. Hift, p. 5.

28. Helen Dudar, "The Sidney Poitier Story."

29. Baldwin, "Sidney Poitier," p. 52.

30. Alan Paton, *Cry, the Beloved Country* (New York: Charles Scribners, 1948), p. xviii.

31. Gary Null, *Black Hollywood: The Negro in Motion Pictures*, p. 164.

32. Bosley Crowther, "Unlimited Humanity: *Cry, the Beloved Country* Made Into a Fine Film," *New York Times*, 27 January 1952. p. 1, col. 8.

33. Edward Margolies, *Native Sons* (New York: J. B. Lippincott Co., 1968), pp. 14-15.

34. Stokely Carmichael and Charles Hamilton, *Black Power* (New York: Vintage Books, 1967), p. 45.

35. *Variety*, 23 January 1952; *Saturday Review*, 2 February 1952.

36. Details of the "Red Ball Express" and its achievements may be found in Ulysses Lee, *The Employment of Negro Troops: United States Army in World War II Special Studies* (Washington: Office of the Chief of Military History, 1966); and John D. Silvera, *The Negro in World War II* (New York: Arno Press, 1969).

37. Ulysses Lee, "The Draft and the Negro," in Schwartz and Disch, pp. 47-48.

38. Bogle, p. 255.

39. Murray Shumach, "Poitier Reflects on Oscar Victory," *New York Times*, 15 April 1964.

40. Hift, p. 5.

41. Frank Daley, "The Black Man's Burden," *Ottawa Journal*, 17 October 1975.

42. Daniel J. Leab, *From Sambo to Superspade*, p. 224.

43. Charles Higham, *Hollywood Camermen* (Bloomington: Indiana University Press, 1970), p. 93.

44. Hall, p. 42.

45. Richard Brooks, "Dialogue on Film," *American Film*, October 1977, pp. 47-48. The continuing controversy between Brooks and studio heads is best suggested by Dore Schary's letter to *American Film* published in a subsequent issue.

46. Bernard Kantor, Anne Kramer, and Irwin Blacker, *Directors at Work* (New York: Funk and Wagnalls, 1970), pp. 35-36.

47. Personal interview with Richard Brooks in Hollywood, 29 November 1966.

48. *Variety*, 2 April 1955.

49. Dowdy, p. 141.

50. *Motion Picture Daily*, 10 April 1956.

51. Royal D. Colle, "Negro Image in the Mass Media: A Case Study in Social Change," *Journalism Quarterly*, 45, no. 1 (1968); 56.

52. Part of a publicity interview in the pressbook for *Pressure Point*.

53. Edward Mapp, *Blacks in American Films: Today and Yesterday*, p. 45.

54. Robert Alan Aurthur's interview appeared in the *New York Herald Tribune*, apparently in February 1957, though the clipping in the Film Study Center of the Museum of Modern Art is undated.

55. *New York Post*, 30 January 1957, p. 66.

56. Robert Ruark, *Something of Value* (Garden City: Doubleday, 1955), p. 87.

57. *Newsweek*, 13 May 1957.

58. *Variety*, 26 April 1957.

59. Robert Penn Warren, *Band of Angels* (New York: Random House, 1955), p. 287.

60. Leslie Fiedler, "The Blackness of Darkness," in Seymour L Gross and John Edward Hardy, ed. *Images of the Negro in American Literature* (Chicago: University of Chicago Press, 1966), pp. 100-101.

61. Rene Jordan, *Clark Gable* (New York: Galahad Books, 1973), pp. 128-29.

62. Music notes to the original score composed and conducted by Max Steiner, RCA, LPM 1557, 1969.

63. Guy Flatley, "Sidney Poitier as Black Militant," sec. 2, p. 15.

64. Killens, in Schwartz and Disch, p. 401.

65. Frank Daley, *Ottawa Journal*, 17 October 1975.

RECOGNITION AND SUCCESS
(1958-1966)

Poitier's search for suitable roles in the late fifties and early sixties dramatically illustrates the two major commitments in his life, one to the civil rights movement and its vision of an integrated, charitable society, and the other to the craft of acting. Poitier struggles in this period for recognition first as a film artist and then as a black American. In a period which witnessed both the decline of the Hollywood studio and the collapse of its much-vaunted star system, and in a period when black identity and manhood were confronted by white hatred and racism, Poitier's twin goals of stardom and freedom made heavy demands on his inner resources, driving him to the analyst's couch and to moments of anger and despair. Much of this *angst* made it to the screen, too, in portrayals that sear their way into the consciousness and the memory. Poitier's art, his public recognition and success, were to help make the American screen free for black artists. His trailblazing efforts would

make it possible for visions as disparate as those of Gordon Parks and Melvin Van Peebles to follow.

Civil rights agitation kept Poitier in the headlines during this period; he was reported picketing construction sites, bailing demonstrators out of jail, conferring with civil rights leaders, addressing fund-raisers, decrying racist policies, and scoring the discrimination in the entertainment business. Poitier was one of the few entertainers who spent as much time on the front page as he did in gossip columns. Dramatic news photos revealed him in court aiding picketers arrested at the South African Embassy, in Africa celebrating native independence, in Berlin representing the United States, and at graveside mourning Kennedy and, later, King.

Like Paul Robeson before him, Poitier became a public figure, a spokesman for his race, a role he did not relish or enjoy and often felt quite uncomfortable in, begging reporters to ask him about his art and not just his race. Occasionally, however, notoriety gave Poitier an opportunity to speak his heart to both blacks and whites. Chatting with Barry Gray, for example, at the time of the violent school disruptions in Little Rock, Poitier could remind all Americans who the real heroes were. Commenting on a famous news photo of one small young Negro girl walking to classes past a threatening white crowd, "a white lynch line," Poitier lauds her unwavering commitment: "I saw the face of this child, the quiet dignity of this fine face—goose bumps raised on my arms, tears came to my eyes—this was a picture of courage—of indomitable spirit." His wife, Juanita, then reminded Poitier of another fact, especially important though not evident in the photo: "Real courage came from her father—who stood in the crowd, and who, a moment before, must have said: 'You must walk through that mob—you must show courage, a belief in God and the Law.' "[1] Juanita knew Sidney was teaching his own daughters that courage, faith, and pride. Through columns like Barry Gray's, but especially in his films, Poitier was embodying a similar "quiet dignity," and, like other civil rights leaders of the day, he was preaching "a belief in God and the Law."

Prejudice and racial conflict were, of course, more than abstract issues of morality for Poitier; they were, he told Frank Quinn in 1958, things "I have to live with and I can help with."[2] For all his attempts to help, Poitier was also required to "live with" discrimination, to cope with awful obstacles to his career. In 1950, he told columnist Archer Winsten his dream of a new Hollywood, a Hollywood which would "integrate Negroes into the American scene, not as Negroes, but as persons."[3] It would be many years until anything resembling that integration would occur. And, while no one can accurately gauge the effect of racism on the development of Poitier's own career, the comments of Hollywood pundit Mel Gussow are worth considering. Looking back on the film *No Way Out*, Mel Gussow feels "One of the most curious things about *No Way Out* and probably the best comment on the discrimination of its time is Poitier's sensitive, disciplined performance—his first in a movie. If he had been white, he would have rocketed immediately to stardom. Instead, he took a back seat for another fifteen years."[4]

Interestingly, this racist backseat prepared Poitier for stardom much as the now declining studios had previously groomed their finest talents in progressively more difficult roles until they were ready emotionally and artistically to carry a whole film or series of films. Like Bogart, Davis, Hepburn, Tracy, Gable, and so many others, Poitier found himself first an apprentice, then a journeyman, and finally a master craftsman; if his films from 1950 to 1957 established his presence, those from 1958 to 1966 made him a screen personality, a recognized success, and, from 1967 on, they finally made him a superstar. Poitier himself understood the old studio system largely as a result of his work with its demigod, Clark Gable, in *Band of Angels*. On set, Poitier admitted he was totally overwhelmed by Gable's professionalism: "I was in awe of him. He was incredibly disciplined, the ultimate professional. He had gone through the years of training actors were no longer getting, and certainly aren't getting now. When we talked at all, it was about acting."[5] Typically, Poitier was trying to learn everything he could any way he could. In 1959, he described himself to the British press as an actor practicing his craft on "the do-it-yourself plan." With no studio to nurture him and with racial barriers impeding him, Poitier actively sought ever more challenging roles; he was literally fighting his way to stardom, cognizant, as he put it, that "an actor has to go after ever part he wants to play" and that, once he has the part, "he has to work on it. He has to do-it-himself indeed."[6]

Opportunities were opening up, however, in the late 1950s for enterprising young actors and ambitious producers. Television, anti-trust actions, and high overhead had weakened the studios, new cameras and films made location shooting easier, censorship standards were loosening, and an age of independent productions was at hand. One of the most socially conscious of the new cinema moguls, Stanley Kramer, offered Tony Curtis and Sidney Poitier a chance to work with him on a project called *The Defiant Ones*, a film which would change all their lives and leave its mark on the whole American film scene.

Kramer had never wanted to be a producer at all, but was tired of the whole "departmental hassle." As he put it, "I became a producer at a time the producer was the boss. He controlled what was made, how it was made, the marketing, everything, and so in order to do what I wanted to do I had to be the boss."[7] Kramer went through valid machinations and chilling financial adventures to bring his product before the cameras. He seemed undaunted by impossible odds, insurmountable obstacles, and hopeless situations. His will overcame it all; despite the worst possible weather conditions and the arduous demands of the script, Kramer pushed Curtis and Poitier through the shooting of *The Defiant Ones* in thirty-one days. Poitier has often referred to this role as his most

Sidney Poitier and Tony Curtis run from the law in *The Defiant Ones*.

physically demanding one; yet, he knows it was his biggest break. Musing on his whole career and the changes in black participation in Hollywood films, Poitier told Martin Levine that "Where I am today is a result of efforts of an awful lot of people, and all of the black actors in films today, much of their opportunities can be traced back to guys like Stanley Kramer who were white and liberal and had a hard time trying to get certain things initiated."[8]

The script for *The Defiant Ones* had, as Sidney Poitier explained in 1958 to Irene Thirer in an article she headlined "Poitier Boosts Screenwriters," been "kicking around from studio to studio for two years." Then Kramer read it at a lunch with the authors, bought it, and sent it to Poitier. Poitier recalled that, within three hours, he read it and made a deal with Kramer because "It was right. It was great—not only for me, but as a picture story with suspense, imagination, realism, and integrity."[9] What Poitier failed to tell Irene Thirer as he "boosted" these screenwriters was

that Nathan E. Douglas was the pseudonym for Ned Young, the blacklisted writer. *The Defiant Ones* began, then, with Kramer and Poitier challenging the blacklist; the result was an Oscar for the script, a small part in the film for Ned Young, whose face appears in close-up under the opening credits in an ironic visual commentary on his pseudonym, and a substantial weakening of the last vestiges of the infamous ideological blacklist.

The Defiant Ones comes perilously close to being too ideological itself. A generous interpretation would call it a fable with symbolic characters; other critiques might be less gentle with its didacticism and predictability. The narrative begins when a truck crashes on a rainy road, freeing two chain gang prisoners, a muscular black named Noah Cullen (Sidney Poitier) and an obstreperous white named John "Joker" Jackson (Tony Curtis). They are chained to each other, so their flight from pursuers must be a mutual enterprise. Behind them are a determined sheriff (Theodore Bikel), some angry civilians, and some well-trained dogs; in front of them is a torturously difficult landscape, with raging rivers and treacherous clay pits, as well as small settlements where vigilante justice is the rule. All the while, Noah and Joker are fighting each other, for Noah's pride and integrity just don't reconcile with Joker's brutal, racist attitudes. Finally, the two of them come to an isolated house where they find a woman (Cora Williams) and an eleven-year-old boy (Kevin Coughlin). The woman separates them, and tries to trick Noah with wrong directions as she plots to run away with Joker. Joker will not desert Noah, however, because their escape has made them partners, and, when he goes to Noah's assistance, the boy shoots Joker. As the posse closes in, Noah must choose between escape on a freight train and staying to help his wounded white buddy. He chooses to stay, and cradles Joker in his arms, singing "Long Gone" as he awaits their recapture.

Stanley Kramer obviously knew he had a "message film" in *The Defiant Ones*. Speaking about the film in a private discussion in Hollywood, he declared that "In *The Defiant Ones*, it was my purpose to stress the idea about all human beings having basically the same nature. To show this, I took two individuals on the lowest possible level in order to tell the glory of the sacrifice for a man, to stress the need they have of one another. This is symbolized by the chain they wear together." Kramer felt there was no reason to fear messages at the box office. As he explained, "The exhibitors and distributors—and the people in general—did not object to social content, only to unsuccessful pictures. Their motivation may be mostly commercial. My problem is to make a film which I myself would like and which at the same time is commercially successful." Commercial success was getting harder and harder in 1958; as Kramer put it, "a 'want-to-see' product is not enough; today, it's got to be 'got-to-see!'" Almost ten thousand theaters closed between 1950 and 1960, and nearly three-quarters of the films released in the late fifties lost money.[10] Fortunately, *The Defiant Ones* proved a "got-to-see"

Poitier comforts Curtis in *The Defiant Ones*.

film, a commercial success that cemented the relationship between Kramer and Poitier which would result in the later films *Pressure Point* and *Guess Who's Coming to Dinner.*

Poitier proved himself a "got-to-see" screen personality in *The Defiant Ones.* At the outset, Poitier's role was considered a subordinate one, and he credits Tony Curtis with insisting they share equal billing: "I don't think I rated it at this point in my career and the producers originally had planned to give Tony star billing by himself. After all, he is a big star and I'm not. He said he didn't want to be up there all alone in this picture."[11] This generous action by Tony Curtis is all the more remarkable when one remembers that *The Defiant Ones* was one of the principal films in which Curtis tried to broaden his repertoire and change his image. As Poitier told Irene Thirer, Curtis was quite eager for this role: "Did you know he wanted to do this role so badly, and didn't want to be considered too pretty in it, so he wears a false nose? He's so fine that nobody will be commenting on his good looks from now on—though he is handsome; they'll always note that he is a good actor." Curtis was never quite able to shake the pretty-boy image despite his fine acting. Ironically, however, the action sequences of *The Defiant Ones* and its close-ups revealed that Poitier himself was more than just a fine actor: he was also a strikingly handsome man. *Time* magazine commented on this years later when they noted that Poitier's screen presence had overwhelmed even the charm of America's two most popular leading men: "A final, and equally inevitable, point about him as an actor is that he is so overpoweringly good looking that he quite literally pales the white actors beside him, even including Paul Newman in *Paris Blues* and Tony Curtis in *The Defiant Ones.*"[12] Media theorists like Marshall McLuhan posited that the black face was more appealing on screen; Poitier was demonstrating this hypothesis in film after film. Poitier was a handsome new screen idol, an athletic and graceful black man dominating a white screen.

All the advertising material for *The Defiant Ones* emphasizes the physical confrontations between white and black, the agonizing fights between Poitier and Curtis. Chained together, facing each other with huge muscles tensed, they seem gladiators in the arena. The copy promised "chained fury" and desperate escapes from "the law and each other." Sometimes the warfare is even pictured in the bedroom, as Noah watches Joker and the woman embrace and "listens for the dogs!" All this material has a subtext, highly reminiscent of John Cogley's quip that movie posters suggest the whole film industry is "simply a highly organized scheme to merchandise French postcards that talk." *The Defiant Ones* so emphasizes the physicality of racial tensions that many critics like Parker Tyler treat homo-erotic themes in the film, or see it, as James Baldwin does, as a none-too-subtle comment on the white man's masculinity crisis; even Pauline Kael calls it *"Thirty-Nine Steps"* in drag."

Viewed as a physical test of black and white, *The Defiant Ones* has a structure quite revolutionary for a Hollywood film: Noah Cullen's stature, as portrayed by Poitier, is constantly growing in relation to that of his white companion. At the beginning, Noah is on the defensive against the aggressive, arrogant Joker. By the end, he dominates the white man completely: Joker is being comforted by Noah. His wounds have made him immobile and broken his spirit. The moral reserves and physical ones are all Noah's as he sings "Long Gone," his voice growing bigger and stronger as he stares at the posse in defiance.

The artists involved in *The Defiant Ones* did not, however, dwell on the tensions in the film. The message, Poitier declared, was a gentle call for brotherhood: "It doesn't pretend to give a cure-all for hate-thy-neighbor but it does say 'I'm going through a hell of a lot with you, and still don't dig everything about you, but in some ways you're not so bad after all.'" Americans in 1958 found both this message and the film "not so bad after all," and *The Defiant Ones* won the Oscar for best picture of the year; Stanley Kramer won the Oscar as best director, and the script was declared best script. In a landmark move, however, something even more dramatic happened in the Academy: Sidney Poitier became the first black ever nominated for the best actor award. Though he didn't win, *The Defiant Ones* brought him to the forefront of American actors.

Around the world, *The Defiant Ones* and Poitier's performance garnered great acclaim. The Berlin Film Festival lauded Poitier with the coveted Silver Bear award for best actor. In Mexico, a hostile, anti-United States audience was quieted by the film. Even in Moscow, where Poitier accompanied the film himself, audiences were, he discovered to his surprise, willing to let the film influence their thinking. As he described the screening at the Moscow Film Festival, it was an emotional triumph: "The thousands who saw the picture—at a dollar a head, by the way—were wholly caught up in the story of a white man and a Negro. They caught not only the picture's statement about race relations but also the idea

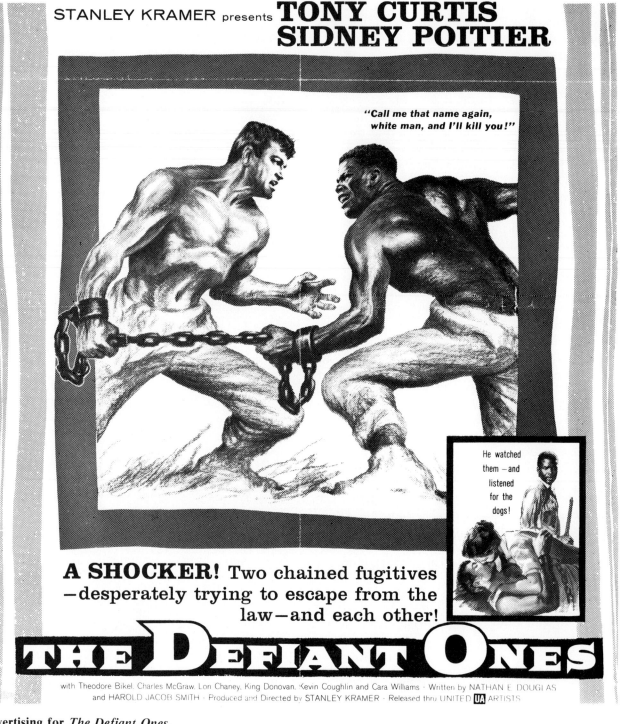

STANLEY KRAMER presents **TONY CURTIS**
SIDNEY POITIER

"Call me that name again, white man, and I'll kill you!"

A SHOCKER! Two chained fugitives —desperately trying to escape from the law—and each other!

He watched them —and listened for the dogs!

THE DEFIANT ONES

with Theodore Bikel, Charles McGraw, Lon Chaney, King Donovan, Kevin Coughlin and Cara Williams · Written by NATHAN E. DOUGLAS and HAROLD JACOB SMITH · Produced and Directed by STANLEY KRAMER · Released thru UNITED UA ARTISTS

Advertising for *The Defiant Ones*.

that such a picture could only be made in a free country, unafraid of self criticism. It was a great, wonderful experience feeling that mass of people surge up to the seats where we were after the showing. It was proof positive of the power of films as international links."[13]

At home, *The Defiant Ones* was also conquering old hostilities. This best picture of 1958 became one of the earliest "cross-over" movies, capable of attracting both black and white audiences. Reporting on the Chicago debut, for example, Walter Lister observed that it grossed over fifty thousand dollars the first week, about ten thousand dollars more than the Roosevelt

Theatre's previous record, and "had a premier audience that was evenly divided between Negroes and whites and is now changing to about 60 percent whites. The audience also includes an unusually large number of women, about 40 percent, for an adventure picture."[14] The effects of Poitier's dramatic role on these record audiences are hard to chronicle, but some indication of his powerful presence and the hope it generated for blacks might be found in black actor Yaphet Kotto's reminiscences that "it was seeing *The Defiant Ones* in which a black actor, Sidney Poitier, costarred with a white actor, Tony Curtis, with such success" that formed his own ambition to be an actor.[15] Undoubtedly, many other blacks and whites were transformed by *The Defiant Ones*.

For 1958, *The Defiant Ones* was a transforming vision and the "best picture"; it must be viewed in the context of the era. Later decades would find America so changed that the film might no longer be an appropriate fable. Interviewed in Hollywood in 1966, Stanley Kramer admitted his work might be "outdated," and acknowledged that he "would not make it today in the same way." Similarly, the innovative educator Richard A. Maynard, in his text *The Celluloid Curriculum*, confessed that "when I saw it in 1958 as a teenager, it genuinely moved me," but seeing it again in 1970 and assigning it to classes generated new insights and problems: "There is something unnerving about that ending. . . . Today's Black kids simply won't swallow that ending. 'Why did Poitier fall off that train? He was free.'"[16] Like many of Poitier's films, *The Defiant Ones* is intimately bound to its day, reflecting social attitudes and sometimes introducing new images. The give and take of racial change in American forms the matrix for his art, and his art in turn transforms its context.

Progressive critics in 1958 did note the rather pyrrhic nature of Poitier's sacrificial victory in *The Defiant Ones*, but the very way they framed their analysis and the blunt replies from the original screenplay writers only accentuate the different perspectives of the liberal fifties and the separatist decades to follow. Commenting on Bosley Crowther's own questions about the ending of *The Defiant Ones*, Ned Young and Harold Jacob Smith wrote the following lines in a letter which Crowther edited and reprinted with no attribution to the blacklisted Ned Young:

> Our simple thesis is that from common struggle toward common goal, man realizes his interdependence with other men. . . . The real triumph . . . lies in the two men overcoming a set of moribund mores learned from an abnormal social structure, which had

originally made them think they were enemies. The song, far from being a senseless one, is sung by Poitier, the Negro, in the opening scenes as an individual gesture of defiance and a source of annoyance to Curtis, the white man. At the end, the song is a gesture of strength and comfort with which the white man identifies. . . . We maintain thematically, the men are liberated—liberated from hate. . . . The question of freedom in its broadest sense can only be resolved by the people everywhere in the land, not by the authors. It is, indeed, today being resolved in Virginia, perhaps, tomorrow, in Little Rock.[17]

As the question of freedom was resolved in Selma and Birmingham, Watts and Newark, *The Defiant Ones* seemed more and more out of kilter with the times.

Poitier's next major film project, *Porgy and Bess*, also seemed to be the wrong film in the wrong decade. But Hollywood patriarch Sam Goldwyn wanted to film the Gershwin classic, and, as Poitier discovered sadly, whatever Goldwyn wanted, Goldwyn got. Poitier obviously didn't want to play a singing cripple, and, to avoid a major contretemps, he took a minor role in the low-budget independent production, *The Virgin Island*. The role had one big advantage for Poitier: it carried him off to the Caribbean and far from the seventy-five-year-old Sam Goldwyn.

For the filming of *The Virgin Island*, Poitier had a chance to return to the familiar environs of the Bahamas and to reassume his native West Indian

Sidney Poitier as Marcus in *The Virgin Island*.

accent. Cast as Marcus, a happy-go-lucky islander, Poitier plays a rather minor role, occasionally aiding the principals of the film, a newly wed couple, in their attempts to flee civilization to their own, private, "virgin" island. In this traditional romantic fantasy, the writer and playboy who sweeps a young British tourist off her feet is John Cassavetes, while the girl is given an uninhibited bouyancy by Virginia Maskell. When they're not splashing around in the nude, the two build a rather sturdy shelter, innocently help some smugglers, and endure the visit of Tina's rather autocratic mother, hilariously overplayed by Isabel Dean. Everything works out well, of course, for Mr. and Mrs. Robinson Crusoe. The stodgy commissioner (Colin Gordon) eventually becomes less menacing, their baby is delivered despite the storm, and Ruth (Ruby Dee) and Marcus are comfortably paired off. The sun then shines as brightly as it always does in travelogues.

For Poitier, *The Virgin Island* was really little more than a paid vacation. Critics all lauded his work, some noting that he did seem to enjoy "sending up" the role. Marcus was Poitier's first comedic role, and foreshadows his later directorial and starring roles in light comedies. Mostly, however, the film was a temporary escape from Sam Goldwyn and a reminder of the dream of "lallygaggin" which haunted his earlier years. Around this time, Poitier was still telling columnists like Whitney Bolton how nice it was to bask in the sun of a tropical island where blacks were free to be themselves and rule themselves:

Have you ever seen Saint Thomas? You must. It is so great. I want to buy property there and build a house. I want my wife and children to know it. It has a native life such as no other West Indian island. It is native to the core. The tourists are a sort of overlay, a plating. They do not disturb the tenor of native life and when the season ends it goes back to being an island for the Negro. Not that it ever stopped. I feel my people have a place, a way, a demonstration there, that we can govern ourselves with dignity and reason and that the burgeoning ferments in Africa and elsewhere in the decade to come will benefit from what is done at Saint

Ruby Dee and Sidney Poitier in *The Virgin Island*.

Virginia Maskell questions Sidney Poitier in *The Virgin Island*.

Thomas. . . . I have a feeling there such as no other place gives me. I am with my own and we work in a common self-respecting destiny.[18]

This feeling of well being and casual self respect obviously animates Poitier's performance in *The Virgin Island*.

No such personal fulfillment accompanied Poitier's performance in the ill-fated Sam Goldwyn production of *Porgy and Bess*. The whole enterprise remains an episode Sidney Poitier would rather forget; he rarely discusses the film at all now. The memories of it are too painful. One can read behind the press releases and news reports and construct a rather clear picture of what happened. It is not a pretty commentary on the power of big money and influential producers in Hollywood.

Porgy and Bess first appeared in a novel by Dubose Heyward, notable only for its local color and the dialect of its black characters: "It sho pay nigger tuh go blin' in des world. . . . Porgy ain't got much leg, but he sho got sense." Porgy the cripple proved, however, to have theatrical legs when Dubose Heyward and his wife Dorothy adapted the novel to the stage in the late twenties. George Gershwin saw the play on Broadway and asked Dubose Heyward and Ira Gershwin to prepare lyrics for a folk opera based on the play. In 1935, after many travails, *Porgy and Bess*, the opera, reached Broadway, where it was a moderate success. Revived successfully thereafter, it finally caught the attention of Sam Goldwyn, who, according to his faithful biographer, Arthur Marx, paid $650,000 cash and ten percent of the gross receipts for the rights to film it. According to Marx, Goldwyn pledged all the profits to charity and intended the whole produciton as a fitting musical and cinematic memorial to George Gershwin.[19]

Black America was appalled at the idea that Catfish Row could be resurrected at this late date. The crap-shooting, whoring, loose-living, lazy world of "I've got plenty of nothin' and nothin's plenty for me" hardly reflected contemporary black people's aspirations. For most concerned blacks, *Porgy and Bess* was, in the words of Harold Cruse, "the classic example of cultural exploitation practiced by whites on the Negro under capitalist culture. Its distorted social and aesthetic values have been projected ever since as the outstanding 'American' musical accomplishment."[20] Harry Belafonte refused the role of Porgy in the film because he didn't want to play "any role on my knees," and that's where most black Americans thought the characters in *Porgy and Bess* were.

Poitier knew Belafonte had turned the role down, and he was also aware that civil rights organizations were opposed to the project; so, as he told Bea Smith, "I read the script. I realized it wasn't the kind of material I do best, and I thought I'd leave it alone."[21] Poitier's public refusal to do Porgy was featured in the *Amsterdam* (N.Y.) *News* which quoted him as saying: "As a Negro I have a certain sensitiveness and as an artist I have certain responsibilities. Certain things I will play, but they must be constructive to my life as a Negro. *Porgy and Bess* is always played in a restrictive range for the actor. There is simply one crap game too many in it." The paper editorialized about Poitier's decision, proclaiming it "a ringing answer to those who say that Negroes are not willing to pay for their self respect and freedom. . . . The Negro race has been dignified by his creed."[22]

On 4 November 1957, Sam Goldwyn announced that Sidney Poitier had been signed to play Porgy, and this in spite of all activities by the Council for the Improvement of Negro Theater Arts to scuttle the project by urging nonparticipation. The confusion deepened when, a week later, on 11 November 1957, the *New York Times* reported that Sidney Poitier had left the film because he had been denied script approval by Goldwyn. Goldwyn was quoted as saying script approval was "out of the question" because "it is my money that is going to finance it and I will decide how it is to be made." Poitier was unavailable for comment, since he was on location for *The Virgin Island*, but he did issue one public statement on 18 November through the public relations firm of Seltzers, O'Rourke, and Sabinson: "*Porgy and Bess* is a classic and Mr. Goldwyn will do it justice. But for me, as a creative artist, I just do not have sufficient interest in the piece. I am not enthusiastic about the part. Still I'm sure Mr. Goldwyn will assemble a superb cast and produce an excellent film.''

The next stages of this mini-war between an Oscar nominee and a legendary movie kingpin are shrouded in mystery. Loyal Goldwyn biographer Arthur Marx describes a meeting between Sidney Poitier and Sam Goldwyn with a sinister simile, but in a generally sugar-coated, tongue-in-cheek rhetoric:

> He [Poitier] wanted to hear Goldwyn's concept of the movie, from Goldwyn's own lips. This was a little like a fly inviting himself to dine with a spider. More stubborn actors than Poitier had been caught in Sam's oratorical web. . . . Sam promised that Porgy would be a great movie, that Poitier would never have a greater opportunity, that he would emerge from it a superstar and his black brothers would be beloved and respected for their courage and dignity in standing up against racial prejudice and its consequent poverty. Suddenly Poitier's resistance crumbled . . . sounding more like a Baptist minister than a Hollywood actor, he said ''I will come to you completely pure, virginal, and unprejudiced.''[23]

Most show-business types and all of Poitier's biographers suggest that Goldwyn's silver tongue brandished more threats than promises. Poitier has made few public statements about the matter, but one can read between the lines in his refusal to be interviewed by Mike Wallace about this meeting and in a *Variety* report that Poitier declined to ''specify the career threats (or the individual who made them) that eventually led to his returning to make a picture that many Negroes regard as a racial slur.'' As *Variety* reported Poitier's attitude, he'd rather drop the matter entirely: ''I feel that is a dead issue and ought to be left alone.''[24] On 11 December 1957, the *New York Times* reported that Poitier was ''to play Porgy after all'' and gave Poitier's new history of his role in the project. Initially, he declared, he was ignorant of the material: ''When Mr. Goldwyn offered me the part, I accepted in good faith. At that time, I knew nothing of the property except what I had heard from friends. I wrote home and asked them to send me the book of the play. Unfortunately, the only thing they could find was an album of records. From the synopsis on the album jacket, I decided that the role was not for me and quite possibly the story would be injurious of Negroes.'' When he was denied script approval, Poitier said, he quit the project because of his fears. Then came the meeting with Goldwyn and director Rouben Mamoulian, where, Poitier reported, ''I discovered

Sammy Davis, Jr., Dorothy Dandridge, and Sidney Poitier in *Porgy and Bess*.

that it was not their intention to injure anyone. In fact, I found them almost as sensitive to the problem as I am.'' Script approval was no longer necessary, Poitier said, because ''I am confident that Mr. Goldwyn with his characteristic good taste and integrity will present the property in a sensitive manner.'' Obviously, this fly had quite a dinner with the spider; even these press statements are a little too ''completely pure, virginal, and unprejudiced.''

Under Rouben Mamoulian, the preparations for *Porgy and Bess* were an arduous affair. Normally eager Poitier complained to Bea Smith that ''it took oh, ages to film. There were so many rehearsals. Then the fire came and everything had to be postponed. Then came the interruptions with the change of directors.'' The fire Poitier mentions completely razed almost two million dollars worth of sets, and occurred just before Goldwyn fired Mamoulian and hired Otto Preminger. The latter action stirred up weeks of trouble with the Directors Guild and precipitated a walkout by Leigh Whipper, president of the Negro Actors Guild of America. Whipper charged that Preminger was a director ''unsympathetic to my people,'' a man who ''insulted the Negro people of

America as a whole.'' Sidney Poitier had his own run-in with Preminger the very first day he came to the set; an eyewitness gave the following account:

> . . . it wasn't like a sound stage—it was like a guerilla war. The thing was the accent—whether the cast would talk in the 'yassuh' Negro dialect of the original script, or whether they could talk in standard English. Now, Preminger has a pretty autocratic reputation and everybody was tensing up. . . . Suddenly I noticed that Sidney's speech was slowly changing from Catfish Row to Mayfair. Everybody followed his cue. Preminger cleared his throat—and Sidney got positively Shakespearean, so much that the script girl said ''My God, they're all crazy.'' Sidney got on his feet . . . and said ''All right, Otto, shall we talk it over?''[25]

All Poitier's struggles and conferences, however, couldn't save this star-crossed project.

Porgy and Bess was shackled by its roots in theater and opera. Preminger shot the whole film in boom shots; some charge this was to keep Goldwyn from editing it. Preminger and Goldwyn never really got along, and disputes over money and technique may have affected the director's work. At any rate, the whole project seems stagey, and this artificiality is accented by the vocal dubbing of the principal roles. Robert McFerrin provides Porgy's voice in the songs, and Adele Addison sings Bess. All the rehearsals in the world couldn't hide lip syncing or being an organic unit back to these characters. And with a fragmented Porgy and Bess, as well as a dramatic rather than cinematic set, the film sinks of its own weight.

Sidney Poitier promoted *Porgy and Bess* at the time of its release with atypical exaggerated praise. He rationalized the use of ''a wonderful voice from the Metropolitan Opera,'' arguing that ''the combination of the two separate talents will be ''much better,'' and constantly proclaimed the work ''one of the classic romances of literature.'' In the

Dorothy Dandridge and Sidney Poitier in *Porgy and Bess*.

fanciest hyperbole of his career, Poitier actually proclaimed Porgy the role of his life: "Other roles may come and go, but I expect the role of Porgy in my new film . . . to stay with me for a lifetime. Ten years from now, somebody will call out 'Porgy,' and I'll stand up and salute and say 'Yes sir.' I don't know why, but Porgy is a role that gets under your skin. . . ."[26] Actually, ten years later, when he was no longer "yes-sirring" Sam Goldwyn, Poitier did tell Joan Barthel the truth: "I hated doing *Porgy and Bess* but pressure was brought to bear from a number of quarters and there was a threat of my career stopping dead still. I toyed with the idea of being steadfast, but I weakened ultimately and I did it. I didn't enjoy doing it, and I have not yet completely forgiven myself."[27]

Poitier didn't enjoy his next role very much either, but it, too, proved another step towards success and kept his career from stopping dead. Actually, Hal Bartlett's independent production is almost exactly what its title suggests, *All the Young Men*, a showcase for the diverse young personalities in the news, all parading as a group of stranded Marines in Korea. There's Mort Sahl, for example, the comedian who, as the cynical soldier, works a whole nightclub routine in between the melodramatics and the battle footage. And there's Ingemar Johansson, the newly crowned, heavyweight champion boxer who plays a soft-hearted strongman and sings sentimental melodies. Even teenage singing idol James Darren is there, as an innocent youth, toting his phonograph everywhere he goes.

All these stereotypes haunt an equally cliched plot, unimaginatively directed by Bartlett. Sidney Poitier plays Towler, a sergeant whose platoon is sent to protect a hill pass high in the mountains. During the mission, the officer in charge is mortally wounded and appoints Towler to succeed him in command. The Marines, especially Kincaid (Alan Ladd), a veteran ex-sergeant recently demoted, and Bracken (Paul Richards), a southern bigot, resent the idea of being under a black. "I'm from a town where black men do the digging," Bracken chides, "They are not born to be in command." Towler gradually wins everyone's respect, however. Rescuing a young newcomer from a dangerous mine field, Towler inspires his men to hold the pass despite winter storms and

The critical transfusion from Sidney Poitier to Alan Ladd in *All the Young Men*.

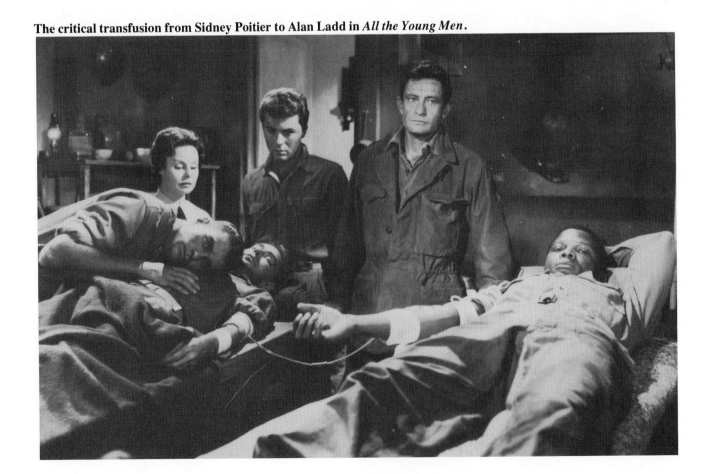

Sidney Poitier, James Darren, and Alan Ladd in *All the Young Men*.

massive enemy attacks. "I have not asked for the job," he reminds them, but he assures them it will be done. When night falls and the men relax, Towler carefully inspects their position in an abandoned farm house, talks cheeringly to soldiers on watch, and hesitantly accepts an American Indian's offer to scout the area alone. Only Kincaid remains hostile and tells Towler, "I'm jumpy and sick of you in my guts"; Towler spits back, "You can go to hell." When the Indian scout is killed, Towler carries him back in his arms and buries him in a very emotional scene. Soon thereafter, he reveals his war weariness to a native Korean: "We have seen too much death and we don't understand why." When racist Bracken tries to rape this woman, Towler intervenes and warns him, "The next time you enter here without direct orders from me, I will shoot you."

Gradually, Towler's superhuman courage, commitment, and integrity mold the platoon into a cohesive unit just in time to repel a massive enemy attack. Kincaid is badly wounded and needs a transfusion after his leg is amputated; Towler provides the blood. Even Bracken is moved by Towler's sacrifices and his steadfast determination

that the unit hold its ground because "thousands of men depend" on the mission. Hopelessly trapped, the unit fights on, saved at the last minute by an aerial attack on Christmas Day.

Sophisticated critics scoffed at all the pieties and heroics which dot *All the Young Men*, with the *New Yorker* critic declaring that "Poitier, a highly gifted actor, does all that could be expected in a role that he should never have got himself into in the first place: he keeps a straight face." Poitier himself was even less enamored of his own heroics and his starring role than were his sternest critics. On this film, he felt, "I was unable to work . . . even on an elementary level, with any degree of imagination. The producer seemed willing to settle for what would have been the first step in a stage rehearsal and print it."[28]

Poitier's experiences with *Porgy and Bess* and *All the Young Men* soured him temporarily on acting and jogged his ambition to produce and direct. Real autonomy would never come, he was learning, as long as he depended on traditional filming arrangements. Blacks just weren't managers on Broadway and in Hollywood, and the contemporary actor was, he felt, "becoming more and more the interpreter rather than the creator, and what creativity he has is subject always to such things as time and budget. The attitude too often is 'We don't want it good, we want it quick.'" This attitude, Poitier told Joe Hyams, made him eager to produce and direct himself, for "If I enlarge my capacity, I may be able to develop a talent which will assure me a place in an area where I want to spend my life. . . ."[29] Poitier's first efforts as a stage and screen director and producer would come in the next decade, but their inspiration came partly from the frustrations that crowded his ascent to superstardom.

Many of these frustrations were dissipated, however, and much balm provided for the insults of Sam Goldwyn, by Poitier's next acting achievement. He was to bring the immensely talented Lorraine Hansberry and her play *A Raisin in the Sun* first to Broadway and then to the Hollywood screen. The original contract for *A Raisin in the Sun* was actually negotiated at Philip Rose's card game, with Poitier the principal agent in assuring that this play by a black woman would come to the Great White Way with the first black director for a Broadway show. Given the overwhelming success

the play garnered and its immediate inclusion in the canon of significant modern dramas, it is worth remembering, as James Baldwin notes, that *A Raisin in the Sun* "would never have been done if Sidney had not agreed to appear in it."[30]

Poitier consciously chose this play because it was, in his words, "exemplary of Negro life" and because it was written by "someone spawned by the Negro community." Lorraine Hansberry's father had bought a house in the middle of a white neighborhood, not far from the black Southside of Chicago. His action and subsequent reactions resulted in one of the most important housing cases ever to reach the Supreme Court of the United States, *Hansberry* v. *Lee*. His daughter, Poitier knew, appreciated the problems blacks faced at work, in their neighborhoods, and at home. Her play, *A Raisin in the Sun* went far, Poitier observed, in defining male-female relationships in the ghetto and in celebrating the matriarchy which resulted from economic pressures. As Poitier told a group of educators, "When things are difficult in a Negro family, a Negro mother can usually find work. And the man cannot. The Negro mother in most instances, consequently, is the wheel of the

Sidney Poitier as Walter Lee Younger in *A Raisin in the Sun*.

family." *A Raisin in the Sun* was, he felt, a "tribute to the black mother."[31]

The framework for this tribute involves a deceptively simple conflict: How should the Younger family use the ten thousand dollars from their father's life insurance payment? Should it go to buy the mother's dream house in a hostile white neighborhood, to pay for medical school for Beneatha, the brilliant daughter, or to finance a business venture for Walter Lee Younger, the eldest son, an impatient, frustrated man? In this drama of a Chicago Southside family, Walter (Sidney Poitier) lives with his mother Lena (Claudia McNeil), his wife Ruth (Ruby Dee), his sister Beneatha (Diana Sands), and his son Travis (Glynn Turman) in a shabby, claustrophobic apartment where he constantly dreams of freedom. Walter works as a chauffeur, but schemes to be an independent businessman. While he adores his mother, loves his wife, and cherishes his sister, he is often rude to them because of all the constant psychological pressures.

His obsession, his dreams, and his gullibility generate the major crisis; he loses all the money his mother has entrusted him with in a swindle, and then is sorely tempted to swallow his pride and sacrifice family dignity by accepting a bribe from the white citizens committee which will pay the black Youngers not to leave the ghetto for a white community. At the critical moment, however, Younger finds a new reserve of black pride, a reverence for his own roots, and promises that all the deferred dreams will be realized. His family, he asserts, will struggle with dignity for their new home and new careers:

> My father almost beat a man to death once because this man called him a bad name or something, you know what I mean? . . . Well, what I mean is that we come from people who had a lot of pride. I mean—we are very proud people. And that's my sister over there and she's going to be a doctor—and we are very proud . . . . What I am telling you is that we called you over here to tell you that we are very proud and that this is—this is my son, who makes the sixth generation of our family in this country, and that we have all thought about your offer and we have decided to move into our house because my father—my father—he earned it.

Walter himself has also earned the respect of wife, sister, mother and son, for, as his mother notes, "He finally come into his manhood today, didn't he? Kind of like a rainbow after the rain. . . ."

A Raisin in the Sun proved a personal triumph for both Sidney Poitier, who electrified audiences with his dynamic performance, and for Lorraine

Advertising for *A Raisin in the Sun* asked "Guess Who's Moving Next Door?" with a jaunty picture of Sidney Poitier.

Hansberry, whose life would be cut short tragically just as she was demonstrating to the world what it was "to be young, gifted, and black." One of the most touching moments in theatrical annals occurred on opening night of *A Raisin in the Sun*. As the theater rang with tumultuous applause, Sidney Poitier leapt from the stage to escort Lorraine Hansberry to the stage; his stardom, he knew, owed much to the fine material she had provided. Given the right roles, he could rise to the top of his profession and engender black pride. Black writers like Lorraine Hansberry must be developed, Poitier knew, if black art was to thrive.

Even with the popularity of the Broadway production and uniformly positive critical reaction, the film project of *A Raisin in the Sun* was fraught with financial risks and physical difficulties. Given American racial attitudes and problems, the film was, as Gary Null notes in his history of *Black Hollywood*, the "first really memorable film of the sixties made about blacks" and a rather daring and unusual product: "Columbia Pictures, which financed the film, knew that it was a risky project. Although Lorraine Hansberry's play, on which it was based, had won the New York Drama Critics Award, the film could be expected to make no money in the South and might be a flop abroad. The risk was taken because Columbia thought that it might prove to be a great film."[32] During the shooting in Chicago, where about one-fifth of the footage was prepared, the crew had major difficulties lining up locations; landlords were threatened, and many contracts were cancelled when the nature of the project was discovered. One student fraternity forbade the use of its name in the film, and even the University of Chicago allowed shooting on campus only after pledges that the university's name would not be mentioned in the film. Back in Hollywood, the black cast found suitable housing almost impossible to procure. Things were so bad that Poitier went to columnist Murry Schumach of the *New York Times* to make his complaints part of the public record. The Schumach article, "Poitier Says Bias Exists on the Coast," which appeared 19 August 1960, offers clear evidence that the housing question, which is so important to the play and film, was much on everyone's mind. Even the daring advertising campaign for the film featured a full-page portrait of a jaunty Sidney Poitier determinedly walking along under the headline "Guess Who's Moving Next Door!" It would be a few more years till Poitier would be "coming to dinner," but *A Raisin in the Sun* put all America on notice that there was a new black pride, a determination based on years of sacrifice. The Younger family and, symbolically, all black families were intent on sharing the good life as equals. As Poitier declared to a startled white racist in his role as Walter Lee Younger: "We don't want to make no trouble for nobody or fight no causes—but we will try to be good neighbors. That's all we've got to say." Similar statements by

Sidney Poitier reveals his anger, despair, and humiliation to Joel Fluellen in *A Raisin in the Sun*.

young activists in the Midwest, including leaders like Father Groppi, were to result in jail terms and violent confrontations.

Poitier still considers the role of Walter Lee Younger one of the most challenging and rewarding in his long career. Discussing his craft as "his life" in a most revealing symposium in the *New York Times Magazine* for 1 October 1961, Poitier outlined the steps he follows in "working on a part" to "bridge the gap between theory and experience." The critical questions, Poitier feels, concern the kind of life a character lives; to act, Poitier argues, you must first totally understand both your character and his milieu. To prepare for the role of Walter Lee Younger, for example, Poitier notes that he began with endless readings of the script: "I read it, naturally, many, many, many times and I knew, generally, after ten or twenty readings, what the circumstances of the play were. I knew what the individual characters were like, generally. I understood my character kind of generally."

The next step, however, is to make all this general understanding more concrete, more specific. To move from vague character type to fully realized individual, you must understand, Poitier urges, all the contributing elements, the "driving forces" of the man: "You must find out what are his political, social, economic, religious milieu and how they contribute to the personality, idiosyncracies or whatever." In the case of Walter Lee Younger, you would find, as Poitier did, " . . . a Negro man 36 years old, living in Chicago on the South Side—which of itself is quite significant in the building of a character, because only a particular kind of Negro lives on the South Side in his particular kind of circumstances, see?" Always, for the actor there are more questions, more probes, more explorations. Poitier insists that, to play Walter Lee Younger or any complex role, the actor must keep digging into motivations and the influence of environment: "Why is this man living here? Is he here by choice? What is his relation to his religion, if he has one? What is his relation to his economic disposition? Is it one in which he finds enough elasticity to function and maintain his manhood or is it a constant badge or remembrance of his inadequacies—you follow?" The answer to all these questions should be in the script, or, if they are not, Poitier feels the actor should find answers which are true to life and compatible with the script. Armed with all this knowledge, Poitier asserts, the actor can move to the final stage, a period of discovery and performance: "Now with this kind of information, I then

Claudia McNeil and Sidney Poitier in *A Raisin in the Sun*.

proceed to familiarize myself with the pros and cons of his life and his wants. I try to experience them, so by the time I'm ready to perform, I don't go in a corner—at least I don't have to go in a corner and concentrate and conjure up some mysterious magic. I walk on the stage and it happens.''

What happened in *A Raisin in the Sun*, on both stage and screen, was one of Poitier's finest moments, truly one of his most moving characterizations. Talking to Joe Hyams, Poitier declared the whole filming process one of the highlights of his life: ''The entire thing was an experience rather than a performance. If I didn't feel good about a scene I played, the director gave me the prospect of doing it again and if necessary again and again.'' And from his fellow actors, Poitier drew rich new inspiration: ''The rest of the cast were truly incredible. I never worked with actors so good. I know every line, every nuance of that show, but when I watched them work I became hooked all over again.''[33] Audiences and critics were similarly

hooked all over again. The reviews of the film all emphasized Poitier's restless energy, a force that seemed to burn its way through the screen; Stanley Kauffman spoke of a ''tigerish, impassioned'' Poitier, moving ''with a marvelous sense of dramatic rhythm,'' who gave *A Raisin in the Sun* ''an agony that is almost too big for it and stretches it at the seams.''[34] The effect this had on general audiences is best reflected by an anecdote in *Ebony* magazine, which quoted one white moviegoer observing that Poitier ''made me feel envious that I wasn't born black.'' *Ebony* also pictured Roderick Mann, the British drama critic, as being so ''struck by the dramatic impact of Poitier's complexion'' that he wrote: ''You forget sometimes how black a Negro can be. Then you see Sidney Poitier and wham! It hits you hard. For that face of his is all African, all Ebony.''[35] Poitier magically transformed the frustration of Walter Lee Younger into his own dramatic achievement, and his powerful physical presence reminded all viewers that black pride was a new reality on the American scene.

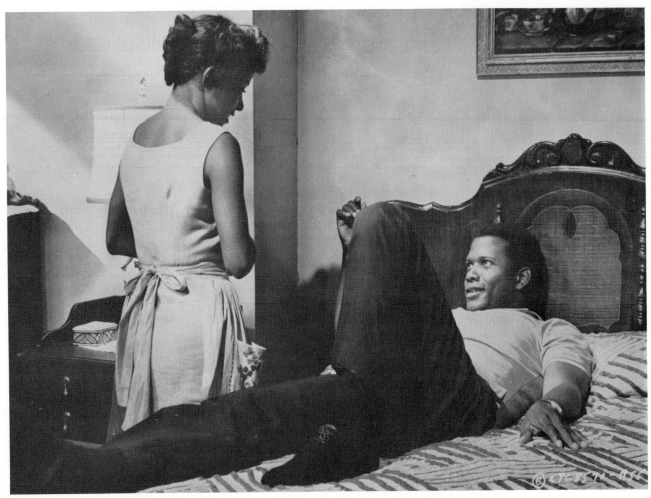

Ruby Dee and Sidney Poitier share a dream in _A Raisin in the Sun_.

By the early 1960s, Poitier was emerging as a full-fledged Hollywood personality, a feature player on screen and in the gossip columns. Even Art Buchwald used the Poitier persona in his hilarious parody of gambling at the Cannes Film Festival. As envisioned by Buchwald, notorious gambler Poitier was a suave, cosmopolitan, but intemperate loser: "Red came up again, and again, and again. Now Poitier tried to get at the roulette wheel and we had to hold his arms. He was so mad he was crushing chips in his hands."[36] Poitier was also in the news because of his public appearance before Adam Clayton Powell's House Committee on Education and Labor. Poitier told the assembled legislators and journalists that he was the "only male Negro among 13,000 members of the Screen Acting Guild who is able to make a living exclusively from work in motion pictures." On Hollywood sets, Poitier reminded his audience, "I am the only Negro . . . except that sometimes there is a shoeshine boy." Despite all his achieve-

ments and his many roles, Poitier declared it was ". . . no joy for me that I am used as the example to prove they really don't discriminate."[37]

Even Poitier's career hit some snags around the time of this testimony, and, as Dennis John Hall observed, "seemed to be plagued with films that never materialized."[38] Poitier was, for example, to have played opposite Spencer Tracy in _The Devil at Four O'Clock_; there were also plans for a western with Harry Belafonte where Poitier would play a black gunfighter. Another project to be directed by John Cassavetes transferred the Othello drama to the context of the famous 99th Pursuit Squadron, an all-black unit of daredevil aviators. Paramount even announced _99th Pursuit Squadron_ as part of their scheduled productions. There was also talk of Poitier doing Shakespeare on Broadway, and of a production of _Brownstone, Brown Girl_ financed by black backers. Poitier was very enthused about this last project, which he described as "a tender and wonderful story about a first and second

Stephen Perry, Ruby Dee, Claudia McNeil, Diana Sands, and Sidney Poitier in *A Raisin in the Sun*.

Sidney Poitier as Eddie Cook in *Paris Blues*.

generation West Indian family in Brooklyn.'' The story was, he pointed out, actually about ''a man who lives with a most unrealistic dream of someday going back to his island.'' Poitier was ready to play that man, and the demise of the project may have robbed film fans of the definitive study of a man caught between two cultures, between his own blackness and the lures of assimilation, a man not unlike Poitier himself.

Themes of assimilation and identity appear in Poitier's next screen appearance as Eddie Cook, an expatriate jazz musician living in Paris, in Martin Ritt's highly commercial, romantic melodrama *Paris Blues*. Most of *Paris Blues* is, however, just what the title suggests, escapist entertainment in the tradition of *American in Paris, Funny Face,* and *Gigi*; much of the time, Poitier and his costars, Paul Newman and Joanne Woodward, do little more than identify landmarks like Notre Dame or walk through quaint streets as an excuse for more moody, travelogue-like footage of the City of Lights. Music, specifically jazz, dominates the action. Louis Armstrong, for example, has a long sequence all to himself, and the soundtrack for this ninety-eight minute film contains a total of fifty-one minutes of Duke Ellington music. Add to this the shots of Paul Newman's band in performance, and one can see the need for advertising posters stressing Joanne Woodward's black negligee, Paul Newman's brass bed, and Sidney Poitier's jazz saxophone, and featuring such heated copy as: "They play their hearts out in a story of young lovers . . . and suddenly the big sound of emotions exploding!"

There may have been bigger emotions exploding in America, however, if Martin Ritt had stayed closer to the original novel or to his own opening footage. The plot of *Paris Blues* starts off hinting strongly at mixed-racial love affairs. Things soon conform to Hollywood convention, however, with a romance between Newman and Woodward, the whites, becoming the film's critical focus, the main love story, while Poitier and Carroll serve as subordinate players, black foils in a secondary romantic interlude. *Variety* noted the sudden shift in plot development in its 27 September 1961 review, declaring that the picture "might arouse some passive criticism from more radical quarters, where it may be felt that a potentially bold interracial theme has been abortively handled and cautiously diluted for mass consumption." As finally released, the development of the romances in *Paris Blues* obviously suits popular taste: at the conclusion, Newman tells Woodward he cannot follow her to America because he must be true to his music. Poitier, on the other hand, tells Carroll he is rethinking his voluntary exile and his expatriate status.

While some critics comment on the fact that *Paris Blues* marks Poitier's first appearance as a romantic lead in a film, the secondary role he and Diahann Carroll play in the film suggests both the powerful appeal of Newman and Woodward to white audiences and the reticence on the part of filmmakers to picture a virile black man and a sensuous black woman. Stanley Kauffmann reminded his readers, for example, that, in the original novel, there is only a black couple; the movie adds the whites. As Kauffman put it, Sidney Poitier is the character "whose story this ought to be."[39] Even in the new conception, there is a

Diahann Carroll and Sidney Poitier as lovers in *Paris Blues*.

marked contrast between the presentation of the two love affairs. With the Woodward-Newman combo, the accent is heavily sexual. In contrast, the pairing of Poitier and Carroll seems curiously platonic and unrealistic. Donald Bogle, a perceptive black film historian, has especially harsh words for Carroll's portrayal. She has become, he charges, "closer in speech, dress, mannerism, looks, and life style to the great white ideal than any black actress. . . . On the screen, not one hair was out of place. Not one word was mispronounced. There was not one false blink of her eyes. So perfectly planned and calculated was she that Diahann Carroll seemed more an automaton—some exquisite bronze Barbie Doll—than a leading lady . . . one more dehydrated and lifeless accruement of a decadent capitalist society."[40]

The only overt political and social commentary in *Paris Blues* revolves around the question of Eddie Cook's flight from America and its race problem. Like James Baldwin, the Poitier character is an expatriate soured on the American scene. The scenes where this issue is discussed by Poitier and Carroll ring surprisingly true, given the unrealistic tone of most of the rest of the film. A good deal of understatement is involved in their critical exchange:

> Eddie: Look! Here nobody says Eddie Cook, Negro musician. They say, Eddie Cook, musician, period. And that's all I want to be.
>
> Connie: And that's what you are here.
>
> Eddie: That's what I am here. Musician, period and I don't have to prove anything else.
>
> Connie: Like what?
>
> Eddie: Like . . . because I'm a Negro, I'm different . . . because I'm a Negro, I'm not different. Who cares? Look—I don't have to prove either case. Can you understand that?

Eddie's comments parallel Poitier's own remarks about his role in *Paris Blues*. The critical question in the film, he argued, was not whether he was black or white, or whether the racial conflict was fully resolved. After all, it was, in Hitchcock's words, "only a movie": "Now, there's no preaching about race, no tub-thumping about tolerance. But we talk it around just like we all do in our living rooms. George Glass and Walter Seltzer

They play their hearts out in a story of young lovers... and suddenly, the big sound of emotions exploding!

Advertising for *Paris Blues*.

(executive producers of *Paris Blues*) said their point of view is that movies are made for entertainment—so that's the way we did this one. Anyone who wants to know which of us is colored and which is white can just look up on the screen and there we are. Nobody is going to get me all mixed up with Paul, so we didn't make a fuss about it."[41]

Audiences couldn't ignore Poitier's blackness, as he well knew; there was always to be a "fuss" about this Negro pioneer. After the unsuccessful attempt to mold a traditional romantic image in *Paris Blues*, Poitier found himself again cast in a "problem" picture where the sociological and thematic concerns were at least as important as the aesthetic issues. Once again, also, Poitier was working for producer Stanley Kramer, whose ad campaign and public statements proclaimed his intentions of making *Pressure Point* the commercial success *The Defiant Ones* was. In essence, *Pressure Point* merely moves the black-white conflict from physical terms to mental ones, from the rough terrain of the South to the equally torturous and uncharted reaches of modern psychotherapy. In *Pressure Point*, Poitier portrays "The Doctor," a prison psychiatrist, confronting "The Patient," a rabid, anti-Semitic, racist fanatic played by teenage recording idol Bobby Darin in a dramatic change of pace from his normal casting. Significantly, all the characters in *Pressure Point* lack names, a clear indication that the dramatic opposition is less between individuals than between general human attitudes and ideologies. Kramer had, in fact, altered the original conception of the analyst from a Jewish character to a black one, hoping, he admitted, to develop "greater explosive qualities through such a switch."[42]

A convoluted narrative structure intensifies the allegorical emphasis in *Pressure Point*, for the film opens with a white psychiatrist (Peter Falk) coming to his black superior, Sidney Poitier, for advice on a

Poitier the jazz musician in *Paris Blues*.

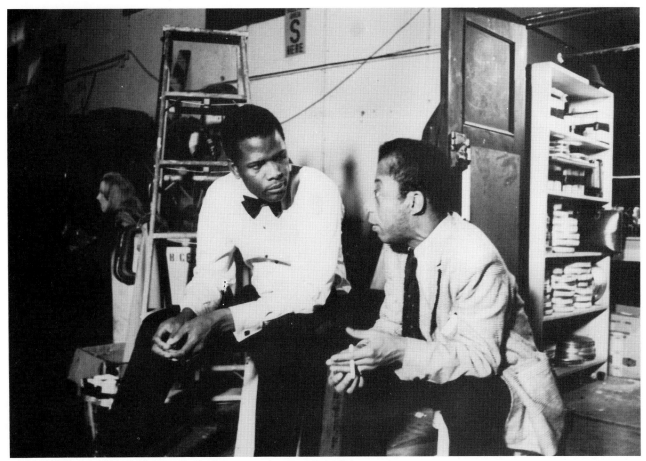

Sidney Poitier and his good friend, James Baldwin, chat behind the scenes.

case. To counsel Falk, Poitier recounts his own earlier difficulties handling Darin's case; given this framework, the main action of the film, Darin's therapy, is clearly labelled a case history, a narrative recounted by the successful Poitier to teach a beginner the tricks of the trade. Told in flashback, the encounter between Darin and Poitier seems a modern parable, a cautionary tale for the Age of Anxiety.

As analyst, Poitier has assumed the white man's burden; his responsibility is to analyze and treat Darin, a despicable young sadist and leader of the German American Bund, who was arrested in 1942 for his Nazi activities. *Pressure Point* pictures the desperate psychological warfare between an aggressive, violent, insulting brute and a composed, self-controlled doctor. Darin has the juicier part: he is all insults and vitriol. Poitier's role is, for the bulk of the film, more constricted: he is all patience and understanding during the treatment. Darin's mental illness mocks Poitier's sanity as the patient reminds the doctor how

society will keep him, too, in a prison of diminished possibilities; Darin warns Poitier, for example, that he will always be a prison doctor since "Psychiatry is an expensive thing. Your people can't afford it, you know. So the best you can be is a prison psychiatrist with the worst office they've got." Darin displays a remarkable capability to goad the doctor about just the problems most American blacks were confronting in the early 1960s. He asks Poitier: "What have you got? What can you do? Can you walk on a bus or a streetcar or a train or sit down with a little dignity like a free human being, like a free man? . . . Can you go to the school where you can get it [an education] best? Maybe you see a house you like and you've even got the money to buy it. Can you live there?" As long as Darin is his patient, Poitier remains cool and professional. Poitier later told Columnist Frank Daley he did the movie *Pressure Point* just to establish that a black could be a real psychiatrist: "I did a very obscure movie . . . because it had to do with a black psychiatrist who

Sidney Poitier as the doctor in *Pressure Point* with Bobby Darin.

was not a caricature. He was a real, honest-to-goodness psychiatrist and I wanted to say that little bit."[43]

Poitier's character, The Doctor, also gets to say his own little bit before the film is over. When his white colleagues reject his recommendation and declare Darin a sane man, Darin comes to the office, an officially cured man, and insults Poitier once more. Freed of his clinical chains, Poitier explodes in a fervent patriotic declaration that "This is *my* country!" and orders Darin to "Get out!" Contemporary audiences were divided on their response to this climactic speech. As Albert Johnson observed in his article "The Negro in American Film: Some Recent Works," the white audience, "dazed and moved by the unusual image of the symbolic Negro as a modern Patrick Henry, roars its spontaneous approval with deafening

applause," while the black audience "is contemplative, tensely moved, and silent."[44] The correctness of Poitier's sentiments and evaluations is reinforced by the next narrative twist, for, when the film shifts back to the present, Poitier appears in his role as teacher and supervisor and reveals that, soon after his release, Darin murdered an elderly man, a tragic proof that Poitier's analysis was correct.

While Poitier's role as "The Doctor" in *Pressure Point* was, as Edward Mapp notes in his *Blacks in American Films*, the "only Negro characterization in a leading role in American motion pictures in 1962," and was well received, Poitier himself wasn't pleased with this reworking of *The Defiant Ones*. The ideas in *Pressure Point*, he thought, were, by 1962, cliches, mere fodder for the box office. "I found it devised strictly for box office potential,'' he told interviewers at the Berlin Film Festival, where he attacked the film rather vehemently: ''In many American films, even those we're doing now, there is a singular lack of truth . . . . Much of what we do in life is built on myths and we seek the wrong things. Basic truths often get lost in our paying court to values that propel us into vacuums . . . such as making films like *Pressure Point*. The kind of character I played in *Pressure Point* was not important. The overall intent of the film was to make money, not to illuminate, to educate, to enlighten anybody. It was a film designed expressly to earn a buck.''[45]

All American movies are, to one degree or another, of course, designed to make money. Poitier was actually facing the same dilemma that the black musician he portrayed in *Paris Blues* had so eloquently described: some films, like *Paris Blues*, tried to picture Poitier as a black and therefore ''not different,'' while others, like *Pressure*

Point, strived to envision Poitier as a black and therefore ''different,'' better, more accomplished. Poitier was tired of proving any case, of being forced to embody either hypothesis. He was actively seeking new material which would allow him greater freedom and a broader artistic range when Ralph Nelson approached him with the most uncommercial property imaginable, a gentle parable of a black handyman and a displaced group of East German nuns stranded in the Arizona desert.

Nelson's religious drama, based on the novel *The Lilies of the Field* by William E. Barrett, was the first feature production venture by Nelson's own independent company, and it entailed considerable risks for all involved. Discussing the project in Hollywood in a 1966 interview, Nelson recalled that he ''had to work very hard to find somebody to finance the project. Practically all the major companies turned it down, because they did not see any commercial chance for such a story about a

Advertising for *Pressure Point*.

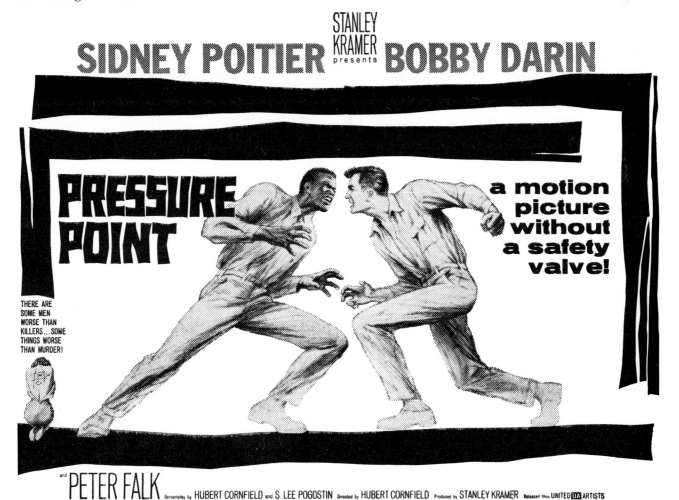

71

Bobby Darin as the racist psychopath confronts Sidney Poitier in *Pressure Point*.

group of nuns and a Negro boy.'' Hollywood was undoubtedly wary of a film treating the two touchiest problems on the American scene: Catholicism and race relations. *Lilies of the Field* may now seem a trivial sentimental fantasy, but its themes were controversial in a nation soon to witness Kennedy's Catholic Camelot and in an America about to suffer the horrors of a Birmingham Sunday.

Finally, however, Ralph Nelson convinced United Artists that his success with *Requiem for a Heavyweight* merited the risk of an investment in *Lilies of the Field*. When United Artists budgeted the film for a paltry $250,000, Nelson accepted the challenge, and set off to convince Sidney Poitier, an actor he had never met, to take a big cut in salary. Their first interview, was Nelson recalls, rather dramatic, for, when Poitier heard the shooting schedule and the budget, ''he was incredulous. He slid right off the sofa and onto the floor

and said 'You're kidding.'" Nelson wasn't joking, and Poitier recognized that the role of Homer Smith in *Lilies of the Field* was a part he had to play. He later told interviewers that he would have assassinated anyone who tried to take the role. Homer Smith, he knew, was the starring role he had been waiting so long to find.

The deal Ralph Nelson and Sidney Poitier eventually negotiated involved a deferred salary payment and a share of the grosses of the film. As Poitier recalls it, when Nelson told him about the funding problem, he immediately responded ''Well, I'll tell you what: Don't give me any money, give me ten percent of the gross.''[46] Nelson agreed and United Artists concurred. Subsequent events would prove this contract one of Poitier's wisest artistic and financial decisions, for *Lilies of the Field* would make Poitier one of America's wealthiest performers and the first black Oscar winner as best actor.

Ralph Nelson always knew this project was "something we could not afford not to do," and he had convinced some of Hollywood's finest talents to work with him, including Earnest Haller, who had done the cinematography for *Gone With the Wind* and *Stella Dallas*. Yet Nelson is the first to admit that "Sidney Poitier was the man who made it possible." *Lilies of the Field* was more than a financial gamble for Poitier; his whole career was on the line. As he told a Variety interviewer on 2 October 1963, *Lilies of the Field* was the first commercial feature where he was "the lone and carrying star." The fate of the film, Poitier declared, "will determine my bankability." Success for *Lilies of the Field* meant stardom and fame; failure would have meant a longer apprenticeship and perhaps obscurity. Poitier went ahead on the project even though Ralph Nelson was not yet one of Hollywood's big names, even though the story, based on a little-known novel, was quite unusual for an entertainment picture, and even though the budget was so small the film had to be shot in two weeks.

Lilies of the Field is, as some critics note, a modern *Going My Way* in blackface, describing the odyssey of a young veteran, Homer Smith (Sidney Poitier), whose used Cadillac is his only fortune. As he wanders through the dusty roads of Arizona looking for a job, he meets five nuns in an isolated house. They have escaped the Communist takeover in Eastern Europe and live under the stern command of Mother Maria (Lilia Skala); their mission is to build a church and to serve the Mexican workers in the area. Invited to share their meager supper, Homer befriends them, and even gives them language classes. All the while, however, Mother Maria schemes to have Homer stay and build a chapel. Homer accepts the challenge, and the film chronicles his victory over the elements, poverty, and himself.

Sidney Poitier as Homer Smith in *Lilies of the Field*.

Lilia Skala and Sidney Poitier match biblical references in *Lilies of the Field*.

Homer builds his chapel in *Lilies of the field*.

When the chapel is completed, Homer departs to the chords of a black spiritual and a triumphant "Hallelujah!"

The charm of *Lilies of the Field* is hardly suggested, however, by its rather trite plot. Its real accomplishment is in the humor and humanity of its small episodes; it is an intimate film, aglow with heartfelt affection and moving sentiments. Most of these small inspired moments belong to Sidney Poitier, whose boundless energy keeps the film bouncing along. There is, for example, a marvelous verbal duel between Mother Maria and Homer as they discuss his lack of a salary for his huge job. Each quotes the Bible in an almost medieval and somewhat incongruous colloquium. This exchange gives the film its title, as a thickly accented German nun declaims to a lovable black itinerant about the glories of Solomon paling before "the lilies of the field." Other episodes include a rather charming ride to Sunday Mass, an encounter in a tavern where it is opined that "I don't think God has sent a black Baptist to Catholic nuns," some hymn singing where Negro spirituals vie with "Ave Maris Stella," and some lively and imaginative language lessons.

At the center of all this activity stands Sidney Poitier as Homer Smith, the black man responsible for the renewed activity and the new vitality. Homer gathers the material for the chapel; he works another job to finance it; he organizes the whole project. He's so dedicated, hard-working, and single-minded that it almost becomes a "one-man chapel"; he has to be convinced to accept any help at all. This chapel is to be his personal achievement, a reflection of his worth and the grandeur of man. When whites obstruct his plans, Homer is quick to respond, chiding one with the comment, "Hey boy . . . you need a good man?" Homer is that good man, and his whole community, the nuns, the Mexicans, the whites, need him.

The most moving moment in the film comes when Homer tries to define what the chapel means to him, why he works with monomaniacal frenzy. Homer declares: "I was going to build it myself . . . . I wanted to really build something. You know? Well . . . well, maybe if I had had an education, I would have been an architect or even an engineer, see? You know, and throw the Golden Gate Bridge across San Francisco Bay and even maybe build a rocket ship to Venus or something." Homer's very speech cadence, his constant small interrogatories are reminiscent of Poitier's own speaking style. It could well be that just as Homer had his chapel, Poitier had this one role to prove it all. The Academy of Arts and Sciences was to praise him with its Oscar, but, even before the award, Poitier declared this his finest role ever. It made him the first actor ever to win the Silver Bear at the Berlin Festival for a second time; his first Silver Bear had been for *The Defiant Ones*.

Bosley Crowther came very close to a perfect description of Poitier's achievement in *Lilies of the*

Lilia Skala baptizes Sidney Poitier in *Lilies of the Field*.

Sidney Poitier in his Oscar-winning role as Homer in *Lilies of the Field*.

Field when he wrote in his 2 October 1963 review of this "disarming modern parable" that "Beneath all his casual bravado, his candid irreverence for the nuns and his air of amused indignation at knowing that he is being used, there is this need for affirmation, this heat of racial pride that puts an aura around him. It is idealistic and sentimental, but it is warm." In 1963, racial pride for blacks was in and of itself a revolutionary statement. In the summer of that year, Harris Polls shows that 85 percent of white Americans believed Negroes laughed a lot, 75 percent believed that Negroes had less ambition than whites, 70 percent believed Negroes had looser morals than whites, 60 percent believed Negroes lived in untidy houses, and a majority believed Negroes had less native intelligence.[47] Poitier's portrayal, his energy, charm, intelligence, and common sense, challenged these prejudices; Homer Smith was a black all audiences could respect and admire.

Stanley Adams, Dan Frazer, Lilia Skala, and Sidney Poitier in *Lilies of the Field*.

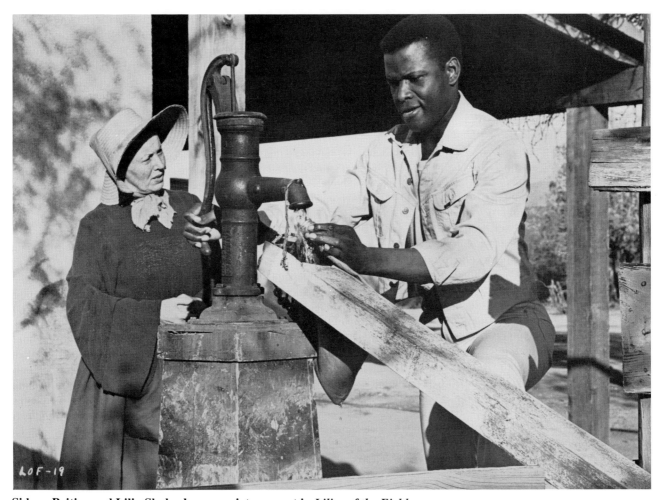

Sidney Poitier and Lilia Skala share a quiet moment in *Lilies of the Field*.

Ralph Nelson knew this personal appeal, this immediate emotional rapport between Poitier and audiences, was the real key to the success of *Lilies of the Field*. It is, he mused in an interview, "through Poitier's personal appeal that the current of sympathy is established. This seems to me, apart from his professional ability as a talented actor, his greatest contribution for better inter-racial relations." Nelson went on to speak of his own litmus test for the film. One of the crew members had mixed feelings about integration and the whole racial question haunting America; he was, in Nelson's words, "a Southerner without special sympathy for Negroes." So, during the first projection of a rough assembly of the rushes, Nelson paid special attention to this man's reaction. When the crew member commented "I liked that Homer," Nelson declared, "I knew we had won the battle." In the battle for the hearts and minds of America, Homer Smith as portrayed by Sidney Poitier was receiving almost everyone's

"Hallelujah!" Blacks and whites praised Poitier lavishly for this positive statement in an age of despair. Nelson reported that privately Poitier told him that "wherever he went, at airports, on the streets, at any public place, people—and not only blacks—were thanking him for his interpretation"; this tumultuous reception, Nelson notes, convinced Poitier of the power of film so much so that Poitier believed "that *Lilies of the Field* has done more for integration than the Washington March." On the record, Poitier himself was more guarded, but he did tell Mel Gussow of *Newsweek* that the Christian affirmation of *Lilies of the Field* was such a magnet largely because it dispelled the dread and despair so evident in a country in turmoil. People were coming in droves to see *Lilies of the Field*, Poitier felt, "to be exposed to a feeling, a reassurance that love is a force in human affairs. They read the newspapers and magazines, which are loaded with the coldest kind of exploration of man's week-to-week evolution and give off antihuman vibrations. They're stone cold, man!''[48] In this icy atmosphere, one remembers the words of Bosley Crowther about this film: "It is idealistic and sentimental, but it is warm."

In his personal life, Poitier was haunted by the "antihuman vibrations" that chilled American in 1963 and 1964. Undaunted, however, by public and private pressures to keep quiet, Poitier gave southern interviewers the same message he gave to all Americans. Civil Rights was his issue, and demonstrators were his heroes. As he told Margaret McManus in a discussion of "Television and Social Responsibility" published in the 20 October 1963 *Louisville Courier*: "It takes a good bit of courage and forbearance to go into a lunchroom in the South and sit down at a counter and be knocked off the stool, and get up, and sit down at the counter again without striking a blow or saying a word." Poitier was displaying a similar courage and forbearance as he tried to move Hollywood to open more of its roles and more technical production jobs to blacks. In an interview with Eddie Kalish, for example, published in *Variety* in October of 1963, Poitier acknowledged that film producers must think of profits and entertainment first, but then he urged they should face up to a "moral" choice and integrate, for "in any time of stress throughout history, the people have turned to their artists and thinkers for answers." If Hollywood sent out the right message, America would respond, Poitier felt. Thus, on all his films, Poitier told numerous interviewers, "I insist on other Negroes being involved in some capacity. That's the most I can do, short of being in production where I would be able to exert large influence. I have not yet had that control." The control would come in a few years; meanwhile, every Poitier performance set a new precedent, and gave him more power to swing open studio gates.

In April 1964, Sidney Poitier experienced what he publicly proclaimed was the "most remarkable night of my life." All precedents were shattered as the first black man ever was named best actor of the year; the most powerful performance of 1963 had come, all of Hollywood agreed, in *Lilies of the Field*. As usual, Poitier was modest about his chances before the actual ceremony, and told interviewers that "I had no idea I was going to win. When Anne Bancroft called my name, it was the likes of which I had never experienced in my lifetime. I felt I had to keep my wits about me or I would pass out. Once I had collected myself, I had to struggle to maintain my composure because I was wandering close to tears."[49] Most of the press found the real news that night in the racial significance, in the incongruity of a black Oscar winner in a country more and more seen as racist throughout the world; Poitier's elegance contrasted sharply with the pictures of poverty and of violence that had clogged television screens. The Academy Awards ceremony was far from the fire hoses, clubs, and dogs, yet Poitier was obviously a civil rights champion. Under the incessant grilling of journalists, Poitier stoically declared: "I have been asked if I think my award has racial significance. I think only that it has democratic significance in this country we live in."

Poitier was angered that his acting achievements were somehow overshadowed by questions of race. For the next few weeks he endured countless interviews, all going over the same questions about his role as spokesman for his race, his ability to achieve despite obstacles, his feelings on politics and national policies; Poitier finally exploded in rage because so little attention was being given to his art. At a large news conference, Poitier reminded the assembled press that "I live close to the skin, everything I do I have to feel with all my emotions. For seventeen years I played nothing but Negro bit parts. And before that I did menial jobs around the theater just so I could be close to actors. . . .Ever since I was 17, I wanted to be the best. At the beginning there weren't even bit parts. I took whatever work I could find just to be able to stay close to the theater. But I knew that someday I would make it. If I didn't I think I would have died trying." And for all that effort, for all those years of work, Poitier wanted more than the charge of tokenism, more than an innuendo that it was the year for a black to win; he wanted to talk about acting, about the role of Homer Smith, about his future in films, about the innumerable other topics that appear in every actor's inverviews after he wins the big prize, the Oscar.

Such a hiatus from his social role was, of course, impossible. Poitier once declared that he had never done an interview where the word "Negro" or "the Negro issue" didn't come up. Speaking to that large press conference, Poitier angrily went through the questions everyone wanted, expected, needed; queried about his affiliations with NAACP, CORE, and other civil rights organizations, he denounced the assembled newspeople for their stereotyped reactions to a black artist:

Sure I belong to them. Why shouldn't I? But this is nothing new to me. I know what is like to be discriminated against. Ever since I won the Oscar the only questions the press seems to be interested in are what my feelings and actions are about civil rights movements. I don't object to being asked about it, but it's the incessant harping that annoys me.

Reporters feel that because I won an Academy Award I'm some kind of political expert. I'm what I always wanted to be—an actor. Why don't they ask me some questions about acting?[50]

Sidney Poitier as Ali Mansuh in *The Long Ships*.

Acting was less on America's mind than civil rights, so Poitier the Oscar winner had to endure an unwanted role as social commentator. Winning the Oscar hadn't, he knew, made him an expert on race relations; it did make him, however, a visible symbol of the new black man and a bellwether of social change. The same year Poitier won his Oscar, Martin Luther King was awarded the Nobel Prize, and the Civil Rights Act of 1964 was enacted. The times were, indeed, "a-changin' " and Poitier was moving with them.

Winning the Oscar made Poitier one of the hottest properties in Hollywood. Like most award winners before him, Poitier signed a number of contracts almost immediately; it was time to cash in on his fame. Years later, Poitier would deeply regret these films, and would dismiss them as works done for "reasons of greed, selfishness, and corruption." Moral judgments aside, it was clear that Poitier did not, as he put it, "gird his artistic loins" for any of his next few roles.[51]

Poitier did acquire some lavish costuming and a totally new hairstyle for his role as Ali Mansuh, a Moorish prince, in Irving Allen's multimillion dollar epic *The Long Ships*, directed by British cameraman-turned-director Jack Cardiff on location in Yugoslavia. *The Long Ships*, an extravaganza designed to capitalize on the success of *The Vikings*, was actually two films in one, a narrative of one Viking captain named Rolfe (Richard Widmark) and his quest for a lost golden bell, "the Mother of Tongues," and a parallel story of Ali Mansuh's attempts to restore this gold, which had been stolen by the Crusaders, to the coffers of Islam. Ali Mansuh first captures Rolfe, then tortures him; Rolfe escapes, is recaptured, and then they join in a united search. After the bell is found, there is a secret Viking raid, and Ali Mansuh dies in a savage battle. Meanwhile, Rolfe plans a new adventure and a new voyage.

Actually, all this plotting just provides an excuse for battle upon battle as Vikings fight Moors, and almost everyone fights everyone else. Judith Crist, in her lengthy reviews, insists the film must have been made in fun since it's "too crazy" to be taken seriously. There do seem to be rather too many rituals, orgies, fights, and shipwrecks for even the most perfervid action-film fan. *The Long Ships*, really one long chase, has enough bumps and grinds, threats and thrills, duels and intrigues to fill another three or four hours. The sense of jumble is exacerbated by awkward cuts and jumps, probably the result of censorship considerations. Enough cheesecake and beefcake does remain, however, to suggest a Cecil DeMille-type fetish for epics sans costumes.

All this might have become salacious were it not for the corny dialogue and cardboard characterizations. Many critics argue that Richard Widmark was playing it for laughs, while Poitier played it straight. Several of their exchanges do suggest that the actors were functioning on different planes, notably their exchanges in the torture chamber, where Widmark finds time to mock his host between Ali Mansuh's clumsy lashes of the whip: "Your ship! I don't mean to be critical, but you Moors don't make very good sailors." Widmark's careful phrasing makes this overly polite understatement a majestic mockery of the whole genre. Poitier, on the other hand, tries to hiss and whisper some chilling threats: "Perhaps a hundred lashes will give you the idea. For the last time, Norseman, where is the bell?''

Poitier's ineffectiveness in these scenes may stem from his inexperience at playing villains. He told *Ebony* magazine interviewers that he had taken the role just for the opportunity to play a heavy: ''It was a very valuable experience. Negro actors have never had the opportunity to play villains before as a result of a widespread tendency in the movie industry to treat Negroes as special, one-dimensional entities. I hope that it is a break-through that applies to other Negroes, too.''[52] Interestingly, Poitier's sharpest critics, blacks like Clifford Mason, do hail his characterization of Ali Mansuh as a breakthrough since it glorifies a separatist stance. As Mason notes, at least Ali Mansuh ''was a fighter—on his own mission, in his own world. . . . He was not killed as a mean, despicable villain, but rather as a noble enemy. Even more important, he was nobody's eunuch or black mammy busting his gut for white folks as if their problems were all that's important in the world.''[53]

Mason overstates his case slightly, but there are some clear indications in the script that Poitier demanded his role have a certain nobility. Explaining his mission to Aminah, his favorite wife, Poitier justifies his temporary vow of celibacy in a rather powerful call for revenge; she must await his affections, he declares, ''Until Allah's Divine guidance leads me to the treasures of Islam. The bell is made of pure gold stolen by the Christian armies when they plundered and raped their way across our cities to the dishonor and humiliation of our ancestors.'' Ali Mansuh then sneers that the ''Mother of Tongues'' rests in a ''*Christian* land.'' His vow is to return it to its proper home. His commitment to Islam and a tradition antithetical to Christianity was powerful material in an age which saw many American blacks turning to Muslim creeds. Poitier's portrayal of a black prince reminded all blacks there had been other civilizations than the one which dominated in American society. Charles Silberman spoke of the importance of such a discovery in his classic work *Crisis in Black and White:* ''Whether African societies were 'better' or 'worse,' 'more civilized' or 'less civilized' than the societies developed by white men, in short, is not really germane. What is crucial is simply the fact that blacks can hold their heads aloft in the knowledge that men of black skin have contributed to human progress, that they have created and maintained societies and civilizations of a high order.'' Poitier's role as Ali Mansuh does recreate Moorish culture with some

dignity. As Aminah tells Rolfe and as the battles illustrate, ''We Moors are invincible in this desert. . . . We are landsmen; you are seafarers.'' Even in death, Ali Mansuh can proclaim victory: ''Well, Viking, my vow has been accomplished. We have found the bell!''

Poitier himself could not feel victorious about his performance. The costuming, makeup, and sneers were all too out of character; the scenes in and around the harem with Aminah and the Viking princess, Gerda, were too awkward and strained. The whole torture sequence with the mare of steel seemed left over from a Fu Manchu adventure. Considered in toto, *The Long Ships*, Poitier felt, was ''a constant reminder that I must never let my head get too big. A complete failure, and I carry a helluva lot of responsibility, not to choose money for money's sake.''[54] As Poitier later told Joan Barthel, ''To say it was disastrous is a compliment.''[55]

Poitier's next screen appearance, a nonspeaking cameo in George Stevens' spectacular biblical epic, *The Greatest Story Ever Told*, was too small to be disastrous, though it hardly ranks with Poitier's most distinguished performances. Like John Wayne, Shelley Winters, Charlton Heston, and almost sixty others, Poitier found himself a victim of the studio's new gambit for box office success, the star-studded extravaganza, a magnum opus upon which the financial health of the whole backlot depended. These projects tended to be conservative ventures, with plots based on established classics like the Bible, and with the numerous feature players as a sort of icing on the cake.

Poitier's role in *The Greatest Story Ever Told* was too pat and predictable, even for this stodgy rendering of Christ's life. Poitier was cast as Simon of Cyrene and helped Max Von Sydow as Christ carry the cross up Calvary. Sophisticated critics like John Simon couldn't resist snide mocking comments on this all-too-perfect, all-too-timely social commentary: ''Here and there the scenarists and director surpass themselves. Simon of Cyrene, who helps Christ carry the cross, is played by Sidney Poitier. His attire is blindingly white, and his face—could it be makeup?—appears blacker than it ever was before. Besides setting race relations immeasurably ahead, this reminds us that the values of the film are, underneath all that orgiastic color, plain black and white.''[56]

Reviewer Bosley Crowther echoes these sentiments in his 16 February 1965 *New York Times* review when he noted that ''Sidney Poitier's Simon of Cyrene, the African Jew who helps carry

Sidney Poitier meets Max Von Sydow as Christ in *The Greatest Story Ever Told*.

the cross, is the only Negro conspicuous in the picture and seems a last minute symbolization of racial brotherhood." In actuality, the idea of casting Sidney Poitier in this role predates the principal civil rights demonstrations in 1963 and 1964. John E. Fitzgerald, the Catholic film critic who was engaged in research on the film in the earliest stages of preproduction, noted in a private interview that Stevens had told him of his choice of Poitier almost at the outset. Interviewed in Hollywood 2 December 1966, George Stevens confirmed the fact of the early engagement of Poitier, and denied emphatically the various accusations by reviewers of opportunist motivations. To treat Simon of Cyrene as a black character was, Stevens noted, both historically and dramatically justified; in fact, some Oriental Christian churches maintain a traditional belief that Simon of Cyrene was a black. Stevens further observed that "Maybe all the other characters have been portrayed too white in my picture and this could have created the contrast some people object to."

In the eyes of some critics, Sidney Poitier's next role, as journalist Ben Munceford in *The Bedford Incident*, made him appear "too white." *The Bedford Incident* was based on a fine novel by Mark Rascovich which used the story of an overly

Sidney Poitier as Ben Munceford in *The Bedford Incident*.

zealous naval commander to make some powerful points about the Cold War. Rascovich is almost too self-consciously literary, constantly comparing his Captain Finlander with Melville's Captain Ahab, and likening the Soviet submarine that Finlander stalks in the North Sea to the evil of the great white whale. Much of the novel is narrated by a devil-may-care, somewhat seedy Southern white photographer and magazine writer, Ben Munceford. Munceford, like Ishmael, is the sole survivor of the holocaust Finlander precipitates, a catastrophe foreshadowed throughout the tense narrative. Finlander makes the political overtones of his mission and of the entire novel clear when he tells Munceford: "I'm giving you the background material, *not* a story, Munceford. This is not a piece of political taffy to be pulled and fingered by pundits and politicians, like they are doing with Berlin and Laos. Those items have at least a certain sticky elasticity. *This* is the hard core, *war* part of the cold war. Here we clash in the privacy of a black, empty ocean with no audience but our own conscience; both parties want to keep it that way because the stakes are such that no compromise is possible."[57] Veteran screenwriter James Poe preserves this exalted sense of mission and of importance, but also manages to emphasize the other theme of the novel, the absurdity of a cold war, a symbolic war, a war of nerves. Even Finlander knows that it "would be sheer insanity to precipitate nuclear war over an incident such as this," but his fellow officers remind him "how rampant insanity is."

Hollywood was exploiting America's fear of creeping insanity in such contemporary chillers as *Failsafe* and in black comedies like the masterful *Doctor Strangelove or How I Learned to Stop Worrying and Love the Bomb*. *The Bedford Incident* was obviously intended to mine the same vein of national insecurity and paranoia; to a large degree, it was a nuclear age version of *The Caine Mutiny*, with Richard Widmark as Captain Finlander taking the Bogart role. Widmark actually put some money into the preproduction, and the film contains what most critics consider one of his finest performances. After *The Long Ships*, Widmark needed this role, even if it was in a film which, as Holis Alpert remarked, might better have been entitled *"Captain Strangefail."*

Poitier also needed his role as Ben Munceford in *The Bedford Incident* to prove a point. All his life, Poitier told Howard Thompson of the *New York Times*, he had been cast "as a Negro actor"; his roles had been "triggered by the Negroness of my own life." Poitier declared that "I'd hate for my

Eric Portman and Sidney Poitier in *The Bedford Incident*.

gift—or whatever—to be circumscribed by color. I'd like to explore *King Lear*, for instance. I don't want to be just an Othello or always linked with *A Raisin in the Sun*."[58] *The Bedford Incident* wasn't Shakespeare, but the role of Ben Munceford was originally conceived of as a white man's role. Casting Poitier in this role and then ignoring all racial questions in the film, even when they are raised through other characters and incidents in the original novel, marked a major change in Hollywood conventions and traditions. Every small scene of Munceford dressing, showering, shaving, drinking, joking, and mugging, filmed without any reference to race or tolerance or any such noble sentiment, distinguishes *The Bedford Incident* from most other film productions of the period. Poitier spoke to Bosley Crowther about the importance of this breakthrough, reminding the critic that opening previously white roles to black actors was an act of courage: "Producers are usually unwilling to cast Negroes in roles that

might normally be filled by white actors for fear of stirring up public prejudice. . . . They don't want to take a chance of using a Negro by play a character that under conventional circumstances would be white. This is a social concession they are not ready to risk."[59] *The Bedford Incident* risked more than filming a naval story without government cooperation; it also risked filming a human relations melodrama where Sidney Poitier was a man like any other man.

This daring innovation in *The Bedford Incident* did not go unnoticed in the Hollywood community. Virtually every trade journal, all the papers distributed to producers and exhibitors, took care to comment on the unique casting. *The Film Bulletin* for 27 September 1965, spoke of proposed screenings "for the Negro press and civil rights leaders to gain support and hype interest because of Poitier's casting in a role which was not expressly written for a Negro performer"; in a similar vein, James Powers noted in the *Hollywood*

A below-deck respite for Sidney Poitier as Ben Munceford in *The Bedford Incident*.

Reporter for 10 October 1965, that Poitier "has an interesting role. It is interesting because Poitier does not play a Negro. He simply plays a man, and no reference to his difference is ever made." Richard Gertner, writing at the same time for *Film Daily*, says almost the same thing: "The picture is also notable for the fact that Poitier, the journalist character, is a Negro never referred to by anyone on board ship. There is no racial comment, as such, at any time in the picture, although it is, of course, implied in the casual manner in which he is accepted. Indeed the handling is so tactful, a reviewer is reluctant to even bring up the subject."

Poitier was obviously aware of the giant step he was taking in *The Bedford Incident* by making his race less of a question than his humanity and ordinariness. His decision to be a man, an actor first and a black second, opened him to vociferous attacks by militant black critics. They would focus on *The Bedford Incident* and several of Poitier's

next few roles where his blackness is either ignored, or hidden behind a telephone, or obscured by another character's blindness, as a betrayal of his race. Poitier the actor and Oscar winner was intent, it should be noted, on working in Hollywood. And as Edward Mapp astutely notes in his comprehensive study *Blacks in American Films*, there was "not a single American motion picture in 1965 which was primarily concerned with the depiction of Negroes and Negro life."[60] The riots in Watts, the assassination of Malcolm X, even the marches of Martin Luther King—all these tumultuous upheavals motivated Hollywood studios to shy away from black themes. Poitier found himself, as he lamented, the "only Negro actor earning a living in movies, the only one"; his hope was that his distinguished performances, even in roles written by whites for whites, would gradually generate an audience awareness that blacks were being excluded from the screen: "But now, if I can work on a certain level, in roles that are treated honestly, and attract attention to what's been habitual—the exclusion of the Negro from the screen except as a stereotype—then people will ask 'Why aren't there more like that? Why is Sidney Poitier the only one?'. . . It's a hell of a responsibility. And if I'm offered some Hollywood part I won't play, I know they'll go out and get a white actor. In a way it's a compliment but it puts down other Negro actors who might be more talented."[61] As his career blossomed, Poitier would eventually achieve a position in production and could bring talented black actors into his projects. In 1965, all his presence on a white screen assured was that black actors wouldn't be totally forgotten and that more starring roles would have to be made available. Blacks were making some headway as extras in films and on television, as civil rights became a chic cause, but Poitier was still the principal feature player, the man with the Oscar.

Poitier's stature as an artist and the audience's preconceptions about his personality and human dignity both contributed substantially to the financial success of his next film project, *A Patch of Blue*. As was so often the case at this stage of his career, Sidney Poitier was gambling, venturing his time and talent on rather unusual materials and in projects with many unknown quantities. *A Patch of Blue* actually began one day when Mrs. Guy Green read a minor novel, *Be Ready With Bells and Drums*, by a little known Australian novelist Elizabeth Kata; Miss Kata's book treated the American scene, although she had lived most of her life in Japan. Despite this unlikely genesis and the rather clumsy title, Mrs. Green did convince Guy Green to read the text; he, in turn, convinced the noted producer Pandro S. Berman to go ahead on the project if they could cast Sidney Poitier in the lead and change the title to one suggested by Mrs. Green, *A Patch of Blue*.

Sidney Poitier as Gordon Ralfe and Elizabeth Hartman as Selina D'Arcey in *A Patch of Blue*.

Sidney Poitier then worked with Pandro S. Berman to update the script, to make it more attuned to his needs as an actor and to the contemporary American scene. As Berman noted in an interview, and as a comparison of the novel and the script indicates, the changes as "very substantial." Pandro Berman put special emphasis, for example, on the fact that "in the book, the girl is racially prejudiced," but she is not in the film. And, while in the book she loses her friend because of her prejudice and white racism, the film changed this completely, for, as Mr. Berman noted: "Nothing of that kind was left in the picture, the meaning of which depended on the fact that she did not mind discovering her friend's Negro origin." Sidney Poitier helped make all these changes; his personal stamp is on the script. As Berman described the preproduction phase, he and Poitier hammered out a new, more contemporary script.

Poitier was, Berman observed, "instrumental in helping me to get the script changed to meet my requirements. We both felt that the original book was somehow out of date, as far as the American situation is concerned. In over twenty years, our interracial relations have evolved quite considerably. Sidney's support helped me to enforce the necessary readjustments."

These readjustments were to receive rather mixed reactions. Poitier and Berman seemed to have had their fingers on the American pulse, for *A Patch of Blue* became an unprecedented success in both the North and, remarkably, the South. In Atlanta, its first two weeks' grosses exceeded the record established by *Gone With the Wind*. *A Patch of Blue* also proved, however, an inviting target for some strong attacks, as black critics and white reviewers lambasted it as a hokey piece of sentimentality, overly pious and totally unrealistic.

A romantic interlude in *A Patch of Blue*.

Sidney Poitier and Elizabeth Hartman explore the world at large in *A Patch of Blue*.

In *A Patch of Blue*, Poitier plays a young newspaper writer, Gordon Ralfe, who works evenings and enjoys spending his days walking in the park close to his home. One afternoon in the park, he spots a young girl sitting beneath a tree, who is apparently troubled by something on the back of her blouse. Gordon aids her, catching the caterpillar which was bothering her, and he discovers she is blind. From that point on, she undergoes a metamorphosis, emerging as a butterfly largely because of his attention. She is Selina D'Arcey (Elizabeth Hartman), daughter of a vulgar prostitute, Rose (Shelley Winters). Selina lives with Rose and Rose's father, Ole Pa (Wallace Ford), in a miserable apartment where Rose abuses her horribly because her blindness is a constant reminder of Rose's degenerate life. In addition to doing all the hard domestic work for her clan,

Selina strings beads for Mr. Faber (John Qualen), a Polish merchant. Mr. Faber, with his young son, Yanek (Kelly Flynn), sometimes takes her to the park, the only place she can feel happy in her share of the sky, her "patch of blue."

Gordon Ralfe expands Selina's blue skies and enriches her life with joy and hope. He shows her a better world, one of greater wealth, taste, beauty, and morality. When racist Rose discovers Gordon is a black, she tries to end his friendship with Selina. It is too late, however, for the girl is in love with the only friendly person she has ever met, and Gordon, who is profoundly attached to her emotionally, decides to salvage her future by sending her to a specialized school, despite the opposition of his own brother, a doctor (Ivan Dixon), who objects to any mixing of black people with whites. The film ends as Selina is carried off

Elizabeth Hartman talks about her life in *A Patch of Blue*.

to her new school, leaving Gordon with a music box symbolic of the emotions they shared and the new world he has opened for Selina.

Some critics see a mirror of Charlie Chaplin's masterpiece *City Lights* in *A Patch of Blue*, but Judith Crist may be a little closer to the mark when she notes that it is the first powerful example of sentimentality being applied to the sordid. Elizabeth Kata's original novel had a bitter, realistic tone; her narrator, Selina, was badly disfigured by acid carelessly slung by one of Rose's lovers, and was so psychologically unbalanced by her tenement environment that she tragically destroyed her one chance for a better life by chasing her "nigger" friend, Gordon, into the hands of a racist vigilante mob. In the film, Selina's accident left smaller scars, and her heart is much more open. She is willing to love Gordon, whereas the Selina of the novel was more interested in making love to him. These changes result in a

rosier, more optimistic film, but, like the happy endings Hollywood screenwriters so frequently tacked on tragic novels, they also glaze over some important considerations. For example, Poitier, as Gordon, has few real answers to make to his brother's warnings not to get involved; all he can say is "Look—on race and politics we don't agree, so let's drop it." But race and politics are central to the film; *A Patch of Blue* would be much less interesting and provocative if Gordon weren't a black from a higher socio-economic class. The whole reversal of roles, the handsome, rich, black man and the homely, poor, blind, white girl, makes the film controversial. Yet, the muddied ending and the platonic drift of much of the footage refuse to confront the deeper issue of miscegenation submerged in this Cinderella story. The film seems torn by its need to picture interracial love and yet to avoid interracial sex. In fact, in the South, even the modest kissing scene, all eight seconds of it, was cut. No wonder Poitier would declare that his lack of a real relationship with a woman in this and several films of this period was driving him crazy. As Poitier put it: "Either there were no women or there was a woman, but she was blind, or the relationship was of a nature that satisfied the taboos. I was at my wits' end when I finished *A Patch of Blue*."[62]

Reviewers revealed no such shortage of a different kind of wit when they tore into *A Patch of Blue*. *Time* quipped in its 12 December 1965 issue that *A Patch of Blue* reduced all human problems to a simple case of "the black leading the blind"; *Newsweek* was equally sardonic in its 27 December 1965 issue, labelling *A Patch of Blue* a "unique motion picture" which managed simultaneously to insult the blacks and the blind by developing new stereotypes so contemptible

that they are just "another way of saying that all Negroes have superb hearing and all blind people love watermelon." For Alexander Walker, the film proved once and for all the lesson that "None are so well integrated as those who can't see."[63] All the reviews of *A Patch of Blue* are larded with these cutting ripostes; the film, which was so popular with America's middle class, the mass audience, alienated its cultural elite. This dichotomy gives some support to the biting analysis of a black activist critic Catherine Sugy. In her review, the title of which suggests the choice she felt American movies had to make, "Black Men or Good Niggers?" published in 1968 in Canada, she labels *A Patch of Blue* the ultimate "feast to the bourgeois sensibility" since that bourgeois sensibility is "on the one hand . . . positively invited to indulge its hatred of its own under-

Shelley Winters confronts Elizabeth Hartman and Sidney Poitier in *A Patch of Blue*.

class—you just love to hate Shelley Winters—on the other hand, it is titillated at the prospect of being told once more that it, at least, is not racist—you just love to love Sidney Poitier—and on the third hand, it is invited to join the consensus of the beautiful people—itself, nice Negroes, deserving poor like winsome, blind Elizabeth Hartmann—against the uglies, the Shelley Winters and the militants and the things that go bang in the ghettoes."[64] Catherine Sugy may be stretching it a bit far to identify the rejection of racists like Winters with a similar rejection of militancy and revolution, but *A Patch of Blue* obviously did want to take a middle road, even to making Poitier's character, Gordon, and his political brother both professionals living in a well-kept, neat apartment, a shining symbol of their economic maturity and their social mobility.

Poitier spoke to many columnists about *A Patch of Blue*, and he constantly emphasized its good features. It was, he reminded Howard Thompson, one of the earliest treatments of a deep personal relationship between an unmarried white girl and a black man; the film explored a "delicate situation," Poitier observed, "with simplicity and warmth."[65] Developing this idea in his interview with Joan Barthel, Poitier reminded all his critics that *A Patch of Blue*, like *Lilies of the Field*, was meant to be a fable, a fictional idealization designed to "warm the heart." Poitier further affirmed his belief that no one "could construe them as representative of American social life." Fables or not, representative or not, the films drew large audiences, seemingly oblivious to the charges of critics like Clifford Mason that white America loved Poitier only because "he's running his

Sidney Poitier as Alan Newell in *The Slender Thread*.

private branch of the ASPCA, the Black Society for the Prevention of Cruelty to Blind White Girls, the BSPCBWG."[66]

The entire plot of Poitier's next film, *The Slender Thread*, revolves around a black man's efforts to save the life of a befuddled, suicide-prone white woman. The similarities to *A Patch of Blue*, with Poitier again bearing the white woman's burden, were highlighted by the fact that both films were released in December of 1965, just in time for the Christmas holidays and just in time to qualify the performers for Academy Award nominations. *The Slender Thread* was meant to be, as they say in the trade, "Academy all the way," and the film gathered some of the hottest talents in America, including Anne Bancroft, who had won the Academy Award for her role as Anne Sullivan in *The Miracle Worker* and who had handed Sidney Poitier his Oscar for *Lilies of the Field* at the awards ceremony. The crew included Loyal Griggs, the cinematographer who had won his Oscar for *Shane*, and Thomas Stanford, the film editor cited for his work on *West Side Story*. Complementing these old pros were newcomers trying to cross over from the television screen to the big screen, including novice film director Sydney Pollack, producer-writer Stephen Alexander, whose wife's article "Decision to Die," a tense, almost melodramatic presentation of an actual "crisis center" case history published in *Life* magazine, was the basis for the screenplay, and writer Stirling Silliphant. Most reviewers felt this television influence was too great and resulted in a film which was merely a "distended teleplay," a film that would have been better in a thirty-minute or sixty-minute format, with commercial interruptions.

In *The Slender Thread*, Sidney Poitier plays a role which, like his character in *The Bedford Incident*, could have been played by an actor of any race. He is Alan Newell, a medical student in Seattle, who, for a few hours each week helps, Dr. Coburn (Telly Savalas) in a crisis center especially designed to reach out to would-be suicides. One evening, Dr. Coburn and his secretary leave Newell alone; everything seems calm. Newell starts reading his textbook. It is 7:46 when suddenly the telephone rings and the real drama begins. "I have to talk to somebody," says a broken, almost whispering voice of a woman who prefers not to tell her name: "Just call me stupid." When Newell discovers that her real name is Inga (Anne Bancroft) and that she has just taken enough pills to put an end to her life, his desperate effort begins, to find out where she is and to keep her on the line, the "slender thread" on which her life depends. On another phone, Newell sends word to Dr. Coburn, asking him to return immediately, and to telephone operators to have them trace the call and alert the police.

The painfully awkward conversation, an agonizing effort on Newell's part, conducted even after Dr. Coburn and his assistants return, reveals in successive flashbacks the circumstances which have pushed Inga to her desperate acts. She has always concealed from her husband the truth about their child: it was not his son. His discovery of that fact, twelve years later, and his harsh reaction have devastated Inga. At this critical moment of her life, she is alone. Nobody but Alan Newell would listen to her. Doctors in the hospitals treated her as one of the vast number of anonymous patients; her son was playing ball with friends, and her office associates all had other engagements.

Throughout this excruciatingly difficult conversation, as he listens to a voice which becomes weaker with each passing moment, Newell unfurls the whole panoply of psychological approaches. Friendly and supportive at first, he reminds Inga she should "Talk to me!" He emanates confidence and charm, indeed almost flirts with Inga. As things become more difficult, however, and Inga wavers about hanging on, Newell switches tactics, arguing with her and goading her for her self pity: "You've been suffered and tolerated? Me, too. O.K.? Times are bad, things stink, the world's a cinder in your eye, but what is the alternative? Now I ask you, Inga, what in God's name is the alternative?" Poitier is, of course, alone on screen as he gives many of these speeches; it's just him and the telephone, a terrible constriction for such a physical actor. Sometimes Poitier is a little too volatile, waving his arms rather too wildly, but, most of the time, his performance is quite engaging. Director Pollack had arranged an actual live telephone wire linking the two stars during the filming. While Poitier talked into the phone on the set, Bancroft answered him from a connecting line off-screen.

Finally, at 8:40 P.M., fifty-four minutes into the phone call, Inga's voice vanishes in an almost indistinguishable "Help me!" Alan Newell despairs, thinking that everything has been lost; there is no answer to his supplications. Then the noise of a door being broken down is heard. The police have found the right room of the motel despite the crowds and confusion of a cattlemen's convention. Inga is saved. At 9:15 P.M. Inga's husband, brought by helicopter, enters the crisis center. There is a quite impressive closeup of

Victory is sweet for Sidney Poitier in *The Slender Thread*.

Poitier looking at this man. Only one of Poitier's eyes can be seen, yet it expresses well both his accusation and his sympathy. When Dr. Coburn asks if he wants to go over to meet Inga personally, Newell says he prefers not to and returns to his telephone station for a new call.

Director Sydney Pollack was evidently, too evidently perhaps, looking for a virtuoso performance from Poitier. He builds all his story around one telephone conversation, with one performer on one set. The result is unfortunate. Instead of a suspense organically generated by interest in the characters, the film grinds out an artificial tension ticked off to the mechanical beat of a clock, which robs the characters of both personality and humanity. Alan Newell and Inga are reduced to automatons answering the demands of a certain time grid.

Poitier's own racial identity is similarly reduced in his characterization of Alan Newell to what Pauline Kael has laughingly called "a living O. Henry Twist," the sort of heavy-handed irony that characterizes juvenile art. As in *A Patch of Blue*, a black man, a medical volunteer, saves a mixed-up white woman, only here Inga never learns that her savior is black. They never meet, let alone kiss, and Alan Newell remains, for Inga at least, the ultimate "invisible man." Given some harsh realities of American life, as British critic Alexander Walker notes, this clumsy twist in *The Slender Thread* seems especially lamentable: "It is one of the commonest neuroses of the black race in America that because a Negro is often 'ignored' by white people, either out of shame or antipathy, he begins to feel he is not there at all, that he is an invisible man. In *The Slender Thread* Poitier institutionalized this phenomenon without perhaps being aware that he was doing so. . . . It is another example of a well meaning film that 'solves' its problem by shutting its eyes to it."[67] Race actually should not have been a problem at all in *The Slender Thread*; the problem was the self-conscious attempt to ignore it and many other human concerns, to compress the lives of two people into one phone call.

Hollywood was ignoring too many questions, both racial and human, to suit Sidney Poitier. In an interview with Sheilah Graham that was widely circulated in 1965 and debated at length, Poitier denounced Hollywood as "the most backward city for racial rights," a stodgy place which was "traditionally backward" and "afraid to take a chance." All his energies were going, Poitier declared, "to see Hollywood get in line with the rest of the country." The key issue, as Poitier saw it, and many commentators and activists agreed, was jobs: "Now I can't believe that I, Sidney Poitier, am the only man of talent for films from among 20 million Negro people. It's simply that Hollywood will not give the people of my race a chance." In prophetic tones, Poitier reminded

Sidney Poitier as Toller in *Duel at Diablo*.

Sheilah Graham and her readers that the pace of civil rights everywhere in America had been far too slow, and that this threatened both the domestic health and foreign policy of the nation. Poitier warned ominously that "If there is no further progress in civil rights, then we are all in trouble."[68]

Poitier's only screen appearance in 1966 was more a conscious plea for civil rights and a black man's right to his history than anything else. Reunited with Ralph Nelson, the producer and director of his Academy Award winning film, *Lilies of the Field*, Poitier took the role of Toller, an ex-cavalry sergeant in *Duel at Diablo*, a mundane Western. Sidney Poitier knew *Duel at Diablo* would not repeat the success of *Lilies of the Field*; to no small degree, he and director Nelson were actually exploiting the success of their earlier film. Poitier wasn't fond of the material in *Duel at Diablo*, but he made it, he told a group of educators, to restore an important piece of history and folklore to black people: "I agreed to make is solely because I would have a role as a Negro cowboy. . . . no one knows the Negro contribution to the building of the West. . . . I also did the film because it gave me an opportunity to give a hero imagery to Negro children who love Westerns."[69] Poitier had loved Westerns himself as a child, but had always wondered where the Negro cowboys were. *Duel at Diablo* was part of his answer to this long smoldering question. If the Western was America's favorite genre, Poitier wanted to put a black stamp on it. Later, in *Buck and the Preacher*, he would expand his influence, using much of the material he read in preparation for *Duel at Diablo*.

The importance of Poitier's achievement in bringing black men into meaningful roles in Westerns might best be appreciated by those who have read Sammy Davis, Jr.'s autobiography. In a key passage, Davis discusses with his agent the roles he could try to get in movies: "Baby, I'll play anything except an Uncle Tom, but don't brush off the Western thing so fast. Aside from the fact that I happen to be better with the guns than most of the Schwabs' Drugstore cowboys they're using, it also happens there were a lot of colored cowboys."[70] Davis may have wanted the role, but it took Poitier to get this kind of assignment first. Even with Poitier as a gunfighter, there was, director Ralph Nelson revealed in an interview, a good deal of audience backlash: "In *Duel at Diablo*, the audiences seemed to have been surprised and skeptical about the presence of a Negro cowboy. Since the famous theatrical model of the Western, *The Virginian*, it was impossible to see a

Bill Travers and Sidney Poitier in an action sequence from *Duel at Diablo*.

significant Negro character in Westerns. But a recent publication by two University of California professors, *The Negro Cowboy*, is there to testify that a good percentage of cowboys were black.''

The book Ralph Nelson referred to, *The Negro Cowboy* by Professors Philip Durham and Everett Jones, was also mentioned frequently by Poitier in interviews and was serialized by several newspapers around the time *Duel at Diablo* was released. *The Negro Cowboy*, a careful, well-documented study, is a powerful indictment of the omissions and oversights of white historians, and a lively chronicle of black personalities like Nat ''Deadeye Dick'' Love, Ben Hodges, the notorious cattle thief and confidence man, Bronco Sam, and Jim Buckworth, mountain man. Durham and Jones argue convincingly that years after the West was won, ''. . .when history became myth and legend, when the cowboys became folk heroes, the Negroes were once again fenced out. They had ridden through the real West, but they found no place in the West of fiction.''[71] Sidney Poitier and Ralph Nelson were intent in *Duel*

at Diablo on bringing fiction closer to fact by restoring the image of the black cowboy.

In *Apache Uprising*, the novel by Marvin Albert which was the source for the screenplay, Toller had been a white man, a gambler, gunfighter, and horse-breaker. So, just as he did in *The Bedford Incident* and several other films, Poitier played a role originally designed for a white actor. Director Nelson was quite happy with the switch in races, for he felt that the black presence in the picture made an additional and quite interesting comment: ''It is a silent comment, about the merciless war between white people and Indians. It shows the absurdity of the war. Even if the whites succeed in eliminating the redskins, there will still be the Negro problem. Without participating in the conflict, Poitier's character contributes to its dramatic significance. The whole impact is due to the mere presence of a Negro actor.''

Poitier underplayed the importance of his impact as a black man in all his interviews around the time of *Duel at Diablo*. For example, when

Sidney Poitier brings a new black presence to traditional western adventure in *Duel at Diablo*.

In a few months, all Hollywood would discover the immense box office appeal of Sidney Poitier. Slowly but surely, he had worked his way into the hearts of all America. In 1967, he was to prove himself not only the principal black star in America, but also to establish himself as the most popular film personality of any race, that year's number one box-office attraction.

asked if there would be any explicit comment on race relations in a conflict between officers and men, Poitier declared that there would be "none of that crap. That's old hat. No, no reference to Negro, to Irish or white. The drama of it is—can they get to Fort Duell in time?"[72] Poitier's star presence in this film was far from "old hat." Audiences responded enthusiastically to all his gestures and jokes; they could read between the lines and feel the dignity and anger Toller balanced in his character. They could easily interpret the subtext in the way Toller "apologizes" after a fight, the way he addresses white officers, or the way he gestures when he receives an official receipt for his horses. Toller was an independent spirit, a man with flair. No one could doubt his words when he ordered the lieutenant to "Shut up, McAllister. You don't scare me none and you sure can't pull no rank on me."

Toller was all man, yet he could be kind to both women and children; he nestles a rescued infant in his arms, observing that "He is very young!" He freely jokes and teases the whites, mocking the commanding officer with the jibe, "Well, what's next, General?" But above all, he is brave; in the final battle with the Indians, he rescues the wounded officer and is hit by an arrow himself. All this, culminating in an emotional shot of Toller saluting his fallen comrades, was especially enthusiastically received by black audiences, who, for the first time, could easily project themselves through Poitier into the Western adventure. Ralph Nelson was pleased to discover that the film did "better in areas with a predominantly Negro population, another proof of Sidney Poitier's box office value for those audiences."

Notes to Chapter 2

1. Barry Gray, "Speaking Out," *New York Post*, 11 September 1957.

2. Frank Quinn, "Crusading Actor," *New York Mirror*, 17 August 1958.

3. Archer Winsten, "Story of a Negro Actor," *New York Post*, 15 August 1950.

4. Mel Gussow, *Don't Say Yes Until I Finish Talking* (New York: Doubleday, 1971), p. 158.

5. Lyn Tornabene, *Long Live the King: A Biography of Clark Gable* (New York: Putnam, 1976), p. 353.

6. Sidney Poitier, "They Call Me a 'Do-It-Yourself' Man," *Films and Filming*, September 1959, p. 7.

7. Paul Mayersburg, *Hollywood: The Haunted House* (New York: Stein and Day, 1968), pp. 58-59.

8. Martin Levine, "Sidney Poitier Sees His Film Role as Historic," *The Record*, 26 July 1974, p. 20.

9. Irene Thirer, "Poitier Boosts Screen Writers," *New York Post*, 5 September 1958, p. 50.

10. Arthur Mayer, "Growing Pains of a Shrinking Business," in Arthur McClure, *The Movies: An American Idiom* (Teaneck, New Jersey; Fairleigh Dickinson University Press, 1971), p. 255.

11. William Peper, "Poitier Gets a Star Role," *New York World Telegram and The Sun*, 2 September 1958, p. 12.

12. *Time*, 24 April 1964.

13. "Sidney Poitier: A Negro Actor With a Full Work Schedule," *Look*, 28 October 1958.

14. Walter Lister, "*The Defiant Ones* Is Launched in Chicago," *New York Herald Tribune*, 24 August 1958.

15. Tom Buckley, "At the Movies," *New York Times*, 10 February 1978, sec. C, p. 6.

16. Richard Maynard, *The Celluloid Curriculum* (New York: Hayden Book Company, Inc., 1971), pp. 156-157.

17. Reprinted and discussed in Gordon Hitchens, "The Defiance in *The Defiant Ones*," *Film Culture*, nos. 50-51 (Fall and Winter 1970), pp. 63-65.

18. Whitney Bolton, "Poitier's Serious Appraisal of Self," *Morning Telegraph*, 21 January 1959, p. 2.

19. Arthur Marx, *Goldwyn: A Biography of the Man Behind the Myth* (New York: W. W. Norton and Co., 1976), pp. 342-343.

20. Harold Cruse, *Rebellion or Revolution* (New York: W. Morrow and Co., 1968), p. 135.

21. Bea Smith, "Stubborn Poitier," *Newark Sunday News*, 13 September 1959.

22. Quoted in John Davis, *The American Negro Reference Book*, p. 844.

23. Marx, pp. 344-345.

24. " 'Lone Black Star' Poitier Rejects 'Good Guy' Role as Race Spokesman," *Variety*, 12 June 1968, pp. 2, 62.

25. Frederick Morton, "The Audacity of Sidney Poitier," p. 109.

26. *Films and Filming*, September 1958, p. 7.

27. Joan Barthel, "He Doesn't Want to be Sexless Sidney," *New York Times,* sec. D, p. 7.

28. Carolyn Ewers, *Sidney Poitier: The Long Journey,* p. 94.

29. Joe Hyams, "Why Sidney Poitier Will Direct," *New York Herald Tribune,* October 1959.

30. James Baldwin, "Sidney Poitier," p. 54.

31. Fordham University Seminar, Summer 1967. Cf. *Pace* magazine in Museum of Modern Art clipping file.

32. Gary Null, *Black Hollywood: The Negro in Motion Pictures,* p. 183.

33. Joe Hyams, "A Happier Poitier Looks Forward," *New York Herald Tribune*, 8 September 1960.

34. Stanley Kauffman, *A World on Film* (New York: Dell Publishing, 1966), p. 153.

35. "Top Actor of the Year," *Ebony,* March 1964, p. 124.

36. Art Buchwald, "Gambling Festival," *New York Herald Tribune,* 23 May 1961.

37. Joel Seldin, "The Bias Story in the Acting Ranks—Starring Sidney Poitier," *New York Herald Tribune,* 30 October 1962, p. 21.

38. Dennis John Hall, "Pride Without Prejudice: Sidney Poitier's Career," p. 41.

39. *A World on Film,* p. 58.

40. Donald Bogle, *Toms, Coons, Mulattoes, Mammies, and Bucks,* pp. 298-299.

41. United Artists' pressbook for *Paris Blues,* p. 9.

42. Quoted in Edward Mapp, *Blacks in American Films: Today and Yesterday,* p. 62.

43. Frank Daley, "The Black Man's Burden," *Ottawa Journal,* 17 October 1975.

44. *Film Quarterly,* 18, no. 4 (Summer 1965), 19.

45. Herbert Feinstein, "Three in Search of Cinema," *Columbia University Forum* (Summer 1965), p. 23.

46. Sidney Poitier, "Dialogue on Film," p. 47.

47. Charles E. Silberman, *Crisis in Black and White* (New York: Vintage Books, 1964), p. 73.

48. Mel Gussow, "From Sidney With Love," *Newsweek,* 11 December 1967, pp. 101-102.

49. "Greatest Night of My Life," *New York Journal American,* 14 April 1964.

50. "Always Wanted to Be the Best," *New York Post,* 22 April 1964, p. 54.

51. "From Sidney With Love," p. 101. Cf. William Hoffman, *Sidney,* pp. 154-158.

52. "Top Actor of the Year," p. 2.

53. Clifford Mason, "Why Does White America Love Sidney Poitier So?" sec. 2, pp. 1, 21.

54. Judy Michaelson, "Sidney Poitier Makes a Choice," *New York Post,* 10 February 1968, sec. 2, p. 26.

55. Barthel, p. 7.

56. John Simon, *Private Screenings* (New York: MacMillan Company, 1967), p. 175.

57. Mark Rascovitch, *The Bedford Incident* (New York: Atheneum, 1963), p. 71.

58. Howard Thompson, "Why is Sidney Poitier the Only One?" *New York Times,* 3 June 1965, sec. 2, p. 1.

59. Bosley Crowther, "Poitier Points a Dilemma Which *The Cool World* Helps Rebut," New York Times, 26 April 1964.

60. Mapp, p. 105.

61. Thompson, p. 1.

62. Hoffman, p. 151.

63. Alexander Walker, *Stardom: The Hollywood Phenomenon* (New York: Stein and Day, 1970), p. 350.

64. Catherine Sugy, "Black Men or Good Niggers?" *Take One,* no. 1 (1968), issue 8, p. 19.

65. Thompson, p. 1.

66. Mason, p. 1.

67. Walker, p. 350.

68. Sheilah Graham, "Poitier Deplores Hollywood Bias," *New York Telegram and Sun,* 9 August 1965, p. 6.

69. "Poitier Shows What Films Teach," *Catholic Standard and Times* (Philadelphia), 28 July 1967, p. 3.

70. Sammy Davis, Jr., *Yes I Can* (New York: Cardinal Paperbacks, 1966), p. 414.

71. Philip Durham and Everett Jones, *The Negro Cowboy* (New York: Dodd, Mead, and Co., 1965), p. 2.

72. Thompson, p. 1.

THE TOP THREE VEHICLES
(1967)

The year 1967 was one of the most tumultuous times ever for all Americans, black and white alike. All the old verities seemed to have come unmoored, and the nation was adrift in a sea of troubles. Racial tension and conflict shattered dreams of integration while the war in Viet Nam haunted the conscience of the young. The duplicity of politicians seemed more blatant than ever before as newspapers reported one nightmare after another. For sensitive, politically active individuals like Poitier, corruption and insanity became recurrent images in their public statements. For a while, it seemd America faced a Hobson's choice of pleading guilty to either collective insanity or inexplicable evil.

Sidney Poitier was especially vocal about the social, political, and moral malaise seemingly so widespread in 1967. His address as keynote speaker at the Southern Christian Leadership Conference Convention in 1967 remains an eloquent catalogue of the numerous manifestations of "the insanity of this old world." To know what was wrong in America, Poitier reminded the delegates, was as easy as turning to "your morning newspaper over breakfast in a few hours. And if that doesn't send you back to bed, try the early morning news broadcast on your television set. And if you are a real bad news glutton you can get another dose from your car radio as you drive to work." Everywhere you looked, Poitier proclaimed, you could find "Greed, selfishness, indifference to the sufferings of others, corruption of our value system, and a moral deterioration that has already scarred our souls irrevocably. On my bad days I am guilty of suspecting that there is a national death-wish active within our borders." On his good days, however, Poitier told the delegates, he saw a hope for the future. For, while the news is "mostly bad tonight," how good it would be tomorrow "depends on how we invest the little love left in our hearts." Activist Poitier placed his faith, both religious and political, in attempts to make "a new world full of love."

Poitier's gospel of love and humanitarianism heavily influenced his thinking about his craft and his choice of film roles. In a lengthy private interview in Hollywood in November of 1966, months after he had completed his work on his next feature *To Sir with Love* but several months before it was released, Poitier emphasized the importance of the emotional effect of movies, arguing that films which preach a regard for the individual enrich their audiences immeasurably. As Poitier saw it then, "certain pictures naturally invoke a certain kind of emotional response from the audience, and the one that the audience feels touches mostly in the area of their sympathy, I think, leaves the longest impression on them. The ones that persuade with love rather than curse with threats or fear are ones I feel that have done the most."

Developing this argument at great length, Poitier equated his own success and his own feelings of self-esteem with the moral, humanitarian themes and effects of his art:

> My satisfaction as an actor is very delicately tied into the reaction of an audience to the work, not so much to the nature of how I work, but to what the statement of the material is, what it says to them. If it makes them feel good, if it enlightens, if it illuminates for them some little dark corner of the human condition, if it touches them in a human way, if it massages their human heart, I like that. I like human beings and I like to say nice things to them. I may use violent ways to say nice things; we may have to use peculiar avenues to get them to see the beauty of human beings. So the films that are best received in this light are the ones that I feel happiest about, because my work is for people. If they are pleased with what I do, I am pleased.

Sidney Poitier was especially pleased with his role as the teacher, Thackeray, in James Clavell's London-based production of *To Sir with Love*. Poitier had read the original novel by E. R. Braithwaite in 1959 and found it "warm, human, ingratiating," exactly the sort of property he would like

Sidney Poitier as Mark Thackeray meets his fellow teachers in *To Sir with Love*.

to be involved in bringing to the screen. The basic plot, as he described it in our interview, involved "a black man who is born and raised in the West Indies, actually in South America in a British possession called at that time British Guyana. He now lives in London, is an engineer by profession but is unable to find a position as an engineer. So he fills in his time, while looking for a job as an engineer, as a teacher in an East End London School, which is a school of slow learners and pretty much delinquent children. The story is how he salvages these children and makes them functioning human beings who are capable of taking part in an organized society rather than going into that society as misfits. That's the whole story." Such a miraculous tale of social regeneration, of an inspired teacher and his success, obviously suited Poitier's predilection for uplifting sentiments in art. *To Sir with Love* was a film project he could embrace because it was a movie that made "you like people," an emotional experience that "made you feel people are kind of marvelous."

Poitier could also embrace *To Sir with Love* because it made such a heartwarming and positive statement about the noble actions of a black man, the very sort of affirmation of black dignity and achievement which he felt aided the cause of integration and racial harmony. Questioned in Hollywood about the impact of his career on race relations in America, Poitier constantly returned to the twin themes of charitable actions and positive images as the key to understanding, sympathy, and love for men of all races. His film portrayals helped integration, he felt, only insofar as the excellence of his craft and the humanity of his portrayals affected audience images of other races:

> I think that every positive action by a Negro person in the United States in whatever area of endeavor makes a contribution to the integration question, if he is a stock clerk or a bus conductor or a movie actor or a singer or a policeman. If he is a Negro and if in his dealings with the white world his behavior in relation to that world is one of a positive, constructive, humanistic nature, then it is a plus factor for the integration question in the United States. So in this light, I think that my career has had some influence on the integration question. And, you know, I have been at this game for some twenty years. I have tried to make the kind of films that would be beneficial to the image of black people in this country. I have tried to be associated with artistic events and involvements that would be healthy and constructive to the black image. I am committed to do the kind of artistic work that would reflect favorably on the black people in this country.

One clear indication of his success, Poitier urged, might be found in the tons of fan mail he received from all over the world. The tone of the mail suggested strongly to him that his message of tolerance and love was having a positive effect on the integration question: "As an example of this positive reaction. . .I have received over the years thousands of letters and I must say that it must be some kind of remarkable record or something, but of probably thirty, forty, or fifty thousand letters I have received, I cannot remember one letter that was not a nice, pleasant, warm, friendly, human letter. I have received letters on all the pictures I have made and the letters come in even now. They come to me at the studios and the studios forward the letters to me in New York, so they come a hundred or two hundred a week. They are all positive." The letters, Poitier observed, came from every country in the world where the films are shown and from every state in the United States. These letters really inspired him: "They make me feel good as an artist first of all, because I try to do the kind of film that people warm to, the kind of film that makes them laugh and makes them cry and makes them feel alive and makes them feel that it is wonderful to be human. Then, on the other side of the coin, I also get the feeling that I show them that the differences of color are incidental and in most cases an accidental condition. That there's really no significance in differentiation between one human being and another. That inherent in the color of one's skin is not one iota of superiority in any area at all."

To Sir with Love was to continue preaching all these lessons, but with a success even Poitier could not have predicted before the film's release. Audiences would crowd box offices waiting to meet "Sir," to learn his lessons of brotherhood and human dignity, and to enjoy the laughing, crying, and loving of this black teacher. Discussing the development of his career with Dorothy Manners, Poitier later noted that the picture which lifted him to stardom may have been *Lilies of the Field*, but it was *To Sir with Love* which literally "flooded me with affection." *To Sir with Love* was the surprise smash hit of 1967, a box office miracle in the age of skepticism. Poitier told Manners that he was overwhelmed by the response to the film; even he hadn't fully realized how desperately America needed films affirming human dignity and the efficacy of love: "I can't tell you the number of letters that poured in—not just asking for an autograph or photograph—but letters from real people with real problems because there is not enough love for them to give—or to take." The success of *To Sir with Love* reinforced Poitier's conviction that films could instill new values in a nation at bay.

Suzy Kendall and Sidney Poitier in *To Sir with Love.*

The success also motivated him to think about playing other roles in the production of films: "I had not done any writing until after I became an actor. But I've made up my mind that if I cannot star in pictures that speak of love and understanding—man to man—if such stories are not on the market—then I will write them."[1] By the end of 1967, Poitier would be filming his own original story, a contemporary romance, *For Love of Ivy,* a project undoubtedly buoyed by the success of three Poitier films in one year.

The genesis of *To Sir with Love* had been considerably more modest, and, as James Clavell remembered it and detailed it in a telephone interview, considerably more shaky. The project began, he recalled,

> back in 1959, when Mike Frankovitch bought the rights of E. R. Braithwaite's book for Columbia Pictures. Carl Foreman was interested in producing

it for some time. Then Jack Clayton, and some others, but things did not materialize. I think that was partially because, at that time, the project would not have been considered a good risk or even a feasible subject for an international market. Then too Sidney was not the star or catalyst that he was in 1967 when the film came out. In 1964 Martin Baum, Sidney's agent whom I had known for six years since the production of *Five Gates to Hell,* asked me if I would be interested in making this film witn Poitier. When I accepted the idea, Baum promised to speak to Frankovitch. Then I called Baum to learn the result of their conference. Baum's associate informed me that Frankovitch was no longer interested. I decided to call Frankovitch directly.

Clavell was to discover that Baum's associate had the wrong information and that Frankovitch was interested in making the picture in England with Poitier; Martin Baum had sold the whole package. Director Clavell is quite lavish in his praise for agent Baum: "I must emphasize the important part Martin Baum played in this affair. It was really a case of an agent proving to be a creative person. He sold me to Poitier and helped to keep things together when there were difficulties."

The principal difficulties in the early stages were financial. As in so many Poitier projects, the film was underfunded and the producer could not meet his legitimate salary demands. Poitier decided to take a calculated risk, and, in addition to a small fixed sum to cover his expenses, he asked for a substantial percentage of the film rentals. His experience with a percentage of *Lilies of the Field* had shown him how lucrative a successful venture could be, and, besides, he was a gambler at heart. Today everyone knows the outcome of his wager. *To Sir with Love* ranks among the one hundred "All Time Rental Champs" compiled by *Variety*. By January 1978, the film had grossed nineteen million dollars in the domestic market alone. *To Sir with Love* made Poitier a millionaire and provided him with the wherewithal to become a film producer.

The financial success of *To Sir with Love* obviously surprised the distributors, Columbia Pictures, for, as *Variety* noted in its trade review dated 14 June 1967, the film's release had been "long delayed." Such a delay, *Variety*, observed, is usually a manifestation of "fear on the part of a distributor who either had a dud on his hands, or doesn't know what to do with a good film." *To Sir with Love* was obviously a good film, *Variety* noted, but it went to market "under the disadvantage of held-back trade evaluation." Still another disadvantage was Columbia's decision to aim the product at a limited market, the juvenile audience and American teachers. Columbia's initial publicity capitalized on the presence of rock singers like "the Mindbenders" and "Lulu" and on the vogue for modish London decors and fashions. In May, both *Seventeen* and *Scholastic Magazine* declared *To Sir with Love* their film of the month, and the first screening was the highlight of the American Film Festival, a convention of educators sponsored by the Educational Film Library Association. By late summer, however, *To Sir with Love* broke the shackles of an ill-conceived sales program and exploded as an all-time champion in neighborhood theaters; Columbia responded by following a record ten-week showcase engagement in New York with an unprecedented return engagement at even more theaters. Meanwhile, Columbia Pictures commissioned a poll to determine the cause for this unexpected success. The survey reported an astounding fact in

The romance between Mark Thackeray and Gillian Blanchard in *To Sir with Love* was softened when the novel became a film.

a year of racial unrest: the most popular star in motion pictures was Sidney Poitier and his name, more than that of any other star, sold tickets.[2] Poitier was not just educating the young and the sympathetic; his message of love was charming all America.

It would be hard to conceive a more suitable vehicle for Poitier's gospel of love and his personal appeal as a man of dignity than *To Sir with Love*. This autobiographical tale of a teacher's victory is based on the inspiring career of E. R. Braithwaite, whose own life has an almost Cinderella-like quality. Born in Georgetown, British Guyana, Braithwaite graduated from City College of New York and received an M.S. in Physics from Casius College, Cambridge, England. At the outbreak of World War II, he enlisted in the R.A.F. as a fighter pilot. After the war, racial discrimination closed off opportunities in physics, so he turned to teaching in a slum school in London's East End. His prose account of his experiences with his recalcitrant students garnered him worldwide attention, and he quickly moved from positions with the Welfare Board in London to the World Veterans Federation in Paris. Eventually, Braithwaite represented his native Guyana at the United Nations. He never forgot his teaching background, however, and frequently visited the set of *To Sir with Love* to talk to the cast about the reality behind their fiction.

In the film *To Sir with Love*, Braithwaite appears under the name Mark Thackeray and is played by Sidney Poitier. The school where he accepts an opening is a particularly challenging one whose headmaster, Alexander Florian (Edward Burnham), is experimenting with new pedagogical methods. Florian favors greater freedom and a reliance on persuasion rather than coercion. Thackeray's colleagues quickly warn him, however, that he is "the new lamb for slaughter—or should I say the black sheep?" The students all come from deprived backgrounds and pose real discipline problems. One cynical teacher warns that, you must not "take any crap from the little tykes. If you don't master them, they'll master and break you." In many ways, *To Sir with Love* reminds one of *Blackboard Jungle*, only the scene is now England and Poitier had taken the Glenn Ford role; he must confront and transform teenagers from a rather rough social environment without using physical force. In Florian's school, he is supposed to master them by a kind of "friendly persuasion."

In the beginning, the confrontation is rather tense. Led by Denham (Christian Roberts) and Potter (Christopher Chittell), the boys try all sorts of tricks. They saw a leg off Thackeray's desk, pelt him with water bombs, and generally disrupt lessons with banging desks and synchronized accidents. Soon the girls join in with their own pranks, and Thackeray explodes in anger. Somewhat frightened by his own violent outburst, he decides to try a new tactic altogether. He will treat his students as adults, and, in place of conventional lessons, he will try a frank dialogue about real day-to-day problems, about love, death, sex, survival, and life. To begin with, he convinces them to take better care of their physical appearance. Then he focuses on common courtesy, demanding they address him as "Sir," call the girls "Miss," and use last names instead of nicknames.

Most of the discussions in class focus on personal dignity and worth; Sir's major lesson is that self-respect demands a corresponding respect for others. Survival in the world, in turn, demands that one make room for others to live. Poitier seems especially at ease sermonizing and makes every lesson as palatable as he can, down to showing the class how to make an edible salad from locally available produce. It might be noted that around the time he was working on this film, Poitier was recording his album *Poitier Meets Plato*, in which he selected passages from Plato dealing with the important issues of the day, "war, greed, lust, hatred, and selfishness." Poiter remarked of the record that he "got a big kick out of messing around with philosophy." He obviously got the same kick out of the down-home philoso-phizing in *To Sir with Love*. His exuberance and joy just radiate from the screen.

In the film, the teacher succeeds in two risky initiatives. The first comes when he takes his class to visit the Victoria and Albert Museum. The effect of this sequence is blunted, however, by the director's uninspired use of montage shots and a pedestrian musical arrangement. The second initiative results, however, in a touching scene detailing Thackeray's emotional victory over the children's prejudice. Seales, one of the students in the class, has a white mother but a West Indian father. When his mother dies, the children collect for flowers, but are reluctant to take the flowers to a colored funeral in a colored section. To Sir's surprise, however, all of them finally do come, reaffirming his faith in the class: love and concern clearly overcome ignorance and racial prejudice.

Surprisingly, the treatment of race relations and prejudice in *To Sir with Love* has drawn sharp criticism. In the eyes of some viewers, the film cautiously skirts all the difficult issues raised in Braithwaite's book, especially those of physical love between white women and black men. Inter-racial sexual relations are a major theme in the novel, with the author charging that it seems "as though there were some unwritten law in Britain which required any healthy, able-bodied Negro resident there to be either celibate by inclination, or else a master of the art of sublimation. . . .We were to be men, but without manhood."[3] The same unwritten law seemed to hold in Sidney Poitier movies. In the film *To Sir with Love*, Thackeray is an immensely appealing, very virile character, and many women are obviously attracted to him, including the lovely, precocious, blond student, Pamela (Judy Geeson), and an equally comely teacher, Gillian Blanchard, played by Suzy Kendall. Judy Geeson would later play quite sexually explicit roles as a teenage seductress in films like *Here We Go Round the Mulberry Bush* and *Three into Two Won't Go*; Suzy Kendall, a honey-blond photographer's model turned actress, would follow *To Sir with Love* with two very explicit features, *Penthouse* and *Up the Junction*. Opposite Poitier in *To Sir with Love*, neither had much of a chance to develop the romantic side of her character. Pamela's story is kept much as it is in the novel; hers is a teenage crush to be discouraged. The film eliminates almost entirely the Gillian episodes in the Braith-waite book. In the original, both teachers fall in love and plan to marry. One chapter chronicling their visit to Gillian's parents could easily consti-tute a major source for *Guess Who's Coming to*

Sidney Poitier dances with student Judy Geeson in *To Sir with Love*.

Dinner. The chapter is pivotal to Braithwaite's theme of tolerance, and provides some of the strongest moments in the text. Dropping this material from the film script constitutes, in the opinion of Clifford Mason, "the all-time Hollywood reversal act. Instead of putting love interest into a story that had none, they took it out."[4]

Director James Clavell deliberately wanted to soften the romantic dimension of the book and, with it, the racial aspects. As he explained in the course of our 1967 interview: "I have made considerable changes in the book. If you read it, you can see that the racial problem is rather strongly underscored. In contrast, the film is not racially 'conscious.' One of its magics is that you forget the color of the teacher's skin, and you are interested in the characters as just teacher and kids. This is due to a very careful scripting and delicate dramatizing of certain details. The color is brought up rather apologetically, as in the dialogue of the girl who says: 'We like him very much, but what will people say?' " By eliminating the issue of a mixed marriage from the film, Clavell hoped to concentrate on his essential motivation, expressed in the following terms: "Reading my novels *King Rat* and *Tai Pan*, one can easily perceive my motivations. I have learned during the war that a man is a man, regardless if he is white or black or another color. Differences are the result of influences we receive from our childhood on. Intolerance starts with wrong teaching. It is not something which comes spontaneously from our nature."

According to Clavell, one of the strong points of the picture and of Poitier's performance is that you start off liking him and hating the children, but you finish by liking them both. In his words, "It was rather extraordinary luck that we could achieve this result. If I had eight million dollars today, I could not repeat it, because Sidney might not be the same and the kids no longer exist as they were.'' The teaching experience, an emerging image of shared growth, remains at the center of Clavell's conception and his film. The plot brings the kids and their teacher so close that he decides to refuse a different job offer and stay at the school. The final heartbreaking touch is a present from the class with a large label, ''To Sir With Love.'' Clavell reports that such a camaraderie had emerged on set between Poitier and the young cast that ''there is authentic weeping, real tears, and profound emotion, which we did not foresee in the script.''

Many major film reviewers and distinguished critics lament the ''authentic weeping, real tears, and profound emotion'' which dominate so much of *To Sir with Love*. In his critique in *Saturday Review* dated 8 July 1967, Hollis Alpert charged that the last half hour of the film has ''so many heart-tugging episodes that the entire crew must have been awash in tears at the end.'' Other reviewers echo the charge of sentimentality. In the London *Observer*, Tom Milne declared he hadn't been so embarrassed for years, while on this side of the Atlantic, Penelope Gilliat in her 17 June 1967 *New Yorker* review opined that the popular accept-

ance of the sentimentality and sententiousness in *To Sir with Love* was a manifestation of a submerged racial consciousness: ''There is no sense in walking round the point. If the hero of this Pollyanna story were white, his pieties would have to be whistled off the screen and his pupils blamed for cringing. The fact that he is colored draws on resources of seriousness in audiences which the film does nothing to earn.''

To Sir with Love does evidence a lack of restraint on the part of James Clavell. Although he was a successful novelist and screen writer, Clavell had only limited experience as a director, and he was unable to create a consistent tone, key, and rhythm for this, his first feature. Despite the evident weakness in direction, Poitier's performance remains quite disciplined even in scenes where the actions of the younger players are too unstructured, uncontrolled, and overstated. The professional restraint Poitier brings to his role as Thackeray highlights the cardinal rule of acting in cinema: everything must be conveyed in small gestures, seemingly insignificant movements, and minute details of body language. Poitier masterfully captures both the temerity and the excitement of a fledgling teacher in his overly cautious posture

The war of wills between Sidney Poitier and his class in *To Sir with Love*.

Christian Roberts, Adrienne Posta, Richard Wilson, Sidney Poitier, Christopher Chittell, Marie Lawrie, Peter Attard, and Sally Cann in *To Sir with Love*.

and rather too formal approach. Poitier's dancing speaks volumes about the generation gap, and his studied movements in the boxing match comment eloquently on his attitudes towards both students and racism. Poitier proves especially good at getting maximum mileage by subtle understatement and precise timing. He is quite convincing in both his lament for the deficiencies of his students, "I feel so sorry for them, most of them can hardly read," and in his anger over his own fit of temper, "The one thing I swore I'd never do, lose my temper." Each of his short sermons on the meaning of marrige and the importance of hard work is pleasantly tempered by some self-effacing gesture that helps to make the moral palatable. Especially notable, however, is Poitier's handling of the racial material in the film. His righteous indignation burns the words of his disappointment onto the screen when his class refuses to go to the black funeral: "Oh. I see. Thanks for making that

clear." This anger dissolves into a beaming smile when the class comes through and overcomes its prejudice.

One of the key achievements, in fact, of *To Sir with Love* in Poitier's eyes was its ability to make audiences remember Thackeray's smile, his humanity, more than his color. Poitier felt, he declared in our interview, that "my most powerful, rather my most effective, films have been those where the question of race never arose." Poitier's constant goal was acceptance as an actor and a man, not as a black: "I have always wanted to be a performer capable of interpreting all parts of different human beings. I always thought that if I have to perform as a Negro always, I would be restricting myself to terribly narrow passages in the artistic realm. . . .It is not that I am not interested in portraying Negroes. I am a Negro. I am quite proud of my heritage and I prefer being a black man in the contemporary world. . . .But, I certainly do not want my blackness to be the determining factor in my artistic life." Poitier was trying to force his audiences to an awareness of individual human worth, a shift which he felt would effectively destroy the barriers of prejudice. He was trying to erase the "good feeling" one can harbor about one's tolerant attitude, a symptom of persistent prejudice, with a more natural sympathy and identification, where one judges on merits rather than race.

Poitier's achievements in films like *To Sir with Love* were carefully noted by civil rights leaders. In the summer of 1967, a summer that witnessed the release of both *To Sir with Love* and *In the Heat of the Night* as well as the advent of pre-release publicity for *Guess Who's Coming to Dinner,* the Southern Christian Leadership Conference lauded Poitier at its national convention. In introducing Poitier to the delegates, the Reverend Martin Luther King, Jr., described Poitier as "one of the warmest human beings that I have ever met. I consider him a real friend. . .a great friend of humanity. He is a man of great depth, a man of great social concern, a man who is dedicated to human rights and freedom, and a generous contributor of funds, time, and talent in behalf of the SCLC. Here is a man who has never lost a basic concern for the least of God's children. Here is a man who, in the words that we so often hear now, is a soul brother."

These sentiments were echoed by Reverend Andrew Young, who detailed some of the specific achievements of Poitier's work. Andrew Young's eloquent praise is a fine summary of the very themes Poitier so often identified as the messages he hoped to convey through his art: "In a country that pronounced God as dead, he made a secular generation sing 'Amen' to the warmth and love in humanity, which is really the ground of all true religion. Amidst the tensions and neuroses of our lives, and of modern life in general, Sidney Poitier has dramatized sensitivity and concern. So that men of prejudice break the emotional shackles that have enslaved them for generations. Children applaud, and men cry, Sidney, for your passionate portrayals of what man really ought to be. Yes, Sidney Poitier. . .you teach us and have taught us what it really means to be a man in our time."

Poitier's vision of man was uniquely positive in an era of negativism. If he was out of touch with the emotional tenor of the intellectual community, he found a deep sympathy within the mass audience. Poitier consciously chose his course, as he explained in an interview: "I believe in positivism. I believe that there are positives and negatives, and I cast my lot, I commit my energies, to positive things. I like people. I like to be helpful to people. I like to be a part of a kind of aggressive, progressive, humanistic trend in politics, in art, in culture." Poitier was acutely aware of the bad news in the headlines; he was committed to bringing good news to the screen in the faith that powerful fiction would soon create more humanistic facts.

Few of Poitier's fictional roles would make a more powerful statement or affect the perception of race in America more dramatically than his characterization of Detective Virgil Tibbs in Norman Jewison's award-winning feature, *In the Heat of the Night.* At the time of the film's release, he told Norma Browning that the role of Tibbs was "certainly the most intense role I've ever attempted and one of the most interesting." In the film, Poitier continued, "There's a lot of social and psychological cross-fire. It's understated but at least it says something." And, for Poitier in 1967, saying something was the central purpose to his art: "You can say more in films to more people than you can in the theater. In my opinion, it's a waste of time to do a play, even the funniest comedy, unless it also has some comment to make on life."[5] The comment *In the Heat of the Night* made, Poitier explained to us, was principally "the relationship between two men who are born of different social, economic, and political fabric but who come to each other in very interesting theatrical terms." The film succeeded, Poitier felt, in integrating a substantial and important theme in a very entertaining story.

While the "heat" in the title of the Academy Award winner as best film of 1967 referred to the sultry evenings in smalltown Mississippi, it might also have referred to the urban riots that were dominating the news headlines the very year Sidney Poitier was ruling the American box office. *In the Heat of the Night* was both an entertainment and a social statement. In this, his most significant role, Sidney Poitier was communicating, as Malcolm Boyd observed, "at deep levels, a number of complex nonverbal ideas about *the* Negro or, rather, about Americans who were Negro" to a nation haunted by black-white confrontations.[6]

In the Heat of the Night features its own explosive black-white confrontation, pitting a paunchy Southern red-neck sheriff against an uppity intellectual Northern black detective, and matching America's outstanding method actor, Rod Steiger, with its emerging black star, Sidney Poitier. Offscreen, Poitier and Steiger were good friends, having met twenty years earlier when

Sidney Poitier as the beleaguered Virgil Tibbs in *In the Heat of the Night*.

Poitier first started working in theater in New York. Over the years, they sought a property suitable to a joint appearance. *In the Heat of the Night* was the sort of package neither could turn down. It offered both of them a complex and fulfilling characterization, and each garnered a nomination for an Academy Award for best performance by an actor for his role in the film.

During the months before the Awards presentation, each of the two principals was actually the other nominee's best publicist. Of Steiger's performance, Poitier would declare: "He gets so involved in a role that after a while he doesn't even look like himself any more. I don't know who else could have gotten just the right mixture of a man who has no use for Negroes but who does have a respect for ability and courage." Steiger's balanced characterization kept *In the Heat of the Night*, according to Poitier's analysis, from lapsing into a trite Hollywood "happy ending": "Steiger doesn't turn into a different man during the film. His police chief doesn't change his mind about Negroes, he just unbends a little bit. So we don't have a happy ending but we have an honest one."[7] Poitier obviously relished the challenge of working with Steiger, and Steiger constantly emphasized the pleasure he found in Poitier's company: "I love Sidney because he has become Hemingway's definition of grace under pressure. He is the prince of twenty-two million people—I mean, the Negroes, do you understand—and he's able not to be prejudiced and he remains, firstly, a man."[8]

In the Heat of the Night involved the sort of professional film crew that Poitier and Steiger knew they could do their best work with. The director was Norman Jewison, fresh from his stunning success in *The Russians Are Coming, The Russians Are Coming,* and noted for his ability to elicit performances from actors and his willingness to tackle controversial material. Ideas and images for a topical film like *In the Heat of the Night* had been percolating in Jewison's mind for some time, as he told Bernard Kantor in an interview for the 1970 volume *Directors at Work:* "There are certain things that I want to say that I have had in my mind for many years. Why I toured, why I hitchhiked to the American South in 1946. . . it was one of my first long stays in America. I went through Arkansas and Alabama and Louisiana and Mississippi and Tennessee. I went to Missouri, where the last lynching was held. Many of the images that stayed with me through all these years ended up in *In the Heat of the Night*."[9]

To convey these images on film, Jewison turned to the inventive camera of Haskell Wexler, who had

Warren Oates corners Sidney Poitier in *In the Heat of the Night.*

Sidney Poitier as a black Sherlock Holmes in *In the Heat of the Night.*

dazzled critics with his work on *Who's Afraid of Virginia Woolf* the year before and who was acclaimed as the master of atmosphere and mood in cinematography. Like Jewison, Wexler was also involved in social and political controversy, and would soon embark on *Medium Cool*, a neglected American masterpiece dissecting the demonstrations of the sixties and the decade's social turmoil. Wexler's cinematography proved the most interesting feature of the film for young British and French critics. Many echo Penelope Houston's praise of Wexler's "almost European concern for the way the film looks," citing especially, as she does, "a spectacular long shot of car and running fugitive high on a towering bridge, a dazzling image of cotton pickers in the fields, and a close-up police examination of a car detailed in a series of engagingly elliptical camera angles."[10]

The script for *In the Heat of the Night* was prepared by Sterling Silliphant, who transformed a rather routine mystery novel by John Ball into an engaging screenplay. Silliphant's screenplay develops all the sociological themes only implicit in Ball's narrative, using the black detective's tedious legwork as a background for a subtle investigation of racial stereotypes, economic inequities, and the psychology of prejudice. Several of Silliphant's changes in the basic narrative of Ball's novel enrich the film immensely. In the novel, for example, black detective Virgil Tibbs regularly works in Pasadena, California. In the film, Virgil is identified with Philadelphia, Pennsylvania, an ironic reference to the "City of Brotherly Love" and a commentary on the flight of blacks from the rural South to the urban North. Similarly, in the novel, the murder victim is a music conductor whose music festival was to be an economic boom to the town of Wells. In the film, the victim is a Northern industrialist who was going to build a major factory employing blacks and whites in equal numbers.

Silliphant offers in his script an economic and geopolitical explanation of racism. Sparta, the town of the film, is Old Gothic South, while Tibbs's background is all new, cultural North. In the film, Sheriff Bill Gillespie and Detective Virgil Tibbs are from different cultures altogether, and their suspicions and fears are paradigms of racial, cultural, social, and economic tensions in society at large. These sociological and psychological elements in Silliphant's script were admirably fleshed out by Poitier and Steiger, whose improvisations generated several additional powerful sequences. The perceptive critic, Vernon Young, for example, finds one of the most powerful episodes of *In the Heat of the Night* in the scene where Poitier and Steiger relax at night over a beer;

Sidney Poitier and the orchids in racist Eric Endicott's hothouse.

they are, he notes, "deceptively at ease with each other until Poitier expresses sympathy and evokes from Steiger the atavistic dread which boils over into snarling hatred."[11] Norman Jewison reported in his interview with Kantor that this "fairly important" scene was "worked out as an improvisation between Sidney and Rod and myself." Such scenes manage, as Moira Walsh observed in *America*, to say a lot "mostly between the lines, about the hows and whys of life in a backward, economically depressed town and about the inter-relationship of economic and social change."[12]

Change in Sparta is threatened, of course, by the death of an industrialist, yet, paradoxically, his murder brings even more cataclysmic confrontation with the modern, technological, and integrated society in the person of Virgil Tibbs, the Poitier role. Tibbs, a homicide expert for the Philadelphia police, visits Sparta, a small Mississippi town, to see his mother. While waiting for his return train at the local station, Tibbs, because of his color, is picked up as a suspect by patrolmen frantically looking for the assassin. After disclosing his identity, Tibbs is drafted by a reluctant sheriff to join the investigation. The sheriff has been badgered into this decision by the widow of the industrialist, a cosmopolitan and liberated woman played by Lee Grant; interestingly, this forceful intervention by an urban female suggests her color-blindness and her interest in expertise, the very attitudes Tibbs's presence will eventually generate in his fellow police officers. The strong suggestion is that racial prejudice and economic backwardness are all symptoms of the same disease. If Sparta is to be accepted in the industrial universe, experts like Tibbs will have to be accepted for their abilities. Tibbs is, figuratively, a freedom rider come to free Sparta from the chains of ignorance and eventually from the economic stagnation they cause.

Poitier's role in *In the Heat of the Night* is interesting on several levels. First and foremost, Tibbs is a professional policeman, a technological Sherlock Holmes, whose intelligence stands in clear contradiction to the superstition and ignorance of Bill Gillespie, who seems overwhelmed by even his office air-conditioner. Poitier is the very image of professionalism, for example, in his examination of the victim's body and his car. Critical clues from these examinations reveal Tibbs's knowledge of plants and anatomy. Tibbs is also a consummate interrogator, discovering everything he needs to know by indirection and careful consideration of psychology. Tibbs is a superior cop and obviously knows it; he is, in the words of Richard Schickel,

Sidney Poitier and Rod Steiger work together in *In the Heat of the Night*.

"just as uppity as he can be."[13] He obviously relishes this opportunity to give some macho whites lessons in criminal investigation.

Tibbs, an efficient though somewhat vain and contemptuous investigator, happens to be a black American, whose color determines in large part the reactions of the whites he encounters. In the opening sequence, Tibbs is accosted and arrested for being a black with too much money. Sam Wood, the patrolman who nabs him, played by Warren Oates, gives Tibbs no chance for explanations. At headquarters, the angry sheriff, Bill Gillespie, also takes the color of Tibbs's skin as sufficient evidence of guilt. Even after his identity as a law enforcement officer is established, Tibbs faces resentment wherever he turns. The other policemen shy away from him, suspects insult him, and a gang of rowdies attacks him.

Tibbs answers all these challenges with his own venom, however. At the police station, he shows real satisfaction in revealing the relatively high salary he earns in Philadelphia, $165.20 a week, and caustically notes that on his turf, "They call me *Mister* Tibbs." This last assertion of black pride touched a responsive chord among black audiences and served as a title for a sequel by Poitier to this film: "Mister Tibbs" was the black man who could find acceptance among blacks and respect from whites. Poitier himself liked the character of Tibbs because he was "a man who lives on his own terms, however high the price may be" and promised interviewers early in 1968 that "There will be other Tibbs movies because a lot of people feel good when I play good solid fellas."[14]

Tibbs is a credible character who reveals his own

Beah Richards and Sidney Poitier in *In the Heat of the Night*.

prejudice and contempt for whites when provoked. When Tibbs meets Endicott, a cotton plantation owner, after having watched black workers in his fields, he is justifiably angered by Endicott's jibe in his greenhouse that "These plants are delicate. They're like the nigras. They need care." Tibbs's resentment shades his questions and, when Endicott senses the insult, he slaps Poitier. Instantly, Poitier slaps Endicott back hard, warning "I will do everything to bring you down from your heights." Endicott's black butler does a double take at this exchange of blows, while Steiger stands gaping in disbelief and finally throws his chewing gum on the ground. Endicott is thoroughly shocked and laments that "there was a day when I could have had you shot for that." Outside, the sheriff can only tell Tibbs, "Why, you're no better than the rest of us." It was a measure of how far Poitier had come as a black star and a militant that, in the era when civil rights leaders like Martin Luther King endorsed nonviolence, Tibbs the black retaliates harshly and violently. This whole scene can be contrasted to a similar incident in his earlier film, *No Way Out,* where Poitier, as a doctor confronting a racist who spits on him, makes no response.

Contemporary audiences, both black and white, had much to learn from Poitier's quick retaliation, and, as an episode Renata Adler relates in her book *A Year in the Dark* indicates, the lessons would take a long time to be assimilated: "When I first saw *In the Heat of the Night,* I sat near two Southern Negro couples who, at the blow that released a perceptible tension in the rest of the audience, simply averted their eyes. It was only when the Uncle Tom Negro butler in the greenhouse did a perfectly timed double-take at what he had seen that the whole sequence was assimilated into a tradition of comedy, and the two Southern couples were as delighted as everyone else."[15] Comedy is critical to *In the Heat of the Night*, but, for a change, one is laughing with the black hero, a far cry from the insults of earlier Hollywood films where blacks were there mainly to be laughed at.

Virgil Tibbs is not a man likely to accept insult; he's black and proud. The quiet calm he demonstrates throughout, which French critic Gilbert Salachas has compared to the chill of marble, communicates a sense of deep tension. In the scene with Endicott, the inevitable outburst comes, the volcano explodes, and centuries of accumulated humiliations come to the surface, burning everything in the way. Then control takes over, and calm is restored. The audience cheers Tibbs' blow for freedom, clearly demonstrating that, in this film, the black is the hero.

The most dramatic acceptance of Virgil Tibbs comes, however, from Sheriff Bill Gillespie, whose uneasy alliance with a black detective is one of the main dramatic themes in the film. When the mystery is finally solved, thanks to Tibbs's shrewd ratiocination, Tibbs and Gillespie separate in a memorable scene. They have what Rod Steiger has called the "fastest handshake in the history of motion pictures." Obviously the two characters have not forgotten their differences, yet it is clear that their attitudes have changed. Virgil Tibbs's display of expertise and courage aids substantially to Gillespie's perception of blacks, a clear and necessary prerequisite for significant change in race relations. As Bosley Crowthers suggests, this understated conclusion shrewdly indicates "that a rapport between two totally antagonistic men may be reached in a state of interdependence."[16]

Images of racial rapport and interdependence in 1967 were powerful pictures indeed. To both black and white audiences, this film, like many other

Sidney Poitier and Rod Steiger wait for the black detective's departure in *In the Heat of the Night*.

Sidney Poitier as Dr. John Prentice and Katharine Houghton as Joey Drayton in *Guess Who's Coming to Dinner*.

Sidney Poitier movies, was saying that color was less important than the quality of the human being. The enormous artistic and commercial success of *In the Heat of the Night* insured that black people could find on the screen images of pride and self-respect. The message was one of harmony, a revolutionary message to an America haunted by a long hot summer.

One small indication of how radical the brotherhood preached in *In the Heat of the Night* must have seemed in the United States in 1967 may be found in the fact that the Academy Awards ceremony which honored the film was delayed for two days because of the assassination of the Reverend Martin Luther King, Jr. At the awards ceremony, Gregory Peck, president of the Academy, praised the fallen civil rights leader, noting that "one measure of Dr. King's influence on the society in which we live is that of the five films nominated for best picture of the year, two [*In the Heat of the Night* and *Guess Who's Coming to Dinner*] dealt with the subject of understanding between the races. It was his work and dedication that brought about the increasing awareness of all men that we must unite in compassion in order to survive." Peck spoke for the whole film industry when he declared that the most fitting memorial the motion picture community could offer to Dr. King was "to continue making films which celebrate the dignity of man, whatever his race or color or creed."[17]

Sidney Poitier recognized quite clearly the intrinsic link between what was happening in the streets in the mid 1960s and his actions on screen.

There was a quite obvious interaction between America's treatment of the race question and the roles blacks played on screen. Discussing this in Hollywood in 1966, Poitier declared that "Rank-and-file people recognize that continued progress in race relations must be maintained in order to avoid catastrophic results in the future. Now, I feel also that the continued progress in this direction does influence the kinds of parts and how I play them. When I say how I play them, I mean if I am going to play a contemporary Negro, I have to understand what is the condition—economically and politically and socially—of the contemporary Negro." As things changed for black Americans, Poitier knew his roles must change.

America in the mid-sixties was, Poitier observed, at a crossroad. Either white America would accept its black citizens as equals, or things would explode in cataclysmic violence. Poitier's language was especially apocalyptic when he spoke about this matter to Roy Newquist, a journalist who followed the whole production of *Guess Who's Coming to Dinner* quite carefully and published his observations and interviews with all the principals under the title *A Special Kind of Magic*. Poitier told Newquist: "Twenty million Negroes in this country are not asking for something unreasonable. They're asking for better education, better housing, and an equal chance at the good life. An *equal* chance—that is not being unreasonable. Either you help them get this equal chance or you repress them. There's no middle way at all, at all, at all. . . .If the white community puts a stop to the progress. . .Negro frustration will find no outlet and will continue to build and build and build to fierce explosions."[18]

Poitier had no time for repression or artistic censorship. He told columnist Francis Melrose of the *Rocky Mountain News* that he had quite a few "provocative things" to say about the need for love and understanding between blacks and whites and that he believed he could say them best in comedy.[19] Poitier was obviously looking forward to both his next film, *Guess Who's Coming to Dinner*, and to his first attempt at directing a Broadway play, the farcical *Carry Me Back to Morningside Heights*. *In the Heat of the Night* had whites laughing with blacks at prejudice; Poitier wanted to continue in this vein.

Only extra-sensory perception could explain how close Poitier's feelings were in 1967 to those of his old friend, Stanley Kramer, the man behind *The Defiant Ones* and *Pressure Point*. Like Poitier, Kramer was preaching a doctrine of positivism to all who would listen and, like Poitier, Kramer was ready to raise new questions about race relations in comic form. Interviewed in Hollywood just before he began work on *Guess Who's Coming to Dinner*, Kramer avowed his purpose was "to tell a story of interracial marriage, trying to examine it with humor." For his film, Kramer helped develop an original script by William Rose. He and Rose recognized that their basic topic was truly iconoclastic, for the merest hint of miscegenation had long been the *bete noire* of American cinema, a taboo dating back to D. W. Griffith's images of a black rapist and his victim among the dark leaves in *The Birth of a Nation*. Griffith's vision, critic James Agee wrote, was one of "the magical images that underlie the memory and imagination of entire peoples" operating on the "deepest level that art can draw on" with a "dreamlike absoluteness."[20] To dispel viewer objections and to handle their theme with taste, Rose and Kramer decided they must cast the three most perfect performers in America in roles that were comical stereotypes of

their traditional parts: Spencer Tracy was to be the proud patriarch too stubborn to accept the black bridegroom; Katharine Hepburn, the willful, dignified mother with enough love in her heart to wish the best for her daughter even if that best included miscegenation; and Sidney Poitier, the charming, accomplished super-hero, too handsome and noble for any family to reject as a son-in-law.

Katharine Hepburn and Spencer Tracy were, of course, in Hollywood iconography the perfect American couple, a pair whose radiant image of love, courage, and wisdom had dominated the screen for three decades in films like *Woman of the Year, Adam's Rib, Pat and Mike,* and *Desk Set.* Hepburn hadn't, however, acted in several years; she was spending all her time caring for Tracy, whose health was failing badly. Neither had any hesitancy, however, about accepting this script. Kramer and Tracy were old friends and had worked together on several films. Besides, Tracy, Kramer, and Hepburn knew, as Hepburn later

Sidney Poitier meets Katharine Hepburn in *Guess Who's Coming to Dinner*.

observed, that the idea of the film was "good and true" and that, while it "will disturb some people and raise a fuss," it was a film she and Tracy and Kramer could be proud of.[21] Throughout the production, Tracy's health was a major concern; it was obvious this would be his last picture, the capstone to one of Hollywood's finest careers. Many of the lines and scenes become especially poignant when viewed in this context, most notably Tracy's climactic monologue when he speaks of his memories of his life with Christina (Katharine Hepburn) as being "clear, intact, indestructible." Tracy was to die within ten weeks of the film's completion, and, as Sidney Poitier noted, it was almost miraculous that Tracy ever completed the film at all: "I doubt if he could have finished the picture except that he was determined not to let down his close and good friend Stanley Kramer. It was a case of his great fighting spirit triumphing over his shattered health. What a man!"[22]

Tracy's untimely death and the presence of Katharine Hepburn in *Guess Who's Coming to Dinner* contributed greatly to its box office appeal. Fans came to see Tracy and Hepburn and the overwhelming presence of these two stars obscured both Poitier's performance and the fundamental issue of the script: the effect of racial prejudice on American marital patterns and practices. It should be remembered, however, that in 1967 and for several years thereafter, miscegenation and intermarriage between races was illegal in many parts of the United States. In Alabama, for example, mixed marriage was a felony punishable by from two to seven years in prison; Mississippi had a similar statute, and the first interracial marriage there in over one hundred years didn't occur until 1970, and then only when the couple went to federal courts after being turned down in state courts. In Massachusetts, Ms. Remi Brooke, daughter of Senator Edward Brooke, made headlines when she announced her engagement to a white. As Milton Mayer observed in his aptly titled article, "The Issue is Miscegenation," there was and is "almost no Negro-white intermarriage in America."[23] The highest reported incidence ever, including all races intermarrying with whites was less than 2.0 percent and in the 1960 census, the last one before *Guess Who's Coming to Dinner?* only .1 percent of all married couples in the country were Negro-white couples.

The infrequency of interracial marriage actually exacerbated white America's fear of the sexuality of black men and women. Ralph Ellison's hero in *The Invisible Man* perceptively notes that in American society ". . .they insist upon confusing the class struggle with the ass struggle, debasing both us and them."[24] Sidney Poitier made the same point in a discussion with Joan Barthel, lamenting that scriptwriters refuse to give black characters full sexual identities: ". . .sexuality is neutralized in the writing. But it's not intentional; it's institutional. To think of the American Negro male in romantic social-sexual circumstances is difficult, you know? And the reasons why are legion and too many to go into."[25]

Stanley Kramer wanted to simplify the issues in *Guess Who's Coming to Dinner*, to define the problem of interracial sexual relations and marriage as sharply as possible with all the emphasis on the prejudice involved. Kramer believed, he told us in an interview in November 1966, that, when it comes to race relations, it all boils down to one issue, because "for all the talk about violence, revolution, and so on, the basic question remains: Do you want your sister to marry a Negro?" In his film, Tracy and Hepburn are faced with one question: Do you want your beautiful, white daughter to marry her handsome Prince Charming, if he happens to be black? One of Kramer's most controversial decisions was to make Poitier so perfect that the only hesitation any parent could have was one based on racial prejudice. Kramer explained to Richard Coe that he found the exaggeration of Poitier's virtues central to his purpose: "The story narrows down to obliterating all questions to this marriage except the one of race. That he's not in an inferior position to the girl and her family is the point, making race the only impediment to the marriage. If he were, like his father, a mailman or a clerk, that would have been a different story involving class."[26]

Kramer's approach can best be described as an argument *ad absurdum*. For his purposes, it was necessary to invest the young hero of the film with every imaginable virtue and accomplishment so his girl's parents could not have any reservation at all about him as a potential son-in-law. The absurdity of color discrimination becomes quite evident in such a situation. Whether one finds this tactic a useful one or not, it is central to an understanding of the film that one recognize that *Guess Who's Coming to Dinner* is not meant as a realistic portrait of an actual incident, but as a cinematic parable where several characters abstracted from reality become visual symbols illustrating a comic discourse about the basic nonsense of racial prejudice.

The sense of unreality and abstraction, of symbol and parable, in *Guess Who's Coming to*

Spencer Tracy meets his prospective son-in-law in *Guess Who's Coming to Dinner*.

Dinner is emphasized by Stanley Kramer's choice of a deliberately theatrical and artifical style and of narrative devices more suited to stage than screen. Almost every commentator on the film mentions some of its more conventional elements. *Newsweek*, for example, scores the whole directorial technique, noting that "the film might have been made a decade or two ago with its painted sunsets, sclerotic photograph, glaucomic process shots, and plastic flowers pummeled by flood lights"; Andrew Sarris makes a similar point in the *Village Voice*, accusing Kramer of doing "everything by the numbers . . . the lumbering machinery of his technique is always in full view of the audience."[27] The 16 December 1967 review in the *New Yorker* seems closest to the mark, however, when it relates all these tired conventions to the tradition of "drawing room comedy," noting that *Guess Who's Coming to Dinner* "observes a strict unity of time and place and circumstance, with, at intervals, conventional rever-

sals of fortune, a conventional Wise Old Man (disguised as a witty, worldly Catholic priest), and a conventional chorus (disguised as a sharp tongued colored cook.)"[28] Over 90 percent of the film is actually shot on one set, the Tracy-Hepburn home, which Robert Clatworthy created on one sound stage and part of another, using about ten thousand square feet of space.

Even more striking, however, than the physical unities and the claustrophobic set, the traditional characters, and the highly formal photography is the number of set scenes in the narrative, intimate interludes between two characters where debates on race relations are repeated and repeated. The film is like a round-robin talkathon, with each dialogue a parallel to the one before it and the one to follow. Almost every character has at least one parley with each of the others: we have, for example, sequences which feature the black boy and the white girl, then the white girl and the white mother, and finally the white mother and the black

Roy Glen, Sr., Beah Richards, and Sidney Poitier in *Guess Who's Coming to Dinner.*

boy, or episodes showing the black father with the black boy, then the black boy with the white father, and afterwards, the white father with the black father, *ad infinitum* and *ad absurdum.*

A short consideration of the narrative structure should give some hint of how artificial, mechanical, and ultimately funny this patterning is. As the credits are shown on the screen, we listen to the rather saccharine lyrics of "The Glory of Love" and watch a hazy airport scene directly out of a travelogue or television commercial which features the handsome Dr. John Wade Prentice (Sidney Poitier) and the puckishly beautiful Joey Drayton (Katharine Houghton) as they leave the San Francisco airport. Everything seems idyllic for this young couple returning from Hawaii; they just radiate excitement. The first breath of chill reality frosts over their warm exuberance when the white cab driver displays his obvious displeasure at the kissing he sees in his rear-view mirror. Much has

been made of this scene; it is the only physical contact these black and white lovebirds are allowed in the whole film and it is seen only through a mirror.

Poitier biographer William Hoffman asserts that many more shots of Poitier kissing Katharine Houghton were "edited out of the film" and that they "are kept in three press books on the third floor of Columbia Pictures' New York office, marked with red X's and the word *Hold,* which means, in no uncertain terms, that no matter how handsome and intelligent and articulate Sidney is, his skin color still clashes with Katharine Houghton's and they must not be seen making love."[29] Some support for Hoffman's provocative charge can be found in a small item which appeared in Irv Kupcinet's column for 10 April 1967: "Movie-maker Stan Kramer reports there'll be no compromise with the script of his current film, *Guess Who's Coming to Dinner.* The opening sequence will show Sidney Poitier making love to a white girl.''[30] The actual opening sequence involves only a kiss, but in the tradition of stage and screen, it does present the audience with a clear problem. If cabdrivers are scandalized, what will their parents think? The rest of the film pursues the answer quite systematically.

First we stop, however, at the art gallery run by Joey's mother, Christina (Katharine Hepburn), where Christina's assistant, Hilary (Virginia Christine), explains that Christina is out for lunch. Hilary's amazed response to Dr. Prentice labels her a racist immediately, and the pattern is complete: both working men in cabs and working women in art galleries are shocked by the pairing of John Prentice and Joey Drayton.

Retreating for a while from this macrocosm, we move to the microcosm of the Drayton home, where the rest of the drama will transpire. Here we witness the first black reaction, from, of all things, the stereotype of a Hollywood "mammy" in the person of the Drayton's maid, Tillie. Miss Matilda Brooks (Isabelle Sanford) has served the Drayton family for more than twenty years and is even more shocked than Hilary was. "I don't care to see a member of my own race getting above hisself," she bluntly tells Joey. This sets the stage for the first confrontation with each set of parents, and we see Joey talking alone with her mother, while John calls his father long distance in Los Angeles. Joey and John both speak happily of their love, but each avoids the color issue. Obviously, this omission prepares for the comic climax of this scene, when Christina is confronted by her future son-in-law. Katharine Hepburn's prolonged reaction, which borders on collapse into catatonic shock, sets the mood for the slapstick to follow. The narrative pace intensifies now as each confrontation is made briefer and characters are shuffled on and off screen hurriedly.

Things really speed up with the arrival of the real protagonist of the film, Matt Drayton (Spencer Tracy), a successful publisher who is in a hurry to keep a golf appointment with his old friend, Monsignor Ryan (Cecil Kellaway). Once Matt breaks through Christina's embarrassed stupefaction and understands the situation, he begins an investigation of John's credentials, muttering, "They don't know what they're doing."

The narrative then reaches fever pitch when John tells both the Draytons that he will not proceed with the marriage without their approval and that he would like their decision that very day. The moment of truth is at hand for these New Deal liberals with their pictures of Franklin Delano Roosevelt and John F. Kennedy. Christina reminds her husband, "We told her it was wrong to believe that the white people were somehow superior to the black people or the brown or the red or the yellow ones, for that matter. People who thought that was were wrong to think that way—sometimes hateful, usually stupid, but always, always wrong. That's what we said. And when we said it we did not add, 'But don't ever fall in love with a colored man'." Her argument is buttressed by Matt's concomitant discovery of what "an important guy" the distinguished Dr. John Prentice is. Matt remains unconvinced, however, and another round of encounters begins, this time between Joey and her mother and between John and Matt.

The chat between John and Matt typifies the humor in *Guess Who's Coming to Dinner*. In an ironic commentary on stereotypes, Matt is pictured in mid-sentence saying, "Well, you say that they don't have any special sense of rhythm?" and Poitier laughingly replies, "That's right." The white editor then finds himself arguing that at dancing "the colored kids are better than the white kids." Poitier demurs with one more careful jest: "I mean, you can *do* the Watusi—but we *are* the Watusi, if you know what I mean."

To sustain this comic prattle, new characters are introduced; Joey invites John's parents to come to dinner, and Monsignor Ryan, the charming, sociable, Scotch-loving clergyman who could just as well have wandered in from the set of *The Bells of St. Mary's* comes round to inquire about the cancellation of his golf match. The monsignor quickly spins off homily after homily about racial prejudice, taunting his buddy Matt for his opposi-

Isabell Sanford insults Sidney Poitier in *Guess Who's Coming to Dinner*.

tion to the marriage: "It's rather amusing to see a broken-down old phony liberal come face to face with his principles."

Matt and Christina try to escape all this confusion and tension by taking a ride downtown for ice cream at a drive-in restaurant. Escape in the world of screwball comedy is impossible, of course, and Matt accidentally backs into a hot rod driven by a black youngster. The youth explodes into a tirade against old folks, a marvelous counterpoint to Matt's unspoken feelings about black folks. The scene is capped by Matt's mock heroic lament: "Less than 12 percent of the people in this city are colored people, and I can't even have a dish of Oregon Boysenberry without running into one of them!"

Similar screwball antics are pictured back at the Drayton house, where Tillie pours her heart out to John while he is changing his shirt. Tillie, the black maid, has some of the harshest lines in the film; the humor comes from the obvious incongruity between the logic of this black mammy and the new ideas of the black doctor. Tillie warns John: "You may think you're foolin' Miss Joey and her folks, but you ain't foolin' me for a minute. You think I don't see what you are? You're one of those smooth-talkin' smart-ass niggers jest out for all you can get, with your black power and all that other trouble-makin' nonsense." This whole sequence is filmed in oblique camera angles which create distorted perspectives. Actually, the material here may have gotten out of Kramer's control, and it is one of the most awkward moments in an otherwise stylized film. Sociologist Standford Lyman considered this scene "one of the most subtly debasing scenes ever to blacks," especially because Poitier covers his shirtless chest when the maid enters his room. In Lyman's opinion, "no white star—Redford, Newman, McQueen—would have been asked to play that kind of comedy."[31] Debasing or not, the scene does sound a sour note in an otherwise carefully orchestrated film.

The arrival of Mrs. Mary Prentice (Beah Richards) and her husband, John (Roy E. Glenn), gets the film back on the track, especially when Mr. Prentice bellows that the two lovers are "behaving like a couple of escaped lunatics." The stage is set for even more heated debates at the cocktail hour

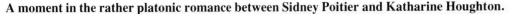

A moment in the rather platonic romance between Sidney Poitier and Katharine Houghton.

118

The black family discovers their son's fiancée is white in *Guess Who's Coming to Dinner*.

which will precede the dinner for the two prospective families. With Christina and Matt split on the issue, Monsignor Ryan on one side and Mr. Prentice firmly on the other, a witty tug of war begins, mingling emotions and laughter in a masterful brew.

One of the most striking exchanges in this predinner combat is a dramatic confrontation between John and his father. Visibly angered at his father's objection to his marriage, John explodes: "You and your whole lousy generation believe the way it was for you is the way it's got to be! And not until your whole generation has lain down and died will the dead weight of you be off our backs! Dad—oh, Dad—you're my father—I'm your son—I love you. I always have and I always will. But you think of yourself as a colored man—I think of myself as a man." Poitier's words ring true in this scene and highlight the seriousness of the topic that has generated such screwball comedy. The emotions Dr. John Prentice gives vent to are remarkably similar to those described by the noted black intellectual Addison Gayle in his moving essay, "Black Fathers and Their Sons." Gayle writes of the "dual contempt" his father

felt, a contempt from the outside world and from his own son: "Though we were the best of friends, and I loved and respected him deeply, he knew that in reality we were enemies. I was the young Hamlet who sooner or later would be forced to thrust the dagger into his heart, forced to stamp out his life in order to be free of the guilt which I felt, and would feel, so long as he lived."[32] Sidney Poitier does a masterful job of bringing this young Hamlet to the screen.

In the last scene of *Guess Who's Coming to Dinner*, the King Lear of the piece, Spencer Tracy, delivers an eloquent monologue, avowing his belief that love is stronger than any question of pigmentation. As he gives this young couple his blessing, he assures them that if they feel half the love for each other that he and Christina have, that will be everything. Needless to say, there's hardly a dry eye in the house when Matt turns and asks a question that must be on everyone's mind after all these lengthy speeches: "When the hell are we going to get some dinner?"

The success of *Guess Who's Coming to Dinner* was immediate; everywhere it played, the film broke box office records. It quickly became

Columbia's all-time top grosser, and reinforced the fact there was a substantial audience for films treating racial matters. In 1967, blacks were going to films in record numbers, and while they constituted less than 15 percent of the population, they accounted for over 30 percent of paid admissions. The number one box-office star in 1967, Sidney Poitier realized over three million dollars from his share of *Guess Who's Coming to Dinner*, money that would help him find eventual artistic and financial independence.

Yet 1967 was to end for Poitier with a sense of muted victory. While audiences flocked to his films, the critics, especially black critics, were treating his roles more and more harshly. Poitier, they charged, was just as much as stereotype as "superhero" as Stepin Fetchit had been as a "coon." Speaking specifically of the Dr. John Prentice role, H. Rap Brown often punctuated his speeches with the joke that "Even George Wallace would like that nigger." Black psychiatrist Alvin Poussaint reported that black children had even made a joke of the film with a little jingle: "Is it a bird? Is it a plane? No! It's Superspade!" Even Poitier's old friend James Baldwin declared that the very professionalism and polish of the film "is meant to blind one to its essential inertia and despair. A black person can make nothing of the film . . .

and when one tries to guess what white people make of it, a certain chill goes down the spine."[33]

Poitier expended a lot of energy defending the film, reminding everyone that it was a comedy, that the film did deal "in a warm, wonderful way with a scary subject," and that "its fairy tale manner" was the best way to invite people to think about interracial marriage without "driving them into frenetic, neurotic reactions." He confided to Martin Levine, however, that for all the good the film did, which he felt was considerable, the charges that he was too smart, too much the super black man with all those degrees, were basically unanswerable: "You can't defend that film against that criticism."[34] The next few years of Poitier's career would evidence his continuing reaction to mounting black criticism, his numerous attempts to mold a new persona more in touch with the militant sense of black identity blossoming in America.

Cecil Kellaway greets Sidney Poitier in *Guess Who's Coming to Dinner*.

Notes to Chapter 3

1. Dorothy Manners, "Poitier Out to Give Love a Hearing," *San Francisco Examiner Chronicle,* 26 November 1967.

2. "To Sir With Love," *Newsweek*, 11 December 1967, p. 101.

3. E. R. Braithwaite, *To Sir With Love* (New York: Pyramid Books, 1966), pp. 95-96.

4. Clifford Mason, "Why Does White America Love Sidney Poitier So?", sec. 2, p. 1.

5. Norma Lee Browning, "Poitier Shuns the Theater to Pursue His Movie Career," *Chicago Tribune*, 20 August 1967.

6. Malcolm Boyd, "The Holywood Negro: Changing Image," *The Christian Century*, 6 December 1967, pp. 1560-1561

7. Roger Ebert, "Sidney Poitier's Hope: True Roles for Negroes," *Chicago Sun Times*, 16 July 1967, sec. 4, p. 1.

8. Gloria Emerson, "Do You Understand, Sweetheart?" *New York Times*, 7 January 1968, sec. 4, p. 15.

9. Bernard Kantor, Anne Kramer, and Irwin Blacker, *Directors at Work* (New York: Funk and Wagnalls, 1970), pp. 143-144.

10. Penelope Houston, "Mississippi Sleuth," *Spectator*, 1 September 1967, p. 251.

11. Vernon Young, *On Film: Unpopular Essays on a Popular Art* (New York: Quadrangle Press, 1972), p. 389.

12. Moira Walsh, "In the Heat of the Night," *America*, 12 August 1967, p. 160.

13. Richard Schickel, "Two Pros in a Super Sleeper," *Life*, 28, July 1967.

14. Judy Michaelson, "Sidney Poitier Makes a Choice," *New York Post*, 10 February 1968, sec. 2, p. 26.

15. Renata Adler, *A Year in the Dark* (New York: Random House, 1969), p. 86.

16. Bosley Crowther, "To Sir With Love," *New York Times*, 3 August 1967.

17. "*In the Heat of the Night* Wins Oscar," *New York Times*, 11 April 1968, p. 52.

18. Roy Newquist, *A Special Kind of Magic*, pp. 125-126.

19. Frances Melrose, "Poitier a Visitor in Denver," *Rocky Mountain News,* 27 June 1967, p. 7.

20. James Agee, *On Film* (New York: Beacon Press, 1950), p. 314.

21. Alvin H. Marill, *Katharine Hepburn* (New York: Pyramid Publications, 1973), p. 120.

22. Dorothy Manners, "Poitier Tells About Tracy," *San Francisco Examiner,* 3 November 1967.

23. Martin Mayer, "The Issue is Miscegenation," in Robert Disch and Barry Schwartz, *White Racism* (New York: Dell Publishing, 1970), p. 209.

24. Ralph Ellison, *Invisible Man* (New York: Random House, 1947), p. 362.

25. Joan Barthel, "He Doesn't Want to Be Sexless Sidney," sec. 4, p. 9.

26. Richard L. Coe, "Kramer Answers Questions," *Montreal Star,* 3 February 1968.

27. "Spence and Supergirl," *Newsweek,* 25 December 1967; "Guess Who's Coming to Dinner," *Village Voice,* 19 December 1967.

28. "Good Causes," *New Yorker,* 16 December 1967.

29. William Hoffman, *Sidney,* p. 10.

30. "Kup's Column," *Chicago Sun-Times,* 10 April 1967, p. 58.

31. Quoted in Paul Dardner, "Hollywood Is Crossing the Last Racial Barrier," *New York Times,* 6 October 1974, sec. 4, p. 13.

32. Addison Gayle, *The Black Situation* (New York: Delta Books, 1970), p. 144.

33 James Baldwin, *Devil Finds Work,* p. 68.

34. Martin Levine, "Poitier Sees His Film Role as Historic," *The Record,* 26 July 1974, p. 20.

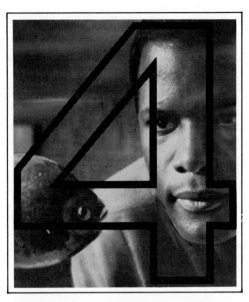

RESPONSE TO PUBLIC CHALLENGE
(1968-1971)

One of the most telling public attacks on Sidney Poitier and his film career appeared as the feature essay in the Arts and Leisure Section of the *New York Times* on Sunday, 10 September 1967, the very time Poitier's charm was dominating the screen all across America. Clifford Mason's articulate and impassioned broadside "Why Does White America Love Sidney Poitier So?" would do more than generate a flurry of letters and other literary responses; Mason's barbs were doubtlessly influential in shaping the development of Poitier's career. Many of Poitier's roles for the next few years may actually be viewed as attempts on his part to rebut Mason's attacks and to refute the arguments of other militant critics. Poitier's portrayals in his next few films are almost too self-consciously designed to erase the ebony-saint stereotype and to enlarge his characterizations, emphasizing his blackness, his virility, and his militancy.

Clifford Mason's thesis was both simple and explosive. All of Poitier's roles over the last two decades were, in this educated black's eyes, "merely contrivances completely lacking in any real artistic merit." In all of Poitier's films, Mason charged, the black star had been an ebony saint, a sad stereotype, "a showcase nigger who is given a clean suit and a complete purity of motivation so that, like a mistreated puppy, he has all the sympathy on his side and all those mean whites are just so many Simon Legrees." For militants like himself and for aggresive young blacks, Mason argues, Poitier's career is stale, hackneyed, and barren, a sort of "artistic NAACPism."[1]

Like most polemics, Mason's diatribe is plagued by overstatements, exaggerations, and some distorted interpretations; twenty years of film appearances cannot be encapsulated in twenty paragraphs of prose, especially when those twenty years have been an era of great change in both film art and American race relations. Nevertheless, Mason's arguments were powerful, and Sidney Poitier was stung by Mason's insults. As Poitier's long-time friend and frequent collaborator, writer Robert Alan Aurthur, observed at the time of Mason's attack, Poitier recognized the elements of truth in the analysis and worried deeply about being a "showcase nigger." Aurthur himself took a rather more practical view, one which recognized the limitations the whole Hollywood system imposed on his friend: "That article hurt him because of the truth in it. But he had one choice, to do 'those' films or not work. What he was creating was a black movie star and there has never been one before. You can't create that by doing black power movies."[2]

Almost all of Poitier's public statements during this period emphasize Aurthur's argument: Poitier found himself the only black in Hollywood, and for him to fulfill the many and sometimes contradictory demands made on him by blacks and whites, by money men and militants, was a clear impossibility. Poitier constantly noted that only when there were more blacks on screen could the whole range of black values be adequately represented. To place the burden of an entire race on one man was too much; as Poitier well knew, it made him an easy target. These few years were, Poitier later confided to Martin Levine, the hardest in his life: "There were so many people whose dreams weren't realized in the kind of films I made, and their frustrations were so overwhelming, in terms of what kind of relief they required, that I became a symbol, a target, and that was a terribly difficult period."[3]

For all the difficulties in this period, however, and despite truly virulent criticism, Poitier's basic arguments remained consistent and convincing. He argued that there must be more room for blacks in films, that there must be a greater emphasis in all films on human dignity, and, finally, that all art must emphasize collective humanity, and he argued these points most eloquently. The elimination of racial barriers in Hollywood was, Poitier told Kathleen Carroll in August 1967, a week before Mason's article was published, the key to breaking stereotypes. When there was only one black on screen, there could be only one vision. America needed more black stars, Poitier complained, but the studios just didn't seem ready for this: "I'm thinking of those twelve first rate Negro actors and ten first rate Negro actresses who can't get jobs. I'm forty years old, and I've spent eighteen years waiting for the situation to change, but it hasn't. I'm certainly not the best Negro actor. There are

many more qualified than I am. The industry just hasn't opened up and I'm discouraged on behalf of others."[4]

In the face of this discouragement and the seemingly impossible odds in Hollywood, Poitier consistently decided to pick the best roles he could and to continue to project the only black presence on a white screen. Sharply questioned by Joan Barthel of the New York Times about this choice and queried whether it really wasn't just a way of playing "the white Establishment Game"—"See Sidney Poitier. See Sidney act. Act, Sidney, act—and show the world how enlightened we are," Poitier roared back that his roles were not "playing along" but were the result of his own decision: "It's a choice, a clear choice. I would not have it so, and if the fabric of the society were different I would scream to high heaven to play villains and to deal with different images of Negro life that would be more dimensional. But I'll be damned if I do that at this stage of the game. Not when there is only one Negro actor working in films with any degree of consistency, when there are thousands of actors in films, you follow?"[5]

Expanding on this idea in a provocative article by Elaine Hamilton, "Why White Women Dig Sidney Poitier," the title of which echoes Mason's famous diatribe, Poitier crystallizes his conception of his responsibility as the only black on a white screen: "As long as I'm the only Negro actor working with consistency, I certainly intend to perpetuate the hero image, until such time as there are sufficient Negroes in films so that we can afford to have good guys and bad guys." Only by demanding black heroes, Poitier felt, could there be real change in Hollywood stereotypes. For example, he knew from his own experience that his presence on screen was a small cause for hope: "Years ago, before I was an actor, I became terribly embarrassed whenever I saw a black on screen. He or she was always devoid of dignity, a funny butler or a comic maid, someone like that. So, since I've been in a position to do so, I've tried to play parts that make a positive contribution to the image of the black people. I want black people in the audience to say 'that's me!' with pride not with shame or uneasiness of any kind."[6]

Poitier's feelings of pride in his own achievement and his recognition that many of his roles did bring new pride to blacks frequently prompted him to even more direct attacks on the underlying, rather monolithic assumptions of Mason's critique. Discussing "black art" with Walter Burrell, Poitier railed at those who suggested there was only one way to be truly black and free. Many roads, Poitier felt, might lead to racial pride and to liberation: "And one thing I truly believe is that we will have made a major step forward when we stop trying to tell other folks how to be black. We're all going toward the same philosophical place. We've simply got to accept the fact that there are many roads leading there—and be tolerant of those travelling those other roads."[7]

Mason's article posited only one truth about black life in American, and this truth was based on several premises which William Grossman attacked a week later in the *New York Times* as fallacies. Grossman argued that Mason falls into at least four major "falsehoods," including the "ethnic falsehood," which argues that a black man should always think of himself primarily as a Negro; "the separate worlds falsehood," which holds that Negroes inhabit a world of their own quite different from whites; "the uncle tom falsehood," that to treat a white man with kindness is to be the white man's nigger; and the "brutality falsehood," which maintains the way to achieve racial dignity is to subject human beings of another race to violence. Falsehoods or not, Grossman does define the key areas where Mason and Poitier would differ. If Mason's critique does assume ethnic separateness, inhumanity, and violence, Poitier's films would never satisfy his criteria. Poitier consciously sought to provide a recognition of all men's common humanity. As Poitier told media maven Lawrence Quirk, "I try to make motion pictures about the dignity, nobility, the magnificence of human life. . . . What we should do is propagandize about being human."[8] And being human was to Poiter much more important than being black or white. Even as racial conflict heated up in America, Poitier spoke of "brotherhood," emphasizing the idea that our common humanity should be the starting point for all teaching: "I believe that a good place for a start is to make a conscientious effort to make universal the understanding that we are all born with the same basic equipment, fronted with an emotional scoreboard. We are all lonely at times, fearful at times, and pained most of the time. Why we do not make use of such kinship rather than ignoring it is a question worth answering."[9]

Poitier's artistic response to Mason and others never blinded him to this notion of kinship. Even in his new militant roles and in his capacity as film producer and director, Poitier acknowledged the need for a comprehensive view of American life and values. As he explained to us in Hollywood, the artist and his society have several important relationships: "I think the artist brings to bear, on every type of work he does, his own value system. And his value system is culled from the values of his society. He may indeed be in advance of his society, but it has been his society which served as the source from which he has gathered his values." As a black American, then, Poitier felt his values are principally American: "The Negro is not a nation unto himself. He does not exist in the United States as a nation unto himself. The overwhelming power structure is that of the whites. The Negro is therefore subject to the rules and regulations and the values of a white society. . . . You have to consider the Negro in the United States as an American first, because he eats the same food and he learns from the same books and the same economic values govern his life. Almost the same, with unfortunately crucial exceptions but generally the same, social values govern his life." As a black performer, then, Poitier felt many affinities with white actors: "When the Negro performs artistically, much of his artistic choices are not unlike those of white actors. The white actor's choices are not too unlike those of the Negro actor because they are both products of the same society. There are fundamental differences, but they do not transcend the overall sameness of the two actors, white and black, functioning in the same familiar society."

Poitier was enough of a realist to know that, as a black actor, he was at the pinnacle of his career. No performer, black or white, had ever had three films jockeying for number one, two, and three in box office grosses. Mason's charges aside, Poitier knew he had to make changes, explore new options, open new areas, for his career would now level off at best, and most likely decline. His choices, as he explained to Martin Levine, could determine the quality of the decline: "I'm a fairly intelligent man. And in 1968, when those three films hit and all year long they were number one, two and three, they were jockeying with each other, I knew then that this was the peak of my career in terms of fame—and stuff. I knew then; obviously it was. I used to sit and evaluate the decline—the quality of the decline, the rapidity of the decline, and the nature of a decline of a career, and how I would try to engineer one with dignity and integrity, so that I could level off, ultimately possibly into oblivion, with grace."[10]

One indication of the seriousness of Poitier's interest in controlling his career was his attempt in February 1968 to direct a Broadway play, *Carry Me Back to Morningside Heights*, a topical comedy about a young Jewish liberal from Greenwich Village who becomes the slave of a black law student to expiate his guilt over racism. Robert Alan Aurthur had originally intended his script as a screenplay, but Poitier convinced him to stage it as a play first. The play was never filmed, largely because it was a failure, yet, for Poitier, it was an important project. As a leading man, a movie star, Poitier is acutely aware of his age; the clock is the enemy of handsome young men, especially when their careers are on screen. While Poiter could joke in 1968 with Guy Flatley that he might have "twenty-five years left" before "age and time and senility" would conspire to bring him to the point where he could not meet the challenge, Poitier had already established the age of fifty as a turning point for his career. Over the next decade, Poitier planned to move into directing, writing, and producing so that, by 1978, he could switch his place before the camera for a position behind it. As Poitier told Guy Flatley, he loved creative work: "It's my life. I hope that the challenge of creating new things is never too much for me."[11] Directing *Carry Me Back to Morningside Heights* was one way Poitier struggled to define his future as a black artist. Its theme touched on the racial problems confronting all America, as Poitier explained to William Glover the Associated Press: "It's a comedy built on the question of guilt. Americans have enormous capacity for guilt, regardless of their color. There is so much about our lives that is guilt-producing in many, many areas. We simply use the confrontation of Negro and white as the most obvious, sharpest, keenest symbol of guilt we have." At the same time, the humorous handling of this racial theme, its artistic realization, proved a process of self-discovery for Poitier: "Failure doesn't frighten me as it used to. If I find I can't direct, my life will go on. But I have to have that information to define myself artistically. I want to know exactly what I am."[12] And, although *Carry Me Back to Morningside Heights* did fail, the play gave Poitier the confidence he needed to make the leap from performer to director, from actor to film maker. The play was contemporary comedy, a mode that Poitier would explore quite successfully later in the seventies.

Still another element in Poitier's deliberate process of self-discovery and redefinition was his determined effort to sharpen his skills as a writer. Given his limited schooling, Poitier had at first shied away from writing, declaring he had no desire to write at all, but gradually he found that he did "have a desire to make a certain kind of film that nobody else was writing."[13] Poitier's first screen story was, in fact, a revolutionary act as he saw it, for, up until the time he prepared his

outline, movies had totally ignored the average black woman. His story *For Love of Ivy*, was meant as a hymn of love to all black women. Poitier had four daughters, and their needs were a large part of his motivation: "They [Poitier's daughters] are black children in a predominantly white society and it's difficult for them, as for all Negro girls, to fashion a sense of themselves from the melange of different values. I want to give them a sense of self that is acceptable to them, and that's hard to come by. For example, the concept of beauty, as presented on, say, television commercials, is not devised from their point of view. Yes, I know there are more Negroes on television now, but 'more now' is not the comment I want to make."[14] The message Poitier had in mind was more fundamental, more down to earth, more in touch with everyday realities: "I found that my daughters were dealing with very intrinsic questions—boy friend, marriage, how many kids?—and I thought I would like to make a film that was in a way a recognition of the Negro woman's existence, and to say that I think she's beautiful."[15]

In terms of his own career, Poitier also wanted to project a new image, that of a "sexy, slightly illegitimate swinger," a rakish black bachelor who was a man about town.[16] Poitier was tired of roles which denied his sexuality, and he wanted, once and for all, to settle the questions of virility and of miscegenation and intermarriage which fascinated his critics. Poitier's attitude was breathtakingly lucid: this black man was interested in a romance with a black woman. Poitier explained his position to Joan Barthel in her unusually intimate interview which was published under the title "He Doesn't

Sidney Poitier as Jack Parks and Abbey Lincoln as Ivy Moore in *For Love of Ivy*.

Want to Be Sexless Sidney": "I've wanted to work with a Negro actress in a man-woman situation that was warm and positive. I'm not interested in having a romantic interlude on the screen with a white girl; I'd much rather have romantic interludes with Negro girls. This is not a put-down of white girls, you follow? But in the lives of most black men are Negro women, and vice-versa. And also because of my feelings about the difficulties of Negro women in contemporary American society. I want them glamorized and idolized and put on a pedestal and spoiled rotten."[17]

Poitier's love story, featuring as it did an average black woman and a sporting young black man, was a subject most film companies were not prepared to undertake. Poitier took his nineteen-page outline, called "Ivy," to the three major companies for whom he had worked and made money, and they all turned him down. In each case, the company offered Poitier an alternate film, one more in keeping with his earlier projects and his old image. As Jay Weston recalled later, each of the studios was "frank to confess . . . fears that a love story between two Negroes might not have the popular appeal necessary to justify the major expenditure of mounting a high style movie comedy."[18]

Finally Poitier and his friend and agent Martin Baum succeeded in selling Poitier's idea to a new film production company, Palomar Pictures International, a subsidiary of the American Broadcasting Company. Palomar launched an impressive number of film projects in 1968, announcing eighteen properties to be filmed. If it hadn't been for Palomar, Poitier told The Film Daily 29 September 1967, he "might still be walking around with the property." In March 1967, while Poitier was still shooting Guess Who's Coming to Dinner and before the release of either In the Heat of the Night or To Sir with Love, Poitier was also working with coproducer Edgar J. Scherick and Jay Weston on the preproduction of the project, by then entitled For Love of Ivy.

With Poitier, the producers chose Robert Alan Aurthur to write the screenplay. Aurthur, whose work on the television project "A Man is Ten Feet Tall" and on the subsequent film Edge of the City had endeared him to Poitier, worked on the script all spring and turned in a full draft in July 1967. All the parties involved loved the material. As Jay Weston recalled it, "We read it with a growing sense of excitement for we now knew that the film story would work and play as we had hoped." Daniel Mann was then signed to direct the project, and the summer of 1967 was spent in script

revisions and in casting the other principal roles.

The key role to be cast was that of Ivy Moore. Almost three hundred actresses tested for the part, including some well known entertainers. Yet, in one of those rare Hollywood Cinderella stories, almost too good to be true, the very last woman to try for the role was selected by Poitier and Mann even before they could schedule a formal screentest for her. Abbey Lincoln was to play Ivy Moore. Few people had seen Miss Lincoln in her only previous film, Nothing But a Man, where she played opposite Ivan Dixon under the direction of Michael Roemer. Nothing But a Man, a moving and authentic story of a real black family, never had a chance to play regular commercial theater circuits in the 1960s.

For Love of Ivy was to be Abbey Lincoln's big break. Almost every commentator mentioned her tremendous skills; some even proclaimed her the new female Sidney Poitier. On the set, Abbey Lincoln and Sidney Poitier worked quite well together; they seemed very comfortable with each other, and many of their best scenes were spontaneous enlargements and elaborations of material in the script. Director Mann was euphoric when he talked about this subtle interaction and communication his principals shared: "There's tremendous rapport in her scenes with Sidney. I find that in working with two Negro artists, an awful lot passes between them that makes me aware how much more they know about the cultural traditions than I do. They do certain things with certain qualities that are quite different. . . . Once, after a wonderful take, Sidney was tremendously impressed by Abbey, and shouted 'Man, she's so colored!' That's why he wanted to make this picture—to present an honest picture of black people in a very real situation."[19]

Abbey Lincoln was equally lavish in her praise for Poitier and for the honesty and integrity of the role of Ivy, which was, after all, originally his creation. Ivy was a real person for Abbey Lincoln: "One reason I enjoy playing Ivy is that for the first time a typical black woman is the heroine of a movie. Like thousands of other black women, Ivy is a domestic. Her problems are typical of their problems. Her battle for independence is their battle and at the same time the film is warm and funny."[20] For Poitier, Ivy was both reality and fantasy. He told many audiences at the time the film was released that, when he was young, he used to fantasize about a certain kind of girl like the girl in For Love of Ivy.

Unfortunately, the realization of Poitier's dreams and, in fact, his whole story line leave

Beau Bridges arranges a date for Sidney Poitier in *For Love of Ivy*.

much to be desired. As numerous critics note, *For Love of Ivy* is a rather mechanical reworking of the thirties' screwball comedy formula, with a dash of Cary Grant in blackface. The film presents a zany white family, the spoiled children, a problem with a domestic, and a whirlwind romance, all by now rather stale and tired conventions. The addition of a new racial angle in the undertaking just isn't enough to spice up the brew.

Several seeming contradictions haunt the film. Poitier's desire to change his idealized image never quite fits in with his attempt to glorify black women. The more he seems the playboy, the less romantic and sentimental the film becomes. Several of his lines make little sense in terms of the total narrative, especially those in which he dramatically compares himself to a piranha who devours little creatures like Ivy. Only a few minutes later, this confirmed bachelor will be a meek supplicant, begging Ivy's hand in marriage. As *Variety* noted in its review dated 10 July 1968, "never made clear are the reasons for Poitier's last-minute about-face after years of defiantly resisting marriage or for the maid's willing capitulation to a man whose values are in striking opposition to her own." Pointing to love as the reconciler of all plot difficulties is just not convincing. Poitier's new image and the old fashioned sentimentality of the tale just don't mix, and, as *Variety* observed, the resultant "sketchy characterizations impose a hardship on Abbey Lincoln and Sidney Poitier."

Still another problem arises because Poitier was so insistent that Ivy be a typical black woman, even down to her employment as a domestic in a white household. America was just not ready for romance in rags, so Abbey Lincoln remains on a pedestal. Despite her status as a maid, she sports designer clothing throughout, parading outfit after outfit that, in the words of some cynical wits, "would charm the false eyelashes off some high-fashion models." A brilliant commentary on this artificiality appeared in the *New York Times* for 1 September 1968, under the title "The Maid Wore Costly Wigs and Dressed Like No Maid We'll Ever

See," a satiric essay by Troy DeBose which parodies the film by having an imaginary character, Beulah, write home to her sister Hattie Mae about the film. Beulah's plot summary and reactions hilariously expose the total lack of realism which mars the film.

Poitier's story as developed by Robert Alan Aurthur drifts so far from any reality into the world of popular culture and genre conventions that some critics like Stanley Kauffmann speculate that Poitier and Aurthur were trying to explode some myths by embracing others: "Under the well-spun floss, it seems to be saying: 'You want integration? O.K., we're going to integrate you out of your minds. We're going to integrate with white America's heritage of twentieth century pop myths.'"[21]

Kauffmann's thesis would explain the almost mechanical, all-too-stylized plotting of *For Love of Ivy*. Like *Guess Who's Coming to Dinner, For Love of Ivy* reveals a narrative structure that seems a bizarre cross between a well made play, a drawing room comedy, and a fable. The opening shots of the film chronicling breakfast at the opulent Austin family home in Long Island, for example, are virtually unvarnished exposition, quickly establishing the importance of the black maid, Ivy, to an inept bunch of virtually moronic whites. Ivy deftly handles the successive appearances at the breakfast table of each individual family member: Frank Austin, played by Carroll O'Connor, the popular and archetypal Archie Bunker from television's *All in the Family*, another fable larded with social relevance; his wife, Doris (Nina Martin); and his teenage children, Gena (Lauri Peters) and Tim (Beau Bridges). This Austin family is, of course, a direct descendant of the rich spoiled family made famous in such classics as *My Man Godfrey*. Carroll O'Connor is cast in a role which, as the critic for New York magazine noted, was a mainstay of Eugene Pallett's career, and the spoiled brats could just as well have been played by Tim Holt and Constance Bennett in earlier decades.

The tenuous domestic peace at the Austin home is ruptured when Ivy announces her decision to quit, and to try at age twenty-six another way of life, maybe a school for secretaries. Mrs. Austin, who struggles even to find the sheets for her bed, let alone to put them on, immediately asks Ivy not to go, reminding her "You're part of the family. We need you. You should take a vacation. . . . We'll send you any place you want to go—Africa?" To Mrs. Austin's exasperated query, "What *do* you want?" Ivy can only reply, "I'm not sure. I just know I haven't got it now."

Amazingly, Ivy's intention so leave the Austin household threatens the equilibrium of the whole house. It's as though the caretaker were threatening to turn the asylum over to the inmates. The Austins go into an even greater frenzy, plotting various strategems to keep Ivy in their employ. If in *Guess Who's Coming to Dinner* the black hero was endowed with almost superhuman qualities, here in *For Love of Ivy* the white family is presented as a bunch of stupid, incredibly inept people, almost subhumans, whose existence is severely threatened by the departure of their maid. The Austins are the butt of all the jokes.

Finally, the younger Austins decide on a far-fetched strategem to dissuade Ivy from leaving. They will introduce her to a suitable black man who can bring romance into her life. Tim, the bohemian ne'er-do-well of the family, blackmails Jack Parks (Sidney Poitier) into dating Ivy. Jack, the owner of a trucking company serving the Austin stores, is at night the partner in an illegal gambling casino functioning in the back of a truck. Tim threatens to expose Jack's racket if he doesn't date Ivy.

Poitier's first appearance in the film highlights the stupidity of the Austin enterprise. While Tim seems a nervous and clumsy blackmailer, Jack is obviously in charge of the situation. His agreement to date Ivy is more a jovial concession to a bumbling acquaintance than anything else. Poitier's amused reactions to this unexpected request are both elegant and funny, as is the gesture he makes when he pays the bill for the drinks when Tim is refused credit at his father's store's cafeteria. Jack is everything Tim isn't, smooth, confident, and independent. The laughs in the scene are again all at the white Austin's expense.

This comic humiliation of clumsy whites continues in the next scene, an awkward dinner at the Austin home, during which Gena and Tim play servants to Jack and Ivy in a comic reversal of roles. The short, simple, honest dialogue between the two blacks again contrasts with the strained, stupid behavior of the white youngsters. The white youths are so gullible and so naively prejudiced about the sexual conduct of blacks that Jack can't resist making them the targets of his pranks. In an inspired scene, Poitier reveals his rich comic talents and his willingness to exploit racial stereotypes in humor as he dupes his two young friends into thinking the aspirin he is taking is a powerful aphrodisiac.

Romance is interspersed uneasily with comedy from this point on, as Poitier begins to pursue

Abbey Lincoln. The scenes between the two blacks are, however, so warm and natural that they seem out of place in a film which has so many grotesque white characters. The more realistic, warm, and engaging the love story becomes, the sillier, and indeed more cruel, the humor of the sequences with the Austins seems. Jack invites Ivy to a Japanese restaurant, where each of them professes a reluctance to be seriously involved in a love affair. This restaurant scene seems contrived and artificial, but does establish Jack's cosmopolitanism, his fluency in Japanese, and his savoir faire. Interestingly, one critic for *Cue* in a review published in the 20 July 1968 issue, found a subtle sociological content in this scene: "Their talking about personal matters as if the Japanese waitress in a restaurant didn't exist is a sly commentary on the way whites usually ignore blacks."

The sociological content in the next scene is equally sly. Jack and Ivy go to an avante-garde theater in Greenwich Village with a bohemian crowd, and immediately they relax and fit right in. Beats had, of course, long identified with black consciousness and black music, so it seems most natural that Ivy and Jack would be at ease. Actually, this was one of the most difficult scenes in the filming because Poitier and his producers wanted to use real Village characters. An open call at the Village Gate, where *MacBird* was playing, drew over a hundred East Village youths, but a riot almost ensued when one was busted for smoking marijuana. Peace was restored when the production company promised legal help. Despite this hassle, Poitier himself told *New York Times* reporters that he had great sympathy with the so-called hippies: "They may be dirty outside, but there are those of us who are dirty inside. If they're sick, it's only to the extent that their parents' society is sick. Give them time, they may come up with something. As long as they hold on to love, they'll be all right." The relative sanity of the beat scene in Greenwich Village, as it's captured in *For*

Sidney Poitier the self-proclaimed playboy in *For Love of Ivy*.

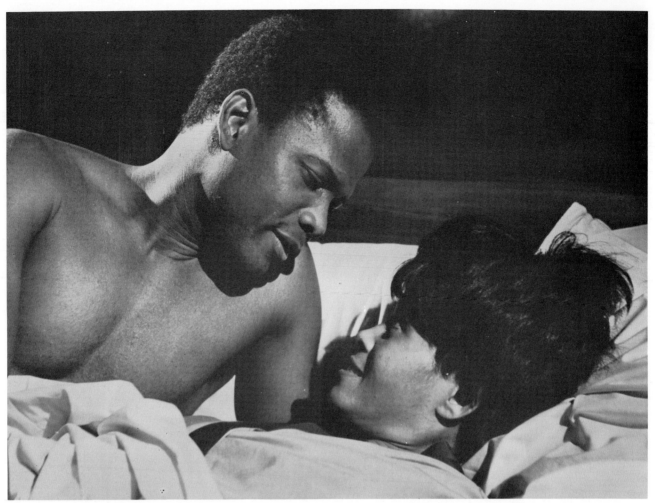

The nude scene in *For Love of Ivy.*

Love of Ivy, is still another pointed commentary on the ludicrous banality and stupidity of the suburban life-style embraced by the Austins.

Jack and Ivy finally leave the crowded Village club and its studied tackiness for the isolation and elegance of his uptown Riverside headquarters, where Jack lives and operates his business. Ivy is impressed by his entire operation, including the casino on wheels, and by Jack's tender concern for some black youngsters, the children of his employees. This whole sequence is quite successful as a prelude to the love scene which follows. Poitier demonstrates great subtlety and tact in his attempt to seduce Abbey Lincoln. He is tender and kind; one feels his growing passion under the mask of external control. Quite overwhelmed, Ivy decides to spend the night. What follows is, unfortunately, anticlimactic. The long-awaited nude love scene between Sidney Poitier and a black woman is, as *Newsweek* critic Joseph Morgenstern skillfully

describes it, a bit of a disappointment, for, despite the fact it is "a hugging, squeezing, kissing and heavy breathing love scene . . . in bed, too, and undressed!" it seems "botched." In Morgenstern's opinion, it seems "more of a tumbling act than anything else, and those black skins which ought to be far more beautiful in color photography than washed-out white, are somehow shied away from."[22]

Whatever one's reservations about this scene, however, about its aesthetics or its frankness, it is a landmark scene in Poitier's career and in the history of blacks in film. Clifford Mason's charge that Poitier never got the girl, or that he never fully expressed his sexuality, could no longer be advanced with any real validity. Poitier had managed to bring an amorous, sexually potent black to the American screen as the hero of a comedy. Stanley Kauffmann is especially eloquent on this point, and his review of *For Love of Ivy* also provides a remarkable insight into the profound effect this nude love scene had on contemporary audiences. In *For Love of Ivy*, Kauffmann feels, Poitier has as a star "entered into that tacit sex dialogue that is a requisite between a star and his audience." Kauffmann saw the film at a matinee and, as he describes it, the show was "attended by lots of ladies of both colors and all ages." At that matinee, Kauffmann notes, Poitier was the real center of attention: "When Poitier stepped out of his car to make his entrance, a sigh went around the theater, an embrace of welcome. When Miss Lincoln visited his *Playboy*-type pad and he appeared in a V-neck pullover with no shirt beneath, there was a puzzled but expectant sign. ('Why so unchic, Sidney? But of course you must have your reasons. Forgive us for doubting. We'll wait and see.') In the bed scene, where he seemed to be naked, I had to switch off my audience radar. Too lurid."[23]

Any lurid vibrations in Poitier's love scene are quickly dispelled in the stylized slapstick which concludes *For Love of Ivy*. Back in the scatter-brained world of the whites, Ivy gathers her belongings and prepares to leave. In one last desperate attempt to dissuade her, the young Austins reveal their blackmail and tell Ivy that Jack acted not out of love for her but from fear of exposure. Ivy's faith in Jack is shaken, and what follows is a comic chase of reconciliation highly reminiscent of the concluding sequence in *The Graduate*. Jack finally displays the wit and personal presence to persuade Ivy of his true love. He even promises "to wipe the thing clean" just as his gambling operation is raided. The film ends with his promise of "the biggest, juiciest kiss you ever had" as the audience waits for the titles and theme music, a fitting parallel to the "they lived happily every after" of traditional fairy tales.

Following the success of Poitier's three previous films, *For Love of Ivy* also made substantial profits. Poitier was surefire box-office as director Daniel Mann explained to Charles Sanders: "I'll tell you how big Poitier stands now. The fellows at the releasing companies don't have to do any kind of selling job on his pictures anymore. They just have to pick up a phone, call a distributor in, say, Cincinnati, and mention Poitier's name. The distributor asks only one question: 'When can I have the film?' Take *Ivy*, for example. We finished shooting it and announced it would be released in July. Within a few days we had something like three hundred theaters asking for it . . . and that was just a starter."[24] Each of these engagements was proving that the earlier judgment of the major studios was wrong: with Sidney Poitier in it, a love story between two black people could be a box office hit, even with predominantly white audiences.

The epic nature of Poitier's achievement in bringing a black romance to the screen as a popular commercial motion picture in the long hot summer of 1968 was not lost on contemporary reviewers. Vincent Canby, for example, in his *New York Times* review dated 18 July 1968, declared that, with so many contemporary events casting a shadow upon America, "it's a De Mille-sized miracle that *For Love of Ivy* is so entertaining and, on occasion, affecting." Canby found the film to be "a slick, funny tranquilizer that, for better or worse, will reassure those people (of both races) who go to the movies to be told that everything is going to be all right." Perhaps the most impassioned and optimistic review of all came, however, not in the entertainment section, but on the editorial pages of the *New York Post* in the column of black activist Roy Wilkins. On 27 September 1968, Wilkins dedicated his whole text to *For Love of Ivy*, musing that "If Sidney Poitier is not careful he is going to undermine the heavy thinkers in the Black Revolution." Wilkins, a distinguished black intellectual, recognized in the film Poitier's studied efforts to confront his critics, and, in Wilkins' view, Poitier was overpoweringly successful: "Already the white and black intellectuals in and around New York are in a tizzy over

Sidney Poitier assumes a new role as Jason Higgs in *The Lost Man*.

131

Sidney Poitier leads his men in a robbery for the good of the organization in *The Lost Man*.

his new film, *For Love of Ivy*." In ways never before thought possible, Wilkins observed, Poitier was bringing the black dream to the screen; Wilkins especially praised the honest writing in *For Love of Ivy*, noting that "the dialogue is often just what the Negro had dreamed ought to be said on the screen."

For Love of Ivy was Poitier's powerful first answer to his critics. In it, he managed to combine a romance between two blacks and some humorous jibes at whites with some rather powerful dialogue. His next film would go further. Poitier would move from the comfortable world of the black playboy to the tense ghetto of the black revolution. His next film would move him to the wrong side of the law, casting him as *The Lost Man*, an urban guerilla on the run.

The Lost Man embodies, in large part, Poitier's answer to the persistent charges that he did not support and encourage black militancy. The narrative was actually based on Frederick Green's novel *Odd Man Out*, a lively story of the struggle for Irish independence which Carol Reed adapted quite successfully to the screen in 1946. Robert Alan Aurthur adapted Green's novel and Reed's film, working not only in his traditional role as writer, but serving for the first time in his life as a director. With his good friend at the helm, Poitier obviously retained much authority himself; the enterprise was a good-natured, collaborative venture.

Poitier and Aurthur shifted the story from Northern Ireland to contemporary Philadelphia, just as Jules Dassin a year earlier had moved John Ford's *Informer* to the black ghetto under the title *Up Tight*. Poitier and Aurthur were committed to authentic location-shooting and to black crews, two decisions which suggest their joint dedication to a serious study of real problems in front of and behind the camera. This first substantially funded, professional study of black militants was shot in the slums of Philadelphia with a great deal of authentic night footage, a formidable undertaking for a tyro director.

In addition, many of the crew and large numbers of the cast were getting their first big breaks. The many picketers and protesters in the film, for example, were amateur film extras but real-life demonstrators. In a dramatic act of allegiance to their cause, Poitier hired the actual militants who had been picketing Girard College for over seven months in hopes of turning aside an old racist bequest restricting admission to poor white youths and gaining admission for students of all races. These Girard College protesters play the roles of activists in *The Lost Man*. Poitier was quite literally taking their cause from the streets to the screen, as well as providing them with salaries and the wherewithal to continue their struggle.

Poitier worked equally hard to see that this film about the black cause had a representative number of black craftsmen in every department of the production. Setting a goal of fifty percent, Poitier approached every department at Universal and requested all the available black help for his film. The result was, as James P. Murray observed in his history of contemporary black film, *To Find an Image*, that *The Lost Man* was a film on which "for the first time in screen history, the technical crew was nearly fifty percent black. Blacks worked as electricians, production assistants, makeup artists, wardrobe assistants, publicists, tailors, grips, and still photographers. There was a black assistant director." Poitier was not only preaching revolution in *The Lost Man*; he was creating one on the set. He knew that liberation would come only when blacks could work together to create their own art. *The Lost Man* marks the earliest stage in Poitier's slowly evolving program of encouraging black artists and craftsmen. In only a few years, Poitier would be producing his own films, projects that would be about blacks and made by blacks.

In *The Lost Man*, Poitier plays the role of Jason

An unexpected gunfight mars the escape in *The Lost Man*.

Higgs, a black militant who orchestrates a daring holdup in order to obtain funds for arrested members of his black power organization and their families. Obviously, Poitier's switch to violent criminal activity marked a major shift in direction for a man who had won an Oscar for *Lilies of the Field* and who had charmed America in *A Patch of Blue* and *To Sir with Love*. A fine artistic indication of how great this shift was can be found in V. S. Naipul's engrossing novel *Guerillas*. Naipul is quite attuned to how influential Poitier's image is, even in the Third World. One of the most poignant moments in the novel comes when one of his most brutal characters goes to a double feature of Poitier hits. *To Sir with Love* moves him to tears of empathy and remorse, but he cannot relate to *The Lost Man* and its image of Poitier as "a man with a gun": ". . . he knew it was made up and he didn't allow himself to believe in it." Many audiences were to have trouble believing in Poitier as Jason Higgs; for them, Jason was too much what Poitier wanted him to be, "a revolutionary." Most of middle America, the so-called "silent majority," was in the grip of a new conservative rhetoric. Blacks became, as sociologist Robert Disch explained in his classic study of *White Racism*, convenient scapegoats: "The Negro has often been forced to assume the role of scapegoat in American history. He has had the society's sins projected onto him and has been considered the cause of the society's problems, a role which previously has been shared by immigrants, 'reds,' 'anarchists,' Jews, and other minority groups. In the present period, signs of the racial scapegoat can be found in the current national obsession with 'violence in the streets,' and the concomitant cries of 'law and order.'"[25] Given the temper of the times, the sympathy for violent opposition and criminal action manifest in *The Lost Man* was quite daring. Poitier was really putting his white audience up against the wall.

The opening sequence of *The Lost Man* is especially disarming and suggests the kinetic energy which characterizes the film, one of Poitier's fastest moving projects. The whole narrative is a prolonged chase through an urban nightmare, and the driving jazz, blaring sirens, and violent lyrics of a child's chant which form an aural collage at the beginning of the film, prepare the audience for the numerous quick cuts and curious juxtapositions to follow. Many of Poitier's most important dialogues occur over the sound of black spirituals sung in the same building his organization uses, so it is only appropriate that, in the first scene, Poitier the committed radical is seen sitting off to the side,

as pickets gather for a peaceful act of civil disobedience and police cars arrive to cart the demonstrators away. As the police officers speak to the black leader, Dennis, excellently portrayed by Al Freeman, Jr., we see Poitier in close-up, his eyes hidden by large sunglasses as he sits in a car near the scene. Poitier is studying the police response; later, we learn he wants Dennis to stage another demonstration to deflect police attention from a bank robbery whose proceeds are to go to "the organization," an unspecified group which some reviewers have quipped seems a curious amalgam of the Boy Scouts and the Mafia.

One of the major achievements of *The Lost Man* is its eye for the realistic details of contemporary urban life. The demonstration which opens the film looks so real that Philadelphia police banned the crew from shooting anywhere the public might see them, for fear the incidents could spark racial trouble. In addition, while many buildings could be included in scenes of robbery and mayhem, no building owner wanted his building portrayed as the target of racial hostility and protest. These scenes were filmed, then, at Philadelphia's Acme Warehouse, away from the eyes of spectators. The footage still seems as though it were culled from television reports. When Dennis convincingly instructs his people, "Everybody down. . .protect yourself, but no violence," and the chant begins, "We ain't gonna let nobody turn us around," audiences are being forced to relive some of the most dramatic moments in contemporary life, seen from the viewpoint of the protestors.

Director Aurthur cuts from the chords of a civil rights chant to the dying words of an old Negro spiritual, "Like a tree that's standing by the water, we shall not be moved," at once establishing the continuity of black protest and the black church, yet highlighting the chasm between a preacher downstairs asking his congregation to "call the beast to you with love" and Poitier, the militant in mod glasses, upstairs preparing the members of his commando unit to rob a bank. The constant counterpoint of hymns and sermon played off against cold, calculated, almost militarily precise commands leads to one of the key exchanges in the film. As the preacher instructs his fold not to be "angry if you can't make them like you want them to be," Poitier mockingly cites the Biblical verse, "Behold the elements, the heaven and earth, for of these all things are created." Queried by a compatriot as to what that means, Poitier explains that "It means everything is the same in the eyes of God, so there's no need in kicking up a fuss." As activist Jason Higgs, Poitier obviously has little time for passive resistance; he's physically and mentally separated from the church and ready to kick up a fuss.

Another key definition of Jason's philosophy comes in the next scene when he tries to convince Dennis, the pacifist, to lead a decoy operation. Dennis is quite skeptical about the whole affair, reminding Jason that "Our guys never pulled anything like this before. And you, man, I remember seeing you on television four or five years back telling people to register and vote, talking love and nonviolence. You sold me!" Jason's answer is bitter and agonizing: "Times change. They beat me up pretty good. They shot me, put me in jail nineteen times. They tried to bury me, brother." Jason goes on to explain the revolution in purely human terms, winning assent even from Dennis's grandmother when he recounts the injustices they had known personally: "My old man was a preacher. He never had a paying job in his life. How long did yours work for the man? Forty, forty-five years? Did he get a nice pension when he retired? Or did he die on the job and get nothing?" Dennis wavers, and Jason delivers his most forceful lines in the film: "Nonviolence is one thing. Passive dying is another. You like being a squatter? A man pays rent on the roof over his head." Just as Jason begins to shake Dennis's resolution, the action gives even more support to his obviously Marxist conception of the need for revolution. Dennis's wife comes in, complaining that the baby is real sick. As Jason gives her money, Dennis tries to refuse, but Jason explodes at him in rage: "It's for medicine, man!" Jason then reminds him that "Tomorrow is for a lot of guys with a lot of sick kids." Dennis reluctantly agrees to go along.

Poitier's one other important encounter in the film is with Cathy Ellis, played by Joanna Shimkus, a white social worker who confesses to him that she "needs to be needed." Cathy attempts awkwardly in their first few encounters to seduce Jason, but he is aloof and distant. Their romance blossoms, however, during Jason's attempted escape from the police, and the two lovers die together at the end of the film, both outcasts in an alien society. Many reviewers note Joanna Shimkus's striking beauty and her refreshing energy in *The Lost Man*; as Guy Flatley notes, she "projects a breathtaking blend of purity and sophistication—half child, half woman; very now, but oddly old-fashioned; sweet but sexy; as nice as Julie Andrews and as naughty as Julie Christie."[26] Sidney Poitier was just as bedazzled by Joanna Shimkus, and an off-screen romance resulted in an eventual marriage.

Sidney Poitier and Joanna Shimkus as lovers in *The Lost Man*.

Poitier's onscreen romance with Joanna Shimkus, as she chases him, emphatically answered all the criticism involving the treatment of his relationship with Katharine Houghton in *Guess Who's Coming to Dinner*. In *The Lost Man*, as Richard Gertner noted, we have an "interracial romance in which osculation goes far beyond the peck on the cheek Poitier gave Katherine Houghton."[27] Both at the Ellis family residence and at the Austin Marina, Poitier and Shimkus are rather intimate. In the last conversation, she tells him that, before they met, she didn't know where to go, and he confesses to her that, in the midst of fear and solitude, he found in her companionship and comfort. They kiss passionately and the scene cuts to Kathy lying on the couch and Jason caressing her face. The two then head for Pier 78 and the one chance of escape. To Jason's question, "Is it still far away?" Cathy answers, "Very far, but I'll come with you." Like the young lovers of Fritz Lang's classic *You Only Live Once*, this interracial

Sidney Poitier's wife-to-be, Joanna Shimkus, shares a joke with him between scenes in *The Lost Man*.

Bonnie and Clyde die in each other's arms, and a dramatic close-up shows their two hands, white and black, united in death. In the background, one hears Quincy Jones's musical lament, drawn from Negro spirituals.

In *The Lost Man*, then, Poitier plays what *Variety* described as "a Malcolm X-type leader," and is shown in passionate love scenes with a white girl. Perhaps even more striking, however, is the fact that he is no longer a successful member of the establishment; he is an outlaw and a loser, a sympathetic villain. Jason Higgs is surely a far cry from the "showcase nigger" that Clifford Mason had deplored. Poitier was changing with the times, for, as he explained to Charles Champlin of the *New York Post*, he felt there was a new audience out there: "The films are finding it necessary to stay on their toes because the audience is thirteen to twenty-five years old and it's hip. They're not

going to be had by old 1940s and 1950s ideas. If they're going to be won, it's going to be by exciting reflections of the world they live in. They're not going to be sold the impression that they live in anything but a multi-racial society. It's a cultivated young generation who ask more questions."[28]

To reach this new generation, Sidney Poitier joined Paul Newman and Barbra Streisand in a dramatic new venture. These three artists formed First Artists Production Company, Ltd., in the summer of 1969, a corporation designed to finance, produce, and distribute the films these three top stars would make. Poitier saw this partnership as a dream come true; he was a black man who would have real control over his own films. There would be no more studio bosses, no more corporate censorship, and no more outside control. The young man who had once been disoriented by the complexity of Darryl Zanuck's operation was now to be a producer, director, and publicist himself. As Poitier signed the incorporation papers, he outlined his ambitious hopes for the future: "We are willing to invest our time, energies, and money not just in our own individual performances, for whatever they may be worth, but in a viable production entity whose sole aim will be the production of quality entertainment. I feel very strongly that we are creating new opportunities not only for ourselves but for many new, young, and diverse talents in the country from all ethnic and minority groups."[29] Poitier's own later productions for First Artists would fulfill this hope.

Before Poitier could develop any material for First Artists beyond the planning stages, however, he was offered the opportunity of repeating the characterization which had brought him such great success in *In the Heat of the Night*, black homicide detective Virgil Tibbs, a role he had long wished to assume again. Poitier's next film, *They Call Me Mister Tibbs!* is not really a sequel to *In the Heat of the Night*; it's more a follow-up feature. The only link between the two films is Poitier's character, and even Tibbs is moved from Philadelphia back to novelist John Ball's original California locale, and is surrounded with a loving, middle-class family, a beautiful wife, and a comfortable life style.

In accepting this rather routine assignment in a totally undistinguished film, Poitier proved, as Vincent Canby indicated in his 9 July 1970 review of the film in the *New York Times*, his "inalienable right . . . to make the sort of ordinary, ramshackly entertainment, very close to pointless movie that a white movie star like Frank Sinatra has been allowed to get away with for most of his career." *They Call Me Mister Tibbs!* and Poitier's next project, another Tibbs caper called *The Organization*, are extraordinary only in their ordinariness. In both of them, Poitier is just another detective plying his trade against a backdrop of dark streets, dangerous thugs, seductive women, and prolonged car chases. The films are pointless, mindless, indeed ramshackle, but they do generate some exciting footage and some glossy stills. *Variety* was right on target when it labeled *They Call Me Mister Tibbs!* a "highly commercial, topical package" that will "attract large audiences, especially in general release in metropolitan areas."[30] Both these Tibbs movies would give would-be producer-director Poitier an intimate exposure to the slick operations of Mirisch productions, a corporation with a good sense of what the public wanted to see.

The script for *They Call Me Mister Tibbs!* was prepared by veteran screenwriter James R. Webb, whose credits included such popular favorites as the thriller *Phantom of the Rue Morgue*, the war epic *Pork Chop Hill*, and the western *How the West Was Won*, and by Alan R. Trustman, whose *Bullitt* was a smash success demonstrating that car chases through the hills of San Francisco could replace a lot of narrative exposition and rivet the audience's attention. Whenever things begin to drag a little in Tibbs's investigation, the film takes to the street for another chase, no doubt designed by Mr. Trustman. The director for all this action was none other than Gordon Douglas, another proven professional who had led various stars through their paces in melodramas like *Tony Rome, Lady in Cement*, and *The Detective*. Douglas was famous for getting things done on time and under budget, with a minimum of delays and difficulties on set.

Like so many of Douglas's later films, *They Call Me Mister Tibbs!* is long on stock scenes, cardboard characters, and sensationalism, and short on logic and insight. Each scene in the film, it seems, is designed to create its own tension and

Sidney Poitier as outcast and underdog in *The Lost Man*.

Sidney Poitier as Virgil Tibbs arrests Juano Hernandez in *They Call Me Mister Tibbs!*

climax; there's little attempt to fit these tidy pieces into a total pattern. One can drop in and out of the film at will, since continuity is so unimportant. This style of film making is, of course, perfectly suited for audiences with short attention spans who are addicted to visceral thrills; it's especially serviceable in drive-in locations. This episodic structure also proves appealing when television networks buy the films; broadcasters can splice as many commercials as they wish in the film and little is lost in the continuity.

The camera work in *They Call Me Mister Tibbs!* has more affinities to television detective shows than to the *film noir* tradition. The opening shot of the film, for example, is a routine establishing shot following an emergency vehicle through a city landscape. The slow movement from wide angle lens to close-up suggests the zoom-in which begins almost every episode of television detective series. In typical television style, the camera then tilts up the side of a building, in through a window, and, as a red light flashes all too symbolically, we witness

disjointed images of the murder of a young prostitute. As in television, all the shots are obliquely framed, and nudity is suggested more than it's presented. The girl's body is then discovered by Juano Hernandez, and the stage is set for an investigation as the sequence ends.

Cut to the police station, and there's Sidney Poitier on the phone with his wife in an all-too-typical slice of life conversation:: "It is Sunday and you have a family." "Can't we go hear Reverend Logan?" "I'm beat." From this point on, the pattern will be the same, a sequence of detective work, a sequence at home, a little chase, then back to detective work, more on the domestic scene, then another chase. *They Call Me Mister Tibbs!* works few variations on this pattern; one of its virtues is its predictability. Early in the going, in fact, it becomes clear that Virgil Tibb's good friend, his spiritual advisor and political ally, the Reverend Logan Sharpe (Martin Landau) is the murderer. The only question is whether Tibbs will be honest enough to arrest him, especially since

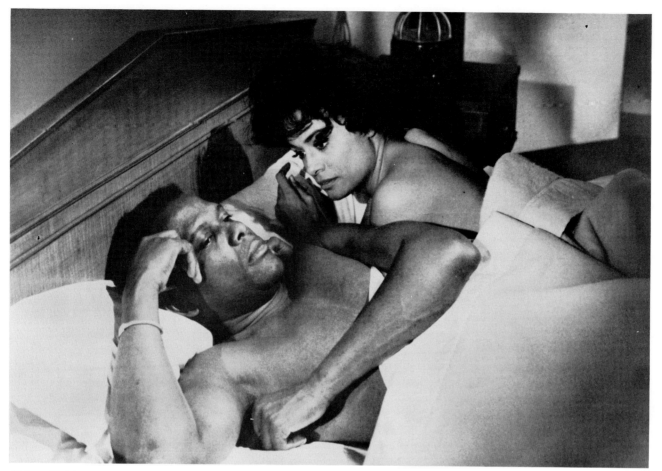

Sidney Poitier shares some intimate moments at home with Barbara McNair in *They Call Me Mister Tibbs!*

Mrs. Tibbs is one of Sharpe's most dedicated supporters and since a critical vote on home rule is about to be taken. Arresting Sharpe would set the movement back many years, Tibbs fears, and even his fellow detectives constantly ask him, "Why don't you pass this one? Don't you and Sharpe sit in the same pew?"

Obviously, Tibbs is too noble to let personal feelings overwhelm his professional responsibilities, and the film suffers somewhat from a lack of suspense and dramatic tension. To replace that energy, numerous exciting scenes are plugged in for little or no reason. There is, for example, a prolonged and dramatic car chase that does little more than give Virgil Tibbs a fine opportunity to puff on his cigar as he listens to squad cars describing it on the police radio; there is also a lengthy chase on foot, again to little purpose, although it does show Poitier's athletic prowess. Similarly, a subplot about drug smuggling enlivens things for a while, as a black prostitute tries to seduce Tibbs; by the time Tibbs brushes her aside, he's ready to demolish some white thugs and to shoot an obnoxious pusher. All of this is, of course, routine adventure fare reminiscent of director Douglas's earlier films.

Finally, Tibbs moves in and arrests Logan Sharpe at his church. When Sharpe tries to explain the crime to his friend, Tibbs is the consummate professional: "I don't want a statement; it's no good without witnesses. Besides, I don't want to hear it." Sharpe collapses in a pew, however, and tearfully describes the agonies of being made to feel "a washout as a minister and then a washout as a man." He begs Tibbs to give him just twenty-four hours until the polls close when he promises to confess. Tibbs can't be swayed, however, as he declares he is "through playing God. Maybe I'll make you a martyr, and maybe not, but I'm not good enough to play fast and loose with the rules." As Tibbs prepares to take Reverend Sharpe into custody, the minister bolts to the street and steps in front of a speeding truck. Newsmen come and Tibbs handles their questions quite professionally,

Sidney Poitier gives some lessons in life to George Spell in *They Call Me Mister Tibbs!*

Sidney Poitier as Detective Virgil Tibbs in *The Organization*.

noting that despite the arrest and subsequent accident, "the case is never solved until the judge declares the verdict." Tibbs then walks off with his family, and the camera pulls back to a street scene and the credits.

They Call Me Mister Tibbs! may be remembered, if it's remembered at all, not for its detective story or its chases, but for the quiet scenes at home with Tibbs and his children. Most reviewers either overlooked or denigrated this aspect, but Poitier obviously gave a great deal of attention to his portrayal of a middle-class, black father. One of the film's finest moments comes after Poitier discovers his son, played by George Spell, sneaking cigarettes with a friend. After making sure it's only tobacco and not pot, Poitier marches the boy upstairs where he forces him to smoke a cigar and "enjoy" some brandy. Poitier is quite intense in this scene as he tries to drive home the point that today there are real opportunities for blacks, "They're looking for you," and that with opportunity comes responsibility: "You'll be on

Lani Miyazaki, Raul Julia, Demond Wilson, Billy Green Bush, James J. Watson, Jr., Ron O'Neal, and Sidney Poitier in *The Organization*.

Sidney Poitier as Virgil Tibbs facing the same adventures found in every celebrity detective film.

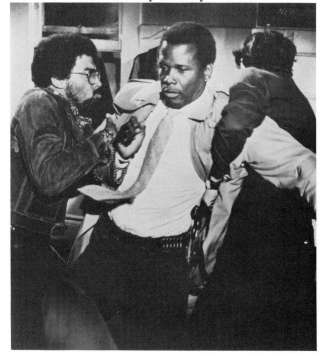

your own, mister.'' This dual theme of opportunity and responsibility will recur in many of Poitier's later films, where it receives considerably more emphasis.

The Mirisch Company obviously had little interest in messages about black opportunity and responsibility, but they were edified with the returns from *They Call Me Mister Tibbs!* Within a year, still another feature based on the adventures of the black detective reached the screen under their aegis. Cryptically entitled *The Organization*, it was, like its predecessor, a commercial entertainment, a fast-paced thriller with flashy women, numerous chases, loud shoot-outs, and bloody brawls. *The Organization* was, in large part, the film establishment's answer to the raunchier blaxploitation entering the American film market.

This time James Webb's convoluted script divides Tibbs's loyalties between his professional responsibilities and his sympathy for a group of young San Francisco radicals who burglarize the headquarters of an international drug syndicate.

Virgil Tibbs in the middle of an assassination scene so typical of early seventies adventure films.

The Organization actually repeats the key elements in *They Call Me Mister Tibbs!*; the major tension and suspense is generated by Tibbs's crisis of conscience. He manages to represent both the law and the good impulses of those who go beyond the law. For a while, in fact, Tibbs is even suspended from the force so he can act just as forcefully, militantly, and extralegally as he did in *The Lost Man*.

Unlike *They Call Me Mister Tibbs!*, however, *The Organization* also relies on a quite complex plot to sustain flagging interest. Three separate crimes are carefully woven into one tapestry, and only when Tibbs discovers the pattern can he close the case and merit reinstatement. The first crime is the drug heist, which the radicals freely admit; the second, however, is the murder of Morgan, the drug dealer, which occurs shortly after the theft. For a long time, these two crimes were viewed as one by the police, and that complicates matters. When the two are finally separated, there is still another double cross to be unravelled, which

centers on the character of the beautiful Mrs. Morgan, played to perfection by Sheree North.

Directed by Don Medford, *The Organization* is slightly superior to its predecessor. The opening six minutes of the film, prior to the actual credits, is a masterful sequence detailing the elaborate heist of the factory which fronts for the heroin operation. The quasi-military nature of the radicals' operation is marvelously captured and mirrored in this carefully lighted, rhythmically edited scene; there is little dialogue, but the fine camera work and impressive jazz background rivet an audience's attention. The professional sheen so evident here might be compared to Poitier's own efforts in later films to mimic this sequence. An especially striking parallel can be found between this footage and the opening moments of *A Piece of the Action*.

Tibb's family almost disappears from *The Organization* because there is so much plot to be unravelled. Poitier's best scenes come in his confrontation with the young radicals. He is wary, firm, professional, yet simultaneously sympathetic

Sidney Poitier flexes his muscles battering white criminals in *The Organization*.

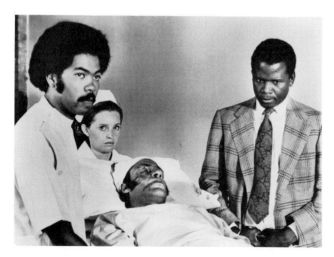

Virgil Tibbs is forced to examine his commitment to the police and to the young radicals in *The Organization*.

Plot complications puzzle all concerned in *The Organization*, a film long on surprises and double crosses.

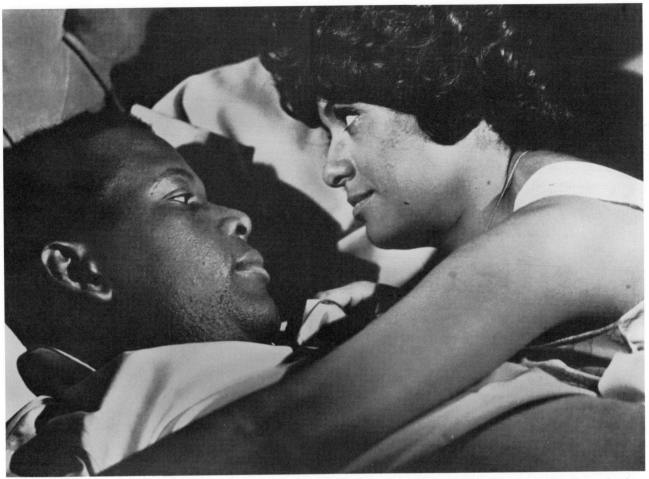

Barbara McNair and Sidney Poitier in *The Organization*.

Wanda Spell and Sidney Poitier in *The Organization*.

and engaging. In these scenes, Poitier is obviously drawing on his own experience as a black activist on the fringes of society. There was, for example, the time he and Harry Belafonte had to take some money to civil rights workers in Mississippi. As Poitier recalls it, "We had to take a small teensy plane to fly us up at night to the rendezvous where we were going to take the money to these Civil Rights workers. We come in on a little airport that is all dark. We see a headlight and it's our guys. Stokely Carmichael and several others were waiting for us." After this perilous landing, still further adventures awaited the northern visitors, who were, Poitier admits, not used to working in the boondocks. To get the money into town, past a truckload of red-necks, they had to sandwich their car between two others. As they drove to town, Poitier recalls, "this truck came up behind the back car and started ramming it."[31] Those hard knocks on the backroads of Mississippi helped shape both Poitier's values and his acting

144

technique. He frequently reminds interviewers that the core of his art comes from his own experiences. If Tibbs in *The Organization* seems at ease with militant radicals, it's because Poitier knows what it is like in underground movements.

Poitier was by now somewhat restless about his participation in purely commercial enterprises. The blaxploitation scene was, he felt, not the answer because the "power was not in the hands of the blacks." The movie industry, he knew after his long years in the trade, was a business controlled by money. The men with the money, the producers with the support of the banks, were the real power brokers. So, between the two Tibbs movies produced by the Mirisch Company, Poitier also found time to begin work on *Brother John*, an unusually inventive and experimental property to be undertaken by his own company, E and R Productions. Under this banner, based on the initials of his parents, Poitier was to enter the next phase of his career. America's only black superstar was to become a remarkably successful black film-maker.

Notes to Chapter 4

1. Clifford Mason, "Why Does White America Love Sidney Poitier So?" sec. 2, pp. 1, 21.

2. Quoted in Mel Gussow, "From Sidney With Love," *Newsweek*, 11 December 1967, p. 101.

3. Martin Levine, "Poitier Sees His Role as Historic," *Record*, 26 July 1974, p. 20.

4. Kathleen Carroll, "With Sidney Poitier," *Daily News*, 27 August 1967.

5. Joan Barthel, "He Doesn't Want to Be Sexless Sidney," sec. 4, p. 9.

6. Elaine Hamilton, "Why White Women Dig Sidney Poitier," *Modern Screen*, August 1968, p. 81.

7. Quoted in James P. Murray, *To Find an Image*, p. 34.

8. Lawrence Quirk, "The Man Who Proved There's Black Magic!" *Screen Parade*, June 1968, p. 54.

9. "Brotherhood," *Newark Evening News*, 9 July 1967.

10. Levine, p. 20.

11. Guy Flatley, "Sidney Poitier as Black Militant," p. 15.

12. William Glover, "Identity Seeking Sidney Poitier Tries Directing a Play," *Courier Journal*, 25 February 1968.

13. Quoted in *This Week*, 21 April 1968.

14. Barthel, p. 7.

15. Gussow, p. 101.

16. *This Week*, 21 April 1968.

17. Barthel, p. 7.

18. Jay Weston, "Care and Watering of Poitier's *Ivy*," *Variety*, 8 January 1969, p. 49.

19. Quoted in *New York Times*, 14 January 1968.

20. "*For Love of Ivy*," *Ebony*, October 1968, p. 53.

21. Stanley Kauffmann, *Figures of Light* (New York: Harper and Row, 1971), p. 94.

22. Joseph Morgenstern, "Maid in the U.S.A.," *Newsweek*, 29 July 1968, p. 80.

23. Kauffmann, p. 95.

24. Charles Sanders, "Sidney Poitier: The Man Behind the Superstar," *Ebony*, April 1968, p. 176.

25. Robert Disch and Barry Schwartz, *White Racism* (New York: Dell Publishing, 1970), pp. 2-3.

26. Flatley, p. 15.

27. "The Lost Man," *Motion Picture Herald*, 14 May 1969.

28. Charles Champlin, "Sidney Poitier: The Burden of a Pioneer," *New York Post*, 3 February 1969, p. 48.

29. A. H. Weiler, "Three Stars Form Film Production Outfit," *New York Times*, 12 June 1969.

30. *Variety*, 8 July 1970, p. 14.

31. Sidney Poitier, "Entertainment, Politics, and the Movie Business," p. 22.

DIRECTOR AND PRODUCER POITIER
(1972-   )

E and R Productions would, Poitier told the press, "make films that show a truer picture of American Negroes to movie audiences." Poitier's first project for E and R Productions was filmed under the working title *Kane*, no doubt an allusion to Orson Welles's classic film, and released under the title *Brother John*.

Brother John was based on an original idea by Poitier and Ernest Kinoy about a man who might be bringing a last message to society, a man who represents different things to different people, a man who had been almost everywhere and done almost everything. This complex allegory was eventually scripted by Ernest Kinoy and directed by James Goldstone, who had just completed *Winning*. *Brother John* was a film with noble ambitions and great aspirations, but eventually it proved a financial failure.

To a large degree, both the noble intentions and financial failure of *Brother John* are a measure of how far Poitier had come in the film business: he was the first black who could risk his career on "iffy" propositions. When Poitier was the only black on screen, he explained to Chester Higgins of *Jet* magazine, he had to play it safe because the establishment was looking for an excuse to exclude blacks: "You know, when a picture of mine didn't make money before, there were always those in the industry to say 'Well, those boys (meaning black, but they would never have to use that word) just aren't commercial.' That's why so many before me—Rex Ingram, Canada Lee, others—didn't get a real shot at film stardom."[1] Now that he was a star, however, and other blacks were appearing on screen, Poitier could take chances, explore new properties, and broaden the range of his roles.

Brother John was, unfortunately, a deeply flawed product, an unfortunate first step for a fledgling producer. The plot at first seems rather straightforward, an amalgam of two stories, the homecoming of John Kane and the intensification of labor agitation in Hacksley, Alabama. In

Hacksley, a black girl dies in the hospital. At her funeral, her long-lost brother, John Kane, is an unexpected guest. Few people know him, and no one quite knows how he knew to come. The police suspect he's an agitator who intends to support the local strike by black workers. Meanwhile, John establishes a romantic relationship with his former classmate Louisa MacGill (Beverly Todd) and revives a friendship with old Doc Thomas (Will Geer). Both these minor characters play important roles in the story. As Louisa, Beverly Todd creates a dynamic vision of a modern black woman, alert, active, and aware, while Geer develops the mystical, quasi-religous aura of the film as he muses on the background, achievements, and travels of the strange Brother John.

The police are equally curious about Brother John, watching his every move and harassing him

Sidney Poitier as John Kane in *Brother John.*

Beverly Todd and Sidney Poitier in *Brother John.*

occasionally. Brother John subdues one racist policeman with a karate chop, but the police search of his room reveals a passport with visas from all over the world and a strange diary with seemingly blank pages. Given all the tension in town, the authorities arrest him, but Doc Thomas helps him escape. Doc Thomas is convinced that John Kane comes from another world as an angel of judgment.

There is an aura of mystery around John, rather self-consciously generated by the camera work of Gerald Perry Finnerman, who uses a soft lighting haze to illuminate Poitier's figure, and by the special wind effects included by director James Goldstone. Major critics all mocked these clumsy devices. Vincent Canby wrote, for example, of "aurorean backgrounds of sunlight" and "close-ups that are so tight you get the sensation that you're looking at Mr. Poitier through some Olympian mail slot."[2] *Variety* was equally harsh when it derided "the now familiar formula interpolation of pretty walks, soulful talks, and the obligatory poptune insert" which characterized the romance.[3] The combination of mysticism and the mundane in *Brother John* finally results in a confusing, seemingly unfinished narrative which combines, as Vincent Canby so aptly declared, "the apocalyptic aspirations of *Samson and Delilah* and the vision of *Search for Tomorrow*."

Despite the fact that the power of the original idea was lost in its transition to the screen, Poitier did see one of his dreams realized on the set of *Brother John*. Long angered by the racism of unions, Poitier told us years before that "Hollywood is the most discriminatory town in the world in terms of job opportunities for minority groups. Hollywood has a complex of unions that are closed shops and many of them absolutely refuse to have

Sidney Poitier as an imprisoned Angel of Judgment in *Brother John*.

even one Negro apprentice come in''; his hope was to open those unions and break the barriers of fear. In the production of *Brother John*, Poitier began his own apprentice workshop for minority trainees in each craft. He and executive producer Joel Glickman recruited these novices, then paid them $150 a week plus their living expenses. Both Poitier and Glickman knew this was not the whole answer, but it was a beginning. They could at least help some apprentices get their union cards; the rest would be up to the unions. As producer Glickman told *Variety*: ''There was still no way this trainee program could overcome the last obstacle, the seniority list, which is an outdated, medieval system that has nothing to do with a man's creativity or skill. Every man with a union card in his pocket in Hollywood should have the right to be employed on an equal basis, regardless of race, creed, or color.''[4] Independent productions, like those of E and R Productions, could provide at least some of the experience so essential for minority craftsmen if they were to compete for jobs in Hollywood.

The restrictive policies of American unions and the prohibitive cost of studio productions combined to force Poitier to shoot his next E and R project in Mexico. For this black western, *Buck and the Preacher*, Poitier joined forces with Harry Belafonte Enterprises, and they both, in turn, borrowed capital from Columbia Pictures. As Belafonte told interviewers from *Variety*: ''We were given a certain amount of money to put this film on screen and we couldn't do it for that price in the United States.'' Executive producer Joel Glickman from E and R Productions agreed, noting that ''you can't do big period westerns in the States anymore. The costs are prohibitive.''[5] Poitier and Belafonte both wanted this to be a big, star-spangled, authentic western; it was their chance to show the large role blacks had played in the conquest of new territories, an idea that had haunted Poitier ever since *Duel at Diablo*. As a boy, he had seen all-white westerns and wondered where the blacks were. *Buck and the Preacher* was his chance to bring those black cowboys to his children and to black audiences everywhere.

The screenplay for *Buck and the Preacher* was prepared by Ernest Kinoy, who had worked with Poitier on *Brother John*, and it was based on an original story by a black writer, Drake Walker, who appears as Elder in the film. Drake Walker, serving as an apprentice director, was also one of the six minority trainees on this project. Poitier continued to employ and train all the blacks he could on his projects; on *Buck and the Preacher*,

Sidney Poitier takes charge in *Buck and the Preacher*.

more than half the production crew, the cast, and the stuntmen were blacks. Nevertheless, there were still racial problems in the production of the film. Poitier and Belafonte had originally intended to use Mexican blacks in supporting roles and as extras. But, as Belafonte explained to *Variety*, the Mexicans just didn't fit the image he and Poitier hoped to project: ''They just didn't look black. They considered themselves black men, but some had blue eyes or red curly hair. It really blew the minds of a lot of people to discover that black Americans don't look like black Mexicans or South Americans.''

Problems with casting were further exacerbated by disagreements over salary. Poitier and Belafonte were paying union scale, but a French company which shot in the area earlier had paid considerably more than scale so local blacks and Mexicans thought the American independent production was trying to cheat them. Needless to say, more than the temperature was hot on the set.

Then there was the problem with the director, Joseph Sargent. Both Poitier and Belafonte had chosen him for the project, yet, as the rushes for the early scenes came in, they were disappointed. Their disenchantment grew, until finally Sargent was released from his contract and Sidney Poitier took over the direction himself. *Buck and the Preacher* thus became the first picture Poitier directed, though he had already extended a helping

Sidney Poitier works behind the scenes with a Mexican crew.

hand on some previous occasions, most notably on *They Call Me Mister Tibbs!*

Sidney Poitier and Harry Belafonte were always most circumspect in their descriptions of their differences with Joseph Sargent, who was a longtime friend of Belafonte. Yet the public statements Sargent and Belafonte made on 17 March 1971 to *Variety* do suggest that it was Poitier's almost monomaniacal devotion to this project and to the integrity of a black vision of the West which was at the heart of the matter. Sargent, for example, declared that Poitier ". . . had breathed and lived with it since its conception. No one knew the material better than he did. He should be the man to put it on the screen. In no way would it work with another director. He had thought it all out beforehand, and whenever I wanted to change that concept, I met with resistance. It's his film. It's as simple as that, and there was nothing racial about it whatever." Belafonte, for his part, emphasized the black aesthetic so central to the project: "If the nature of the subject wasn't such that it's working and dealing as deeply as it does

with the black psyche, it might not matter. But Joe came up with a style for this film that had both Sidney and I concerned whether the style was going to fulfill the purpose of the film when we saw the footage."

There were few neutral observers of all the conflict on the set of *Buck and the Preacher*. Even the *Look* reporter assigned to cover the project, George Goodman, penned an article, "Durango: Poitier Meets Belafonte" with the subtitle "Two Wary Rivals Patch Up a Fight to Make a Movie Together," which prompted both Belafonte and Poitier to appear as the only guests on a ninety-minute interview program to refute his charges. Goodman's article does offer, however, the only explanation of the specific differences between Sargent and his stars. Goodman quotes costar Cameron Mitchell as saying that Sargent was fired because "he was shooting the picture like a television show." Despite the limited funding Columbia had provided, neither Poitier nor Belafonte wanted *Buck and the Preacher* to be another routine programmer. For Belafonte, *Buck and the Preacher* was his major chance to achieve a goal that had always eluded him, recognition as a black actor rather than as a nightclub entertainer. And, for Poitier, this project was his chance to redeem himself as an independent producer, to overcome the failure of *Brother John*, and, with the exit of Joseph Sargent, to establish himself as the first black director of the seventies, a star before and behind the camera.

Directing had, of course, long been on Poitier's mind. Even at the peak of his career, when he was making *Guess Who's Coming To Dinner*, he spoke with Roy Newquist on the set about the need to take control of his own career, expand his talents, and move behind the camera. Poitier was quite aware that the career of an actor is frequently short and often unrewarding artistically. Actors, Poitier knew, and especially black actors, are forced into "types." Even in 1967, Poitier himself was wearying of his acting chores and looking for the escapes and new opportunities producing and directing could provide. The genesis of Sidney Poitier, film maker, may well be found in the laments of Sidney Poitier superstar: "Once you become successful in this game, a certain kind of image becomes the personality that is the bankable product in this industry. I'm considered to be a certain type of personality, and I'm hired more often than not for that type of role. Even though I've had great opportunity and diversity in the parts I've been offered and the parts I've accepted, I still find myself in a circle that reminds me I played this before, I played that before." Poitier was anxious, he told Roy Newquist, to break that circle. He didn't want to spend the next twenty years repeating himself as a successful actor, but wanted new challenges and greater involvement. One place he knew he could find that chance for artistic growth was as a director. Poitier explained to Newquist the artistic contribution a good director could make: "The director has an enormous opportunity for expression because he has almost complete control over all the contributing forces—the actors, the writers, the set designer, the technicians and . . . the cinematographer. All these people are guided by him, so he weaves all these creative contributions into a total. A total that comes from his own imagination, his own concept. The style and fabric of the completed work is largely the director's and that has to be an enormous satisfaction."[6]

The director's job is, of course, as demanding as

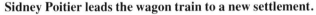

Sidney Poitier leads the wagon train to a new settlement.

it is satisfying. *Buck and the Preacher* was a rather awe-inspiring project to be undertaken by a tyro director in a foreign country with foreign crews and performers, for it involved a good deal of outdoor shooting, stunt work, and action sequences. Poitier later told a group of would-be film makers at Greystone, the center for advanced film studies run by the American Film Institute, about his first day on the set directing *Buck and the Preacher*: "The self-doubt that must be faced came up for me then. I had seen the camera, and I knew what it was about. I knew lens sizes. But how to use the camera as an instrument of your own creative process was all new to me. I felt the panic building up in me when I made my first setup. I had very sympathetic actors to work with, and they were very nice, but I felt my setup was organic to the material, even though I was scared." Finally, as the images took shape in front of him, Poitier could begin to feel at ease because things looked so right: "I began to watch the actors unfold in the frame I had structured, and they began to make sense. They seemed to be real. What they were doing had some kinship to my view of reality, and I began to relax."[7] Poitier's confidence grew as he moved from scene to scene, and the resulting footage is a truly revolutionary reworking of traditional western materials in a new black perspective.

In *Buck and the Preacher*, Poitier explained to Gil Noble during a provocative interview on the ABC-TV program "Like It Is," which was later transcribed and edited for publication in the leftist film quarterly *Cineaste*, the black star was finally "given the opportunity to make a film that really got down to the creation of the black heroes of another time."[8] Poitier knew, as James Baldwin had so eloquently written in *The Fire Next Time*, that the key to a black future was the rediscovery of the heroes and realities of the past. Like Baldwin, Poitier knew that American blacks were products of the American experience and that their roots were in American soil. *Buck and the Preacher* may profitably be viewed as Poitier's artistic musing on Baldwin's theme in *The Fire Next Time*: ". . . the Negro has been formed by this nation, for better or for worse, and does not belong to any other—not to Africa and certainly not to Islam. The paradox—and a fearful paradox it is—is that the American Negro can have no future anywhere, on any continent, as long as he is unwilling to accept his past. To accept one's past—one's history—is not the same thing as drowning in it; it is learning how to use it."[9]

Buck and the Preacher uses some authentic stories and characters to create new heroes. Central to the film is the wagon master, Buck, played by Sidney Poitier, who guides a group of black ex-slaves, emancipated after the Civil War, to the new territories in the West. These blacks not only face the hardships of the trail, but are savagely attacked by white mercenaries employed by Southerners anxious to maintain the old master-slave relationship. Helped by an unorthodox con man, a role played with relish by Harry Belafonte, and aided by some Indian warriors, Buck finally does provide his pilgrims safe passage to the promised land. The movement in *Buck and the Preacher* is largely symbolic, then, an odyssey from enslavement to freedom, from repression to liberation, a timely parable for American blacks seeking reaffirmation in their own struggles.

The film opens with a series of sepia stills, taken against western backgrounds, as the titles unfurl. Alex Phllips, Jr., the director of photography,

Harry Belafonte and his stained teeth in *Buck and the Preacher*.

Sidney Poitier and Harry Belafonte team up in *Buck and the Preacher*.

manages a skillful transition from these stills to the opening scene as the sepia gradually switches to color. The technique here was no doubt heavily influenced by features like *Bonnie and Clyde*, where similar devices established the mythic quality of what was to follow. In *Buck and the Preacher*, there is the constant balancing of the idealized and the real, the legendary and the authentic. Thus, when Poitier first appears on screen as Buck, he seems larger than life as he dismounts gracefully and gestures broadly to the black settlers that "this is your land." Accepting his wages, he then wishes his charges well and rides off through the desert. All these grandiloquent images and gestures prompted Vincent Canby to write that the soul of the movie "is on the plains once ridden by Tom Mix, whom Poitier, astride his galloping horse, his jaw set, somehow resembles in the majestic traveling shots given him by the director."[10] Canby is too gracious to note that the director is, of course, Sidney Poitier himself, an actor not above making himself look handsome and heroic on film.

Wagon-master Poitier no sooner leaves the settlers, however, than the villains appear. A gang of white renegades led by former military man Deshay (Cameron Mitchell) overruns the camp and questions their victims about Buck's whereabouts. Having introduced the good guy and the bad guys in a matter of moments, *Buck and the Preacher* begins to exploit every convention of the western, only this time it's not the sheepherders against the farmers, or the railroads versus the pony express, or even the cowboys against the Indians; it's free non-whites against the oppressors, white men who would be masters.

Interesting as the conflict in the film may be on sociological grounds, there is an artistic tension just as rich and complex. Not only was Poitier using old conventions to treat new material; he also found himself doing curious, double duty on each side of the camera. His first directorial assignment involved controlling the most volatile leading man of all—himself. Poitier told the young film makers at Greystone that directing yourself is not impossible to do, but it does help if you're a trifle crazy: "I think it takes a touch of schizophrenia to be able to do it well, because there's a sentinel up here that's overseeing all of it. It's uncanny. You're in a scene with three or four other actors, and you can hear whether they are working well. You can hear it. You can feel it. And, at the same time, you can hear yourself, as you're feeding them lines, and you're responding to lines from them. If you are a bit schizophrenic, it's a big help. Believe me when I tell you that."

Sidney Poitier and Harry Belafonte begin a profitable partnership in *Buck and the Preacher*.

Some of this schizophrenia can be felt in the next scene of the film, as director Poitier skillfully moves actor Poitier, the hero of the film, through some quite athletic maneuvers, all with considerable grace and aplomb. When Buck arrives home, he finds himself ambushed by Deshay's men, who use Ruth, his wife (Ruby Dee), as a shield. Poitier captures beautifully the tension and sense of danger in Buck's approach to the house. Then, there is an impressive close-up of his cold stare from behind his horse and his tiger-like leap to safety when the first shot is fired at him. Looking for cover behind trees and fences, he manages to escape, only to be chased in classic western style by the gang as Benny Carter's galloping music plays in the background.

Director Poitier is especially kind, however, not to his character Buck, but to Preacher, the role played by Harry Belafonte. The two men are good friends off screen, and some scenes in the film are actually light-hearted practical jokes, while others are all seriousness. Poitier's one jest at Belafonte's expense is the nude scene where Buck meets the Preacher for the first time. After a whole night running from Deshay's men, Buck rides off the trail into the woods and discovers a fine, healthy,

Ruby Dee joins Sidney Poitier and Harry Belafonte in *Buck and the Preacher*.

well-rested horse tied to a tree. He quickly dismounts and switches horses, only to be chased by the real owner of the animal, the Preacher, who had been bathing in a nearby river. The Preacher runs naked after Buck in a futile effort to save his horse.

Indians and blacks prove natural allies in *Buck and the Preacher*.

This nude scene bothered Harry Belafonte, so Poitier had to make special arrangements with Alex Phillips, Jr., to photograph Belafonte quite discreetly. Nevertheless, Belafonte still protested about the whole episode to Wanda Hale, the newspaper columnist: "Sidney is my best friend. But he was the director. I don't believe in nudity, on screen, stage, anywhere. I'm not a prude, but not even my wife has seen me completely undressed. Sidney made me do it. He treated me like John Huston abused Walter Huston in directing him in *Sierra Madre*." Belafonte continued his protest and his analogy to *Sierre Madre* when he further complained about the way his teeth were stained for the role of Preacher: "I have my own teeth, so I had no dentures to remove as John made his father do. But Sidney made me stain my teeth. And it had to be done every day." Sidney's answer to this latter charge speaks volumes about the problem of low-budget movies. He told Wanda Hale in the same interview that they stained Harry's teeth with dark makeup pencil covered with clear nail polish; their makeshift approach contrasted, he thought, with the techniques the major studios could employ on big projects: "Twentieth Century Fox hired a dentist to stain George C. Scott's teeth for the Patton role, but we didn't have that kind of money. All we had was ingenuity and a makeup kit."

Buck and the Preacher also had Poitier's intuitive good sense about using his actors. Belafonte's protests are actually part of the friendly banter that characterized the whole project, for he knew, as did all the cast, that Poitier had great respect for the needs of actors, having come to directing after a long career in acting. Having been an actor, Poitier recognized, he told Judy Michaelson, "what goes on in their heads, how they're reacting, and how IM.POR.TANT their ego is, you know."[11] The critical task, Poitier explained in an interview in Hollywood, was to balance the needs of all the artists involved and to elicit the fullest contribution from each individual. In his view, a film was really the sum of all its parts, and true achievement came as a result of collaborative and cooperative efforts: "The continuation of the creative process requires that each contributing force be at least elastic enough to encompass or incorporate the creativity of the other contributing forces. So that a writer's work is of no value if it is not performed by very gifted actors. And gifted actors truly can never function at their best if they are not under the guidance of a very imaginative and gifted director. . . . So that each contributing force has itself a special contribution to make, but at the same time each force has to remain elastic in order to complement each other."

If Poitier makes any mistake at all in *Buck and the Preacher*, it is in giving Harry Belafonte too much latitude. In most of the scenes between Buck and the Preacher, Poitier the director favors Belafonte over Poitier the actor. He gives Belafonte almost all the comic moments, including a classic scene when he tries to acquire some liquor, and virtually all the key lines in the dialogue. Belafonte has a real showcase for his rather

Blacks find roles in Westerns as Harry Belafonte and Sidney Poitier explore the diverse facets of a familiar genre.

Romance in *Buck and the Preacher*.

histrionic performance, while Poitier the actor spends much of the time in the shadows once Belafonte enters the film.

A good example of this favoritism towards Belafonte comes after Buck and the Preacher team up, plan a new caravan, negotiate help from the Indians, and then execute an attack against Deshay and his men in Madame Esther's (Nita Talbot) bordello. Belafonte is absolutely sensational in his oration before the gang, a mock sermon designed to distract them long enough for Poitier's surprise attack. Buck and the Preacher then rout the gang in a dramatic shootout and make a daring escape as they jump to their waiting horses and disappear in the dark. The whole sequence is directed with real bravura, excellent visual effects, dynamic timing, and a great sense of humor, yet it is Belafonte's sermon which sticks in the memory.

Belafonte shines again in his next exchange with Poitier, as next morning Buck and the Preacher count the money they took from the gang. Belafonte casually eyes Poitier up and down, as he tells him "that is what they were going to pay me for delivering you." Now the only delivery to be made is that of the new caravan. Buck and the Preacher stop to pick Ruth up, then hurry on to hold up a bank to get some money for the settlers. The holdup sequence, excellently staged by Poitier, culminates in a beautiful chase across the desert and another encounter with the Indians. The Indians aid the black caravan in the battle against the white mercenaries, the most exciting sequence in the film, but they refuse to give the blacks either guns or ammunition. Their chief (Enrique Lucero) reminds the blacks that his tribe will "need our guns for our own fight," lines that seem especially relevant for an era which witnessed the advent of militant Indian activism.

The spectacular battle in the desert culminates in a black victory, and the beleaguered caravan finally reaches the green pastures of the promised land. Buck, the Preacher, and Ruth leave the group now, and the last shot of the film, of the three riding away, freezes into a sepia portrait, bringing the audience back to the static universe of the titles, a device which distances us from those legendary heroes and preserves them forever in the world of myth.

In making *Buck and the Preacher,* Poitier achieved several important goals. He established himself as an competent director and cemented his links to the black community. Even normally hostile militants like Donald Bogle were swayed by this film. Bogle declared it "one of the more pleasant surprises of the new decade," noting that "Here the fine American actor attempts to redeem himself and re-establish his roots with the black community. . . . His character not only questions the inhuman white system and his white oppressors, but also takes direct action against them." As a result, Bogle observes, Poitier regained the audience his recent films had been alienating, the young urban black audience: "Black audiences openly screamed out in joy, and *Buck and the Preacher* emerged as a solid hit with the community."[12] Poitier had created a new black hero, this time within the framework of Western mythology, a hero who not only contributed to the conquest of the West but who accepted considerable personal risks to protect a black community from white aggressors.

Poitier's next film, *A Warm December,* brought him back to the contemporary scene, but to a cultured circle where whites were considerably less important. Poitier directed *A Warm December,* the first project he undertook under the banner of the First Artists Production Company. There had been considerably publicity when Steve McQueen, Paul Newman, Barbra Streisand, and Sidney Poitier first entered this joint venture in 1969, but it was two years later before the company cut through all the red tape and went public. Twenty-five percent of the shares were offered to the public; the rest were held by the stars, Creative Management Associates, National General Pictures, and the directors and officers of the First Artists Corporation. Two years after the stock offering, Poitier was advanced enough capital to film his first project on location in England with the fine cinematographer, Paul Beeson. *A Warm December* was designed to be a highly commercial property, a dazzlingly beautiful black version of *Love Story* which also contained a few echoes of Hitchcock's adventure *The Man Who Knew Too Much. A Warm December* aimed neither at the significance of *Brother John* nor the relevance of *Buck and the Preacher*; all eyes were on the box office.

Again, Poitier was directing himself, only this time he was in a familiar role; he played Matt Younger, a distinguished doctor, a widower who might have walked right off the set of *Guess Who's Coming to Dinner.* This time, however, the doctor wasn't chasing the lily-white daughter of an

Sidney Poitier as Matt Younger and Esther Anderson as Catherine in *A Warm December.*

Director Sidney Poitier explaining his conception to actress Esther Anderson.

Sidney Poitier and Esther Anderson bring elegance and style to the black romance in *A Warm December.*

American family. His romantic interest was a black princess, the heiress of a long line of African royalty.

The opening shots of *A Warm December* picture Matt Younger flying from Washington to London with his ten-year-old daughter Stefanie (Yvette Curtis). They are met at the London airport by Matt's friend Henry Barlow (George Baker) with whose family Stefanie will stay while her father registers in a posh hotel. Matt intends to use part of his vacation to pursue cross-country motorcycle racing, his hobby. As he enters the hotel, Matt encounters a mysterious and attractive black girl half-masked by big sun glasses and clad in a stunning fur coat. The girl uses Matt as a shield to avoid two strange-looking men who are following her, and then safely reenters the Embassy of Torunda, a fictional African country. From this point on, Matt struggles to find out who she is.

His reaction seems very natural, because the girl, Catherine, played by Esther Anderson, is almost preternaturally beautiful. Poitier told Wanda Hale that for the film he wanted a beautiful girl so he "looked and looked and looked. And I looked and looked and looked and I looked and looked and looked." Reminded that this was nine times he looked, Poitier laughed heartily and rejoined: "And that was just the beginning. I looked nine times nine before I found her, a Jamaican girl, out of London, with very little experience." Poitier always had an eye for women and a bit of a reputation for womanizing, but Esther Anderson stands out as his most attractive costar. She provides the perfect fairy-tale beauty for this fluffy reaction of Erich Segal's tearjerker. The screenplay for *A Warm December* is credited to Lawrence Roman, but its roots reach deeply into pop culture and what Pauline Kael has called "crumb crushers."

A chance meeting at the theater, where black

An intimate close-up in Sidney Poitier's black version of *Love Story* — *A Warm December*.

Sidney Poitier as Matt Younger discovers the pigeons in London.

Sidney Poitier and Esther Anderson as seemingly happy-go-lucky tourists out for a day in the park.

artists perform, allows Matt to meet Catherine, the niece of the Torundan Ambassador George Oswandu (Earl Cameron). The film then develops in three directions: sightseeing in London, motorcycle racing, and the chase after Catherine. The sightseeing with daughter Stefanie fills the film with too many travelogue-like sequences and postcard style shots of famous spots, but it also allows Poitier to ham it up quite a bit. He dances gracefully to pose for the inevitable snapshots and has a fine comic scene in Trafalgar Square, where he is surrounded by pigeons which perch on his head and arms. Meanwhile, the race sequences provide some fine action footage, which counterpoints the mystery generated by the chase after Catherine. She seems plagued by awkward guards and equally inept personages who follow her every step.

Little by little, these three plot elements begin to merge. Catherine is included in the sightseeing after she and Stefanie meet and become good friends. They both attend some of Matt's motor races and then join him for a weekend in a beautiful old country cottage.

Then comes the unhappy twist. Just as the romance between Matt and Catherine blossoms, he discovers her secret: she is the victim of sickle-cell anemia and thus under the constant vigilance of embassy employees. This revelation proves the undoing of the film, because it deflates all the mystery Poitier worked so hard and long to create, and yet doesn't intensify the romantic interest sufficiently. Instead of tragedy, the love affair of Matt and Catherine becomes a case study, a sophisticated public health message on the horrors of sickle-cell anemia. *Variety* was right on target when it observed that Catherine's disease seems too little a motivation for all the cloak and dagger machinations which had preceded it; it was as though director Poitier fell in love with the aura of mystery and forgot that style had to be justified by substance. As *Variety* notes, Catherine "is shadowed unendingly by mysterious people, from whom she is usually fleeing with Poitier's help. To go on so long with this artifice is eventually self-destructive to the film. . . . Audiences will likely feel more exploited than satisfied."[13]

A Warm December does have, however, its pleasing aspects, most of them resulting from the physical beauty of Esther Anderson and her handsome suitor, Sidney Poitier. Their elegant surroundings, impeccable taste, and commitment

A temporary escape to the country for Sidney Poitier and Esther Anderson in *A Warm December*.

to black culture, combine with the stunning color photography to create a glossy, idealized, but enchanting vision of a truly warm encounter. There is, for example, the poetic interlude early in the film at the British Museum, when they stroll through the Divine Kingships in Africa exhibition, and the black-tie African gala at the Drury Lane Theatre, where they are entertained by accomplished black dancers. Other quite romantic episodes take place in the red twilight of a discotheque and the hazy candlelight of an elegant restaurant, where Matt and Catherine occupy a richly set table of exotic and attractive food. At the restaurant, Matt wears a stylish dark suit and Catherine, a glorious gown. Each is shown in close-up listening intently to traditional Swahili chants performed by an African folk group and singer Letta Mbula. Their wistful expressions, as Julian Fox observes in his *Films and Filming* review, "appear to express a yearning back to the courage and dignity of their pre-slave ancestors with a

heartbreaking intensity that is startling in its impact."[14] This intensity, dignity, courage, beauty, and elegance is obviously the effect director Poitier was seeking. *A Warm December* was his demonstration that black was beautiful.

The film ends with the most beautiful gesture of all, a noble sacrifice on Catherine's part. She is torn by her obligations to her country, her recognition of Matt's commitment to community health programs, her love for him, and the burden of her fatal disease. At first she tells her uncle, "It's December for me, and I know there's not much time left, but I want a husband and a child before I die," and she resolves to go with Matt. Her uncle dissuades her, however, with his reminder, "The man already lost one wife and the child one mother." Catherine forsakes her beloved out of love, and her last words to Matt are in Swahili: "*Kwaheri, mume wangu, ah sante kwa disemba Tamu*" ("Goodbye, my husband, thank you for a warm December"). The film ends as the tearful Catherine walks back to her elegant reception and the duties of the Embassy and Matt Younger flies back to America, carrying his memories of a warm December.

Poitier was to turn from tears to laughter in his next film, from romance to high jinks, from high society to the raunchy confines of the urban ghetto. *Uptown Saturday Night* was to fulfill another life-long dream. Poitier finally felt self-assured enough to make a film about blacks starring blacks which laughed at black foibles. As Poitier saw it, blacks "had not had an opportunity to laugh at themselves very much, particularly with material they would invite other people to join them in laughing at themselves. Blacks have to feel terribly secure to laugh at themselves in public and allow others who are not black to laugh too."[15] By 1974, Poitier felt secure enough to undertake such a "cross-over" comedy, and he read his audience quite well, for both blacks and whites were ready for some raucous comedy.

Uptown Saturday Night had been percolating in Poitier's head for a long time. He told many of his intimates that he had a vision of a large group of characters who intrigued him, and he was looking for a framework dynamic enough to contain them, yet with plenty of room for lively music, dance and slapstick humor. The theme of the film was to be corruption in modern life, but its main focus was to be entertainment. Poitier knew it was easy to catch an audience with honey, and *Uptown Saturday Night* was his salute to the sweet side of the black experience, the wenching, drinking, gambling, conniving, and hell-raising.

For this original comedy Poitier gathered a truly distinguished cast, headed by his costar in *Buck and the Preacher*, Harry Belafonte. Belafonte and Poitier had long worked together on civil rights fund-raisers, and now their independent productions under the control of First Artists were enriching their own considerable bankrolls. Now that the two of them no longer needed money, having escaped from desperate poverty, they stumbled on an almost sure-fire formula for instant wealth, low-budget films by blacks and for blacks, which also appealed to the white audience. They could do their own thing and still make money in the American market; their joy at this discovery is evidenced in their bouyant performances on screen. Poitier and Belafonte are living it up, and their energy enlivens the whole project.

The real explosion of joy comes, however, from the other major actor in Poitier's three later comedies, Bill Cosby, an acknowledged master of

Director Sidney Poitier prepares for the African songs in *A Warm December*.

Sidney Poitier hard at work preparing his comedy *Uptown Saturday Night*.

Comedian Bill Cosby, whose antics enriched *Uptown Saturday Night* and challenged the abilities of director Poitier.

Director Sidney Poitier discusses an upcoming scene with Lee Chamberlin who plays Zenobia, the operator of an after-hours club.

the one-liner, who broke the color barrier on television as a daffy secret agent in the "I Spy" series. Poitier and Cosby are long-time friends, yet Poitier finds Cosby the most difficult person of all to direct in films. Cosby's comedy flows from his personality, and he just can't stand planning or rehearsing. As Poitier explained to some visitors to the set of *Uptown Saturday Night*, "Each performer is an individual and you have to direct them accordingly. Bill Cosby, for instance, is a wonderfully spontaneous actor, so I didn't rehearse him too much because I didn't want to drain his energy. With him, spur-of-the-moment stuff is the best once the point of a scene has been decided on." The hang-loose mood Poitier achieved on the set gives *Uptown Saturday Night* a bouyancy and excitement that radiate from the screen.

Poitier's plans for *Uptown Saturday Night* were huge, and, to complete his cast, he employed, as James L. Limbacher observed, "just about every black actor now residing in Hollywood or New York City."[16] Poitier was noted for his generosity

by other actors; the larger his success became, the more he was willing to share the limelight. Among the talented black performers involved in *Uptown Saturday Night* were luminaries like Flip Wilson, Richard Pryor, Roscoe Lee Brown, Calvin Lockhart, Rosalind Cash, Lee Chamberlin, and Paula Kelly. Poitier was actually forming his own stock company, a cadre of talent from which he could draw for his future projects. He did the same thing on the technical crew also, recruiting professionals like Pembroke J. Herring, writers Timothy March and Richard Wesley, designer Alfred Sweeney, and, later, cameraman Donald Morgan.

Uptown Satuday Night was designed by Poitier as a light comedy, with little serious content, unless you count the fact that most of the corrupt politicians are given names of white statesmen like Lincoln and Washington. To a considerable degree, *Uptown Saturday Night* was Poitier's mellow response to the blood and gore of the black exploitation films which had shocked much of America. Most of all, however, *Uptown Saturday*

Sidney Poitier and Bill Cosby in their frantic quest for assistance in *Uptown Saturday Night*.

Sidney Poitier and Bill Cosby as working-class heroes in *Uptown Saturday Night*.

Night was Poitier's most comic valentine to what he conceived of as his constituency, the hard-working blacks of America whose lives had little to do with pimps and drug pushers and even less to do with white fantasies. Poitier was very forthright about his constituency in a powerful interview with the white columnist Bernard Drew of the White Plains, New York, *Reporter Dispatch*: "I don't make pictures for you, Bernie, or the *New York Times* or the *Post* and all the rest. You keep slamming them but black audiences flock to them anyway. I don't say they don't read you, but they don't listen to you because you're not criticizing from their point of view. They have specific needs and the white director is not answering those needs, nor does the white critic understand them. I would like to please you and other critics but at all costs I am bound to take care of my constituency."

To prepare the comic script suited for his fans, Sidney Poitier worked on his original ideas for *Uptown Saturday Night* with playwright Richard Wesley, a young black whose last work, *The Last Street Play*, had brought him a great deal of notoriety. Poitier told the seminar at Greystone that he selected Wesley because he was a writer who was "able to put his ego in his pocket." Wesley and Poitier worked very closely on the project. Poitier would suggest moods, feelings, and images, while Richard Wesley labored on reducing them to dialogue and placing them in a coherent structure. Richard Wesley had the job, Poitier told the young film-makers, of putting on paper what Poitier already saw in his head: "There is a rhythm in my head even before the writer ever puts anything on paper. It's not that he has to write to that. I give to him and he gives back to me. We

Bill Cosby threatens to break a bar into pieces in *Uptown Saturday Night*.

kind of meld together. So I respect the writer because what I spew out to him I can't put on paper, even though I have it in my head." Most directors who worked this closely on the preparation of a script would demand at least a partial credit. Poitier does not list himself as a writer, however, because he feels that to have a film which announces itself as produced by Sidney Poitier, directed by Sidney Poitier, starring Sidney Poitier, and written by Sidney Poitier, would be too ostentatious. Poitier is, in fact, however, the main creative force in all three comedies he's produced for his special constituency, *Uptown Saturday Night, Let's Do It Again,* and *A Piece of the Action.* He envisioned these projects, drafted their rough outlines, cast them, directed them, played in them, and arranged many of the details of their distribution. And, for all his attention to black ticket buyers, the charm of his productions has also drawn a large white audience, making him the first black film-maker successful in the total American market.

The script Richard Wesley and Sidney Poitier prepared for *Uptown Saturday Night* bears a slight resemblance to Rene Clair's classic, *Le Million.* In each film, a winning lottery ticket has been lost in a jacket and the owner has to recover it. In *Uptown Saturday Night*, the lottery winner is an innocent factory worker, Steve Jackson (Sidney Poitier), who loses the ticket when he and his friend a taxi driver named Wardell Franklin (Bill Cosby) sneak away from their wives to visit a fancy after-hours club which houses a gambling den and bordello, managed by Madame Zenobia (Lee Chamberlin). No sooner are they inside, enjoying the fancy drinks, the gambling, and the stunning women, than some masked thugs come in and clean out all the guests' jewelry and belongings. The thugs are quite professional and thorough, but Poitier can't resist a joke even during the holdup. All the victims are told to hand over their valuables and strip to their underwear. One very attractive young woman, when told to take off her expensive dress, protests she has nothing on under it; the thieves don't believe her until she takes the dress off, and then they are flabbergasted. Poitier's inspiration here is no doubt the widely reported theft after one of Muhammad Ali's title defenses where engraved invitations lured big spenders to a supposed party. Inside, all the guests were stripped of their belongings and herded into the cellar. Poitier's thieves are considerably more modest, and the whole theft seems an ironic retribution for the machinations Steve Jackson and Wardell Franklin engineered to fool their wives.

Harry Belafonte, Sidney Poitier, and Bill Cosby in *Uptown Saturday Night*.

The day after the robbery, Jackson reads the newspaper and discovers that the lottery ticket he had been carrying around in his now stolen wallet was the fifty-thousand-dollar winner. Jackson quickly summons Franklin, and these two inept bunglers start their scatterbrained attempts to recover the wallet. First stop on their ill-conceived odyssey is the office of Sharp Eye Washington (Richard Pryor), a nervous lawyer who seems to be left over from the cast of "Amos and Andy." All Sharp Eye can manage to do is swindle Jackson and Franklin, cheating them out of their last few dollars. The scene with Sharp Eye is one of the film's highlights, however, as Richard Pryor, a leading nightclub and television comedian, is given wide leeway to emote by director Poitier. Pryor created his own problems on set, as director Poitier recalled at Greystone: ". . . with Richard Pryor, you can't get your work done. You play a scene with Richard and it's dynamite! You say, 'Terrific. Now, I want close-ups and I want another angle.' He does a different scene! You say 'No, Richard,

Extensive makeup transforms Harry Belafonte into a Godfather look-alike in *Uptown Saturday Night*.

Harry Belafonte as a hoodlum in disguise makes a comic exit in *Uptown Saturday Night*.

Roscoe Lee Browne and Paula Kelly, part of Sidney Poitier's acting company in *Uptown Saturday Night*.

it's the *other* way!' and you won't get it. Next time I work with Richard, I'm going to put multiple cameras on him so I can cut it.'' The performance Poitier did capture, however, is quite memorable, and suggests the frenzy that Pryor brings to all his work.

After Sharp Eye Washington dupes them, Jackson and Franklin go to their congressman, a representative named Lincoln, played by Roscoe Lee Browne in a satiric vein which makes the *National Lampoon* seem the soul of discretion. Disappointed by lawyers and lawmakers, our gullible heroes turn to the mob, finally contacting the Godfather, Geechie Dan Beauford, after a series of misadventures. In their confrontation with gangsters, Poitier and Cosby have some marvelous routines all aimed at projecting a supercool, supertough image right out of *Superfly* and *Shaft*; needless to say, they crumble hilariously when the first real tough guy appears on the scene. Geechie Dan Beuford, played by Harry Belafonte, whose features are obscured by makeup and whose face seems puffed up as though stuffed with cotton, is an amazingly fine parody of Marlon Brando playing the Godfather, a role which had its own elements of exaggeration and parody. Belafonte obviously enjoys this improbable impersonation, and Poitier must also have relished it, because Geechie Dan Beauford dominates almost every scene he is in, right down to a hilarious chase in which he, disguised as a woman, eludes the police. A good part of the humor in this climactic chase depends on the wild incongruity: what audience could resist laughing at Harry Belafonte, the attractive black singer, imitating an aging Brando playing a Mafia don, running from the police in a fancy woman's dress, lifting his skirts up as he tries desperately to hold on to his wig?

The humor in *Uptown Saturday Night* almost defies description. Many critics tried to explain it by declaring that Poitier had finally found "soul," but Vincent Canby was probably closer to the truth when he said that the film is "so full of good humor and, when the humor goes flat, of such high spirits that it reduces movie criticism to the status of a most nonessential craft."[17] Stuart Byron echoed these sentiments when he observed that "There are some pictures which give off such a feeling of togetherness that you become convinced that they must have been shot on a 'happy set.' *Uptown Saturday Night* commands this aura. The ensemble playing seems a result of each actor or actress trying to impress the rest with the ultimate in funkiness and soulfulness . . . you get the feeling that everyone in the cast found it a liberating release to return to ethnic roots. *Uptown Saturday Night* seems like one long block party."[18]

Sidney Poitier's next project, *The Wilby Conspiracy*, was less a block party and more a warm reunion. Poitier turned his attention for a moment from his own projects and from his directing to work for his old friend and agent Martin Baum in Baum's very first independent production, an adventure film to be directed by Ralph Nelson, the man whose work on *Lilies of the Field* made Sidney Poitier's best actor Oscar possible and who had also worked with Poitier on *Duel at Diablo*, the western which foreshadowed *Buck and the Preacher*.

The Wilby Conspiracy was based on a best-selling novel by Peter Driscoll with a screenplay by Rod Amateau and Harold Nebenzal. The action is set in South Africa, although, for obvious reasons, the actual footage was shot on location in Kenya while the studio scenes were done at Pinewood near London. Interestingly enough, President Jomo Kenyatta, the mastermind of Kenya's independence whose story played such a large role in *Something of Value*, personally invited Poitier to film in his country and provided considerable help to the whole production of *The Wilby Conspiracy*. Neither the novel nor the film is out-and-out propaganda, but the comments, both direct and indirect, on life in South Africa and on the apartheid policy are quite clear. Poitier and company spent seven very difficult weeks on location in Kenya, communications with the outside world were poor, the diet was very limited, and the perils very real. All the physical strain shows on screen and gives the film a startling authenticity.

Both producer Baum and director Nelson clearly wanted *The Wilby Conspiracy* to work both as entertainment and as a political tract. Baum, for example, told interviewers, that "we recognize that there are many South Africans who reject apartheid completely, but the film *is* against any system which creates second-class citizenship in whatever form or for whatever cause.'' Nelson, on the other hand, stressed the positive side of the message, the idea that men need each other; he saw *The Wilby Conspiracy* as "a film about man's humanity to man which, in the course of entertaining, may also make people think.''

In some ways, the plot of *The Wilby Conspiracy* is really a reworking of *The Defiant Ones*. *The Wilby Conspiracy* shows two men, one black and one white, forced by circumstances to aid each other in their desperate flight from the police. The

Sidney Poitier as Shack Twala in *The Wilby Conspiracy*.

whole film is an arduous physical chase across desolate terrain and through teeming cities; audiences are treated to one hair-raising episode after another in an adventure which is almost too relentlessly harrowing.

Poitier plays the main role, that of Shack Twala, the Bantu chairman of the radical Black Congress Party, who punches a police officer shortly after his attorney, Rina (Prunella Gee), successfully defends him on another charge. As a result of the assault, Shack Twala must escape arrest, and he is aided by Rina's lover, Keogh (Michael Caine), an English mining engineer, who is caught up unexpectedly in all the excitement.

Their escape is thrilling, largely because they stumble accidentally on a plot to recover some stolen diamonds which were to be used to finance an anti-apartheid conspiracy. In the dark underworld of smuggling, thievery, double crosses, and political ferment, Poitier and Caine meet one seedy character after another and never know whom to trust. At the same time, they need help from everyone to escape. Always behind them, too, dogging their every step, is Major Horn (Nicol Williamson), a sinister figure, articulate and cunning, who hopes the fugitives will lead him to the head of the black conspiracy, Wilby (Joseph De Graf). Horn is probably, as Pauline Kael argues, the most interesting character in the film. For all his villainy he does capture what she calls the "dire earnestness of apartheid."[19]

In *The Wilby Conspiracy*, Poitier gives an earnest performance, though it is rather obvious that he feels he has done this all before. At this late date, of course, he can be more sexually active than he could in earlier films, and he is afforded an almost ludicrous opportunity to show off his sex appeal when he is hiding in a closet with the gorgeous dental assistant Persis Ray (Persis Khambatta). Apparently, the heat inside the closet, the fear of being discovered by the police, and the profuse sweat covering their bodies prove an irresistible aphrodisiac and they form a liaison which has important ramifications later in the film.

Apart from this new sex angle, however, *The Wilby Conspiracy* is the sort of routine heroic saga Poitier favored earlier in his career. He has fine opportunities to display his physical fitness and daring, and, once again, can identify himself with a militant cause, yet most critics and the popular audience knew this was all a bit frothy by now. Only the background, as Nancy Schwartz of the *Soho Weekly News* notes, was new and daring, for "the adventure never completely overshadows the *mise-en-scene* . . . the film offers a rare and fascinating vision of South Africa, that oft-forgotten colonial dictatorship . . . we see an unromanticized, almost unbelievable land of stratification and repression. 'The police are busy tonight,' remarks Michael Caine.' 'In a police state,' replies Poitier, 'the police are always busy.'"[20]

For Poitier, who was returning to Africa for a fourth time, *The Wilby Conspiracy* continued the commentary he had begun in *Cry, the Beloved Country* and continued in *The Mark of the Hawk* and *Something of Value*. Poitier could see in Kenya the changes he wanted for all of Africa. Maybe the most subtle comment of all in *The Wilby Conspiracy* is a sly piece of casting. One of Kenya's best loved and most revered statesmen, Joseph Murumbi, plays the village elder who is humiliated and debased by the South African security police led by Nicol Williamson. For African audiences, Murumbi's role is an obviously symbolic one.

Poitier's excursion to Africa in *The Wilby Conspiracy* was, for all its nostalgic pleasures and political commentary, a bit of a detour in his career. Poitier was consciously trying to put acting behind him and dedicate all his energies to directing and producing. Even his role in First Artists couldn't relieve him of financial obligations, however, so, once again, he found himself

The police state and rebel armies form the backdrop to *The Wilby Conspiracy*.

Sidney Poitier as Clyde Williams in *Let's Do It Again*.

both starring in and directing his followup to *Uptown Saturday Night, Let's Do It Again*. Poitier complained to *Cue* magazine that it was "hard to direct myself, and I'd rather not. But I've had to act in my films as part of the packaging."[21] Without Poitier the star, Poitier the director had little opportunity to work.

Let's Do It Again actually involves many of the black performers involved in *Uptown Saturday Night*. The most notable holdover is Bill Cosby, the player Poitier felt was most responsible for the amazing financial success of the film. *Let's Do It Again* is not a sequel, but is is a stylized attempt to mine the same anarchic vein of ethnic humor, while attracting both whites and blacks. Once again Poitier's eye was on the box office and on the concept of a "cross-over film," a product which served his black audience without alienating other patrons. In *Let's Do It Again*, Poitier almost outdoes himself: it is by far the funniest, most

remarkable film in his comic trilogy, a film which had major critics comparing Poitier to Woody Allen and other important comedians. Just about the time Imamu Amari Baraka was satirizing Poitier in his vicious polemic *Sidnee Poet Heroical*, Poitier was changing the whole equation radically. He was doing more than bringing a black star to the white cinema; he was bringing white audiences to a black cinema, a cinema aware of its roots and self-assured enough to laugh at old stereotypes.

Let's Do It Again opens with an engaging sequence picturing factory worker Billy Foster (Bill Cosby) leering at a young secretary in a miniskirt, only to find himself challenged by a co-worker to a boxing match which Billy finally manages to dissolve in a warm embrace. Billy is obviously a lover, not a fighter; a con man, not a hero. Billy then joins his milkman friend Clyde Williams (Sidney Poitier) for a meeting of the Sons and Daughters of Shaka congregation. It is worth

Bill Cosby, Denise Nicholas, Sidney Poitier, and Lee Chamberlin in *Let's Do It Again*.

Bill Cosby and Sidney Poitier on the run in one of the better slapstick moments in *Let's Do It Again*.

noting that Poitier mirrors his own constituency in his films: his heroes are working class, and their principal recreation is found in the context of the lodge and the church.

The Sons and Daughters of Shaka have a problem which is all to reminiscent of reality: the city of Atlanta has refused to extend their lease, so, in six weeks, they need at least fifty-five thousand dollars to finance a new building. Billy and Clyde develop an ingenious scheme to raise cash; borrowing two thousand dollars from the treasury, they plan to pretend they are big spenders, travel to New Orleans, and generate big money in the big town for their little church. They want to "look like we have millions" to negotiate thousands from others. Poitier and Cosby make this scheme seem more hilarious than it is by their excited gestures and facial expressions, beautifully captured in extreme close-up by Donald M. Morgan, the cinematographer on the project.

Morgan and Poitier worked together very carefully on *Let's Do It Again*, and it is obvious that Poitier was able to direct Morgan to achieve just the results the now more confident director desired. Morgan also worked on *A Piece of the Action*, and the collaboration between him and Poitier will probably continue in the future. The more projects Poitier directed, the more assured he became in his camera style, and the more insistent he was on a special rapport with his cinematographer. For example, Poitier spoke at great length in his seminar at Greystone about his liaison with Morgan; Poitier noted that he would tell Morgan exactly the tone and mood he wanted for a scene, then Morgan would work out the details of the lighting. Usually Morgan's lighting would complement Poitier's conception, and, when it didn't, it was, in Poitier's words, only "a matter of a few adjustments here and there." Morgan was, Poitier felt, a very low-key lighting man who went for deep, rich colors. This suited *Let's Do It Again*, Poitier noted, for all but the most comic scenes, when the director ordered the cameraman to come up more and provide a bright rather than deep color.

Morgan and Poitier worked especially hard on the color scheme of *Let's Do It Again*. So much of the project involved the fancy clothes and lush decors associated with smart money and fast women that Poitier and Morgan worked out even the details of wardrobe and set decoration. As a result of all this preplanning, both Poitier and Cosby literally bedazzle audiences in the scenes where they're trying to impress gangsters and fast-buck operators. Poitier, for example, is especially resplendent in a flowing cape that emphasizes his height, and Cosby is the embodiment of the flashy hipster in his plaid cap and streamlined sunglasses.

In New Orleans, our artful dodgers, Billy and Clyde, register in the Royal Orleans and escort their lavishly bedecked wives to a fancy meal in an even fancier restaurant, a fantasy world obviously

Bill Cosby and Sidney Poitier try disguises in *Let's Do It Again*.

Sidney Poitier and Bill Cosby plan their own version of the sting in *Let's Do It Again*.

designed to amuse and titillate the urban blue-collar audience for the film. Inside, they overhear a conversation between a gang of big-time bookies about a forthcoming boxing match between an unknown, Bootney Farnsworth (Jimmie Walker), and the champ (Lee Hayden). Farnsworth is a hopeless case, a rank outsider, according to all reports. Billy and Clyde immediately recognize their opportunity: they must engineer an upset, for the long odds are just what they need to multiply their temple's meager treasury into an endowment for the new building project.

Billy and Clyde next appear at Bootney's workout, a pathetic display of cowardice and ineptitude. Actor Jimmie Walker has one of his best roles in this film; his portrayal of Bootney creates a memorable scrawny sad sack, all arms and legs and nerves, with no muscle or skill. Bootney is so pathetic he's funny and so nervous his excess energy seems contagious. The audience is soon as craven as the challenger, looking for a way to get out of the ring without getting hurt.

Billy and Clyde follow Bootney to his hotel, where Clyde uses his hypnotic skill to persuade Bootney he is a tiger and will win the championship. Poitier and Walker have another wonderful scene here, as Poitier portrays a rather low-key Svengali and Walker becomes an athletic, if somewhat uncoordinated, Jekyll and Hyde. Pure slapstick follows as Billy and Clyde escape out the window on a rope of bedsheets only to drop into a window on the floor beneath where they surprise the house detective making love to a lady guest. Poitier works in the great Abbott and Costello-Laurel and Hardy tradition here, right down to a wonderful sight gag as Cosby's beard is caught in the caresses of the two lovers.

Similarly inventive gags occur in the sparring session next morning with Bootney still under hypnosis. Bootney destroys everyone and everything around him, wrecking the ring, and punching the big bag across the room and out the window. Clyde and Billy quickly make their bets and the whole fight sequence which follows is deftly

Bill Cosby and Sidney Poitier outwit the bookies in *Let's Do It Again*.

A rather anxious payoff for Bill Cosby and Sidney Poitier.

A rather anxious payoff for Bill Cosby and Sidney Poitier.

captured in a stylish montage; Bootney wins in a slow motion knockout, the bets are paid, and the two heroes leave town, all to the rhythms of Curtis Mayfield.

At this point, the plot of *Let's Do It Again* actually runs out, and it is as though someone on the set, overjoyed with the fine footage that had already been shot, did call out, "Let's do it again." What follows is almost literally a rerun of the first half, reminiscent of Keaton's mirror structure in his classic comedy *The General*. Where Keaton repeated his train journey, Poitier and his crew set up another boxing match and betting coup. Gangsters force Billy and Clyde to return to New Orleans for more hypnosis. And, as Clyde declares in a powerful close-up, "I'd rather go to New Orleans than to a cemetery." What follows is

Bill Cosby and Sidney Poitier back at their lodge, the Sons and Daughters of Shaka.

Sidney Poitier at the premiere of *Let's Do It Again*.

another excellent mixture of black humor and fantasy, fancy clothes, and wild chases. One of the best chases comes when the gangsters follow Billy and Clyde to a building labelled "Turkish Bath," which happens to be a police precinct house; here they have to contribute to the Police Community Fund in order to avoid arrest for gambling. Meanwhile, Billy and Clyde ride back to Atlanta, musing on the next bout, an epic confrontation between Muhammad Ali and a hypnotized Sammy Davis, Jr.

Let's Do It Again proved to be one of the top-grossing films of 1975, a major success in every market, black and white, urban and rural, Northern and Southern. Poitier had established a new type of film, the so-called cross-over film, his own answer to earlier problem films by whites for blacks and the blaxploitation films by blacks against whites. His cinema was for all the people, yet had black casts and crews, black material, and black comedy.

Poitier knew it was good business to make cross-over films, but he also spoke to Frank Daley of the *Ottawa Journal* in late 1975 about the universal nature of their humanity and their all encompassing comedy and laughter: ". . . if you use black actors as I tried to do, you should also try to make sure that the theme is universal; that what you are saying is said to mankind, to people everywhere. Because the circumstances that make up the film as a whole are familiar to everyone—to white people and to black people—it has appeal. . . . I want to make a film where I use what is culturally black but has universal under-pinnings."[22]

Poitier was, as Pauline Kael observed, doing something he profoundly believed in when he made *Let's Do It Again*, and he managed to give the black audience, in Kael's words, "entertainment that it wants and has never had before."[23] Yet Poitier revealed to Frank Daley in a very candid interview that his real sense of accomplishment came from the fact that he was providing opportunities for young black actors. All the years alone in Hollywood were justified, Poitier felt, and all the old charges were answered; he had done it, he had

Sidney Poitier as Manny Durrell and Bill Cosby as Dave Anderson in *A Piece of the Action*.

made room for blacks on a white screen: "Now, I tell you, the feeling of accomplishment is rather overwhelming because I look around and I see so many guys and women who have followed in my footsteps that the loneliness was all worth it." Things hadn't been easy, Poitier admitted to Daley, but the promising talent in *Let's Do It Again* was the fulfillment of his dream, the vindication of his lonely struggle: "Inside, I felt lonely. I had only to think, however, of how important it was for me to persevere. Survival for me at what I was doing was terribly important to a lot of people in my picture, *Let's Do It Again*, who at that time, when I began, were either unknown or didn't even know themselves that they wanted to be actors."[24] Poitier had come a long way from the days of *No Way Out* to First Artists Productions and *Let's Do It Again*, and his successes were victories for all black actors and actresses.

Success brings its own burdens, of course, and, even in 1975, Poitier couldn't ignore the popularity and profits of *Let's Do It Again*. His power in the film industry was established, yet there were con-siderable pressures to continue in the same vein, to pursue ethnic comedy again. As he told Frank Daley, even freedom from financial worries has its complications: "Certainly there will be pressure built up at the studio for my next project to be a comedy, but certainly it won't be my sole means of expression from now on. I don't know what will come next. Since I can do what I want to do, I don't know what I want to do, now that I don't have to worry as much about the kind of things I should do."

In fact, the inspiration for Poitier's most recent film, *A Piece of the Action*, came from a rather unexpected quarter, an incident between Poitier and a young man dating one of the actor's daughters. Poitier happened upon the boy and his daughter one day, and the boy said, "Hey, what's your man?" Poitier was appalled, for he was of a generation that spoke reverentially to adults, with polite "Yes, sirs" and "No, sirs." This incident inspired Poitier to explore the mores of urban youth and the decline of civility. *A Piece of the Action* is his cinematic plea for courtesy and

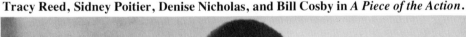

Tracy Reed, Sidney Poitier, Denise Nicholas, and Bill Cosby in *A Piece of the Action*.

consideration, his attack on the decline of civility, the failure of the social system, and the resulting juvenile delinquency and unemployment problems in this country.

A Piece of the Action is, then, a film with a little more substance than his earlier comedies, but Poitier never loses sight of the need for entertainment. As he warned young filmmakers at Greystone, the artist must put entertainment first and message second, for, without an audience, there is no meaningful communication: "I will never start out to make a movie that I know is not going to make any money. I made a movie once—and I've made a lot of bombs—that didn't even get back the negative cost. . . . I mean, how important can the comment be? You just spend a million to say something? Spend a million, have a lot of people come and see it, and then make your comment."

It is rather too evident that commercial success dominated Poitier's approach to *A Piece of the Action*. One has the feeling of a calculated gamble, where the gambler has stacked his deck with all the "sure-fire" devices experience has taught him were successful at the box office. As Newsweek noted in its 31 October 1977 review, just about every commercial base was touched: action, comedy, romance, and sentimentality.

The highly improbable plot of *A Piece of the Action* involves the history of two successful criminals, Manny Durrell (Sidney Poitier) and Dave Anderson (Bill Cosby), forced by retired policeman Joshua Burke (James Earl Jones) to support a community center for black ghetto youth, which was the favorite project of his late wife. While Cosby, attracted to the charming Lila French (Denise Nicholas), the community center director, evaluates the management and fundraising aspects of the center, Poitier gives a helping hand to the principal teacher, Sarah Thomas (Hope Clarke), who must transform a surly, disenchanted group of thirty adolescents into civilized, well-behaved, employable graduates. For all the added incidents, the complications of concealed identities, and the incursions of gangsters chasing Cosby, *A Piece of the Action* is little more than a reworking of the basic situation in *To Sir with Love*; only this time the locale is America and the students are black.

The film does have some highly charged moments as the kids begin to tell their personal experiences, and there is one truly dramatic episode when the toughest ghetto girl denounces the prim black teacher as a "poverty pimp" who has forgotten her people and her heritage.

Actor Poitier actually relates better to this group of adolescent costars than he did to those in *To Sir with Love*; he seems much more relaxed, confident, and sure of his screen presence. Interviewed after the filming, all the young members of the cast commented on Poitier's patience as a director and his generosity as a costar. *A Piece of the Action* proved a fine showcase for some aspiring black talent largely because Poitier was willing to give the younger members of the cast their own important scenes and to showcase their lines. Even in the scenes where he is teaching the class, Poitier turns his camera on the youngsters, using reaction shots instead of close-ups of his performance.

Poitier manifested a similar respect for the comic talents of Bill Cosby in *A Piece of the Action*. Poitier the director made Cosby the actor the real center of the film. His jokes, his romance, and his adventures occupy the bulk of the film. Poitier and Cosby were such good friends, and Cosby was such a joker, that Poitier actually barred Cosby from the set when he was filming serious sequences. In retaliation, Cosby went around telling the columnists that "This director doesn't know what he's doing. I am only doing this to help him make a living." In his more serious moments, however, Cosby commented on one of the most striking features of the film, the romance between him as Dave Anderson and Denise as Lila French. Few critics mention this plot line, but, as Bill Cosby well knew, it was a quiet revolution on screen for two blacks to embody the romantic fantasies of the popular audience. They weren't particularly sexy, just normal folks in love, but after years of emasculated black males and fast black women, it was enough. As Cosby saw it, this aspect of *A Piece of the Action* was most encouraging for all black performers: "It's an important thing that happens between these two characters in the movie. They are a couple of people who discover each other and like what they have discovered. It's a nice, clean relationship to see on screen—with dinners, dances, concerts, and a little disco thrown in. There is something very new and different, with a great potential."[25]

This great new potential for all black filmmakers and black performers came directly as a result of the efforts of Sidney Poitier. For almost thirty years and in over three dozen films, he had paved the way as performer, star, and entrepreneur. In a project like *A Piece of the Action*, Poitier told reporters, he began with his original idea, then "worked for many months with the screenwriter. And then I had to make the picture,

Bill Cosby and Sidney Poitier learn they're being blackmailed in *A Piece of the Action*.

direct it, and act in it, and once it was finished, I had to edit it, oversee the scoring, and supervise all the manifold details attendant on getting a picture out.''[26] This was arduous labor for a man who once· said he only wanted to make money from films so he could "lallygag." At the age of fifty, after almost three decades in the movies, Sidney Poitier decided to take a sabbatical to rest his bones and restore his juices. For the year of 1978, he decided to cruise round the world with his family, write his autobiography, and plan his next project. During this hiatus, his last film, *A Piece of the Action*, garnered the National Association for the Advancement of Colored People's Image Awards for best screenplay and for best director. Poitier had come a long road to the top, as both actor and film maker, and he had met his responsibility to his audience.

Notes to Chapter 5

1. Quoted in James P. Murray, *To Find an Image*, p. 29.
2. *New York Times*, 25 March 1971.
3. *Variety*, 24 March 1971.
4. *Variety*, 17 March 1971.
5. *Variety*, 17 March 1971.
6. Roy Newquist, *A Special Kind of Magic*, pp. 121-122.
7. Sidney Poitier, "Dialogue on Film," p. 34.
8. Sidney Poitier, "Entertainment, Politics, and the Movie Business," p. 19.
9. James Baldwin, *The Fire Next Time* (New York: Dial Press, 1963), p. 95.
10. *New York Times*, 29 April 1972.
11. Judy Michaelson, "Sidney Poitier Makes a Choice," *New York Post*, 10 February 1968.
12. Donald Bogle, *Toms, Mulattoes, Mammies, and Bucks*, pp. 335-336.
13. *Variety*, 18 April 1973.
14. *Films and Filming*, July 1973, pp. 52-53.

15. Quoted in Frank Daley, "The Black Man's Burden," the *Ottawa Journal*, 17 October 1975.

16. James L. Limbacher, "Blacks on Films," *Journal of Popular Film*, 4, no. 4: 373.

17. *New York Times*, 17 June 1974.

18. Stuart Byron, "Sidney Poitier finds the Ticket to Soul," *Real Paper*, 24 July 1974, p. 24.

19. Pauline Kael, "Bigot," *New Yorker*, 15 September 1975, p. 93.

20. Nancy L. Schwartz, "Rebels and Causes," *Soho Weekly News*, 11 September 1975, p. 28.

21. *Cue*, 26 November 1977, p. 31.

22. *Ottawa Journal*, 17 October 1975.

23. *The New Yorker*, 11 March 1975.

24. "The Black Man's Burden," *Ottawa Journal*, 17 October 1975.

25. *Amsterdam* (N.Y.) *News*, 3 September 1977.

26. *Reporter Dispatch*, 27 October 1977.

CONCLUSION
POITIER'S ACHIEVEMENT AND FUTURE PROJECTS

The door closed. Wait a minute. The sign went on. The motors revved up. The
plane shook. I shook too. It taxied to the runway. It was taking off without Sidney
Poitier. But they had promised me. He would be there. He would ride in. In a
pumpkin seed. To take care of me. To hold my hand. And when we land to dance
me up the Plantation Stairs in Dem Golden Slippers. They'd lied. He
didn't show up. If my voices lied about Sidney Poitier, then they
could have lied about the plane's credentials.

— Dory Previn, *Midnight Baby*

Asked to define success in Hollywood, Humphrey Bogart once said, "It's very simple, kid. Success is still being around after twenty-five years. Just be a survivor. Out-endure the other sons-of-bitches. You'll be more famous than any of them. It's the guys who are still around who get the awards." Sidney Poitier is definitely still around today; he has had more than his twenty-five years, and his awards are still coming at the box office.

This past year witnessed the announcement of his autobiography, a long-awaited work which had been promised years ago in a poker-game agreement with Lyle Stuart. It also saw the publication of a lavishly-illustrated fan book by Alvin H. Marill, with interesting stills and clippings on each film and very comprehensive credits.

Yet Poitier's success extends far beyond the covers of a book or his portrayals on screen. His career is truly remarkable for its unique change in direction: after achieving a status which very few white actors attain and which no black performer ever had, Sidney Poitier refused to be boxed in or to rest on his laurels. Instead, he decided to use his immense popularity and his considerable financial resources in pursuit of other creative ventures as a writer, director, and producer. In this way he managed not only to prove himself in the face of new challenges, but he also gave other blacks real opportunities to take their places in the American film industry.

His films became the center of an entirely new sector of the American film industry, opening new

Sidney Poitier at home behind the camera

doors for black people on all levels of film making, allowing them active participation and sharpening their skills in the profession. Few critics have understood or noted this important fact about Poitier's recent productions. The box office success of *Uptown Saturday Night, Let's Do It Again*, and *A Piece of the Action* has assured that black people finally have the opportunity to make films aimed at a wide audience.

What is next? Only Sidney Poitier can answer that question definitely, though he did give some clues in an interview with *Cue* published a month before his sabbatical began: "I feel I'm at a good place in my life. I'm more relaxed because I've grown. A lot of work is behind me, much that I'm pleased with, much that I'm proud of, and not much that I regret. I don't think I'll continue to act. . . . But I'm going on to direct more films and write screenplays and novels." Among the projects already in the planning stages are: a production of *Sizwe Banzi is Dead;* and *The Island;* a science fiction film written by Jason Starks; a woman's picture from a black woman's point of view written by Richard Wesley; Poitier's own version of the life of Paul Robeson, an interpretation focussing on his relationship with Eslanda Goode Robeson, his wife. This wealth of projects suggests that some of Poitier's greatest achievements lie in the future.

FILMOGRAPHY

NO WAY OUT (Twentieth Century Fox Film Corporation, 1950). *Director*: Joseph Mankiewicz. *Producer*: Darryl Zanuck. *Screenplay*: Joseph Mankiewicz, Lesser Samuels. *Photography*: Milton Krasner. *Music*: Alfred Newman. *Editor:* Barbara McLean. *Art Direction:* Lyle Wheeler, George W. Davis.

Cast: Sidney Poitier (Dr. Luther Brooks), Richard Widmark (Ray Biddle), Linda Darnell (Edie Johnson), Stephen McNally (Dr. Daniel Wharton), Dots Johnson (Lefty), Don Hicks (Johnny Biddle), Ken Christy (Officer Kowalski), Harry Bellaver (George Biddle), Stanley Ridges (Dr. Moreland), Amanda Randolph (Gladys), Rubie Dee (Connie), Ossie Davis (John), Mildred Joanne Smith (Cora Brooks), Frederick O'Neal (Dr. Clark).

CRY, THE BELOVED COUNTRY (Lopert Films Release of a London Films Production, 1952). *Director*: Zoltan Korda. *Producer*: Zoltan Korda. *Screenplay*: Alan Paton, from his novel. *Photography*: Robert Krasker. *Editor*: David Easy. *Art Direction*: Wilfrid Shingleton.

Cast: Sidney Poitier (Reverend Msimangu), Canada Lee (Stephen Kumalo), Charles Carson (James Jarvis), Joyce Carey (Margaret Jarvis), Geoffrey Keen (Father Vincent), Michael Goodliffe (Martens), Edric Connor (John Kumalo), Charles McCrae (Kumalo's Friend), Lionel Ngakane (Absalom), Vivien Clinton (Mary), Albertina Temba (Mrs. Kumalo), Bruce Anderson (Farmer Smith), Bruce Meredith Smith (Captain Jaarsveldt), Berdine Brunewald (Mary Jarvis), Ribbon Dhlamini (Gertrude Kumalo), Stanley Van Beers (Judge).

RED BALL EXPRESS (Universal Pictures, 1952). *Director*: Budd Boetticher. *Producer*: Aaron Rosenberg. *Screenplay*: John Michael Hayes, based on a story by Marcel Klauber and Billy Grady, Jr. *Photography:* Maury Gertsman, *Art Direction:* Bernard Herzbrun, Richard Riedel. *Editor:* Edward Curtiss.

Cast: Sidney Poitier (Corporal Andrew Robertson), Jeff Chandler (Lt. Chick Campbell), Alex Nicol (Sgt. Ernest Kallek), Charles Drake (Partridge), Hugh O'Brien (Pvt. Wilson), Frank Chase (Higgins), Jack Kelly (Pvt. John Heyman), Judith Braun (Joyce McClelland), Cindy Garner (Kitty Walsh), Jacqueline Duval (Antoinette DuBois), Howard Petrie (Gen. Gordon), Bubber Johnson (Pvt. Taffy Smith), Robert Davis (Pvt. Dave McCord), John Hudson (Sgt. Max), Palmer Lee (Tank Lt.), Jack Warden (Major).

GO, MAN, GO! (A Sirod Productions Film Released by United Artists, 1954). *Director*: James Wong Howe. *Producer*: Anton M. Leader. *Screenplay*: Arnold Becker. *Photography*: Bill Steiner. *Art Director*: Howard Bay. *Technical Director*: Harry Hannin. *Editor*: Faith Elliott.

Cast: Sidney Poitier (Inman Jackson), Dane Clark (Abe Saperstein), Pat Breslin (Sylvia Saperstein), Edmon Ryan (Zack Leader), Bram Nossen (James Willoughby), Anatol Winogradoff (Papa Saperstein), Celia Boodkin (Mama Saperstein), Carol Sinclair (Fay Saperstein), Ellsworth Writht (Sam), Slim Gaillard (Slim), Frieda Altman (Ticket Seller), Mort Marshall (MC), Jean Shore (Secretary), Jule Benedict (First Bathing Beauty), Jerry Hauer (Second Bathing Beauty), Marty Glickman (Announcer No. 1), Bill Stern (Announcer No. 2), Lew Hearn (Appraiser), Ruby Dee (Irma Jackson), and the Harlem Globetrotters as themselves.

BLACKBOARD JUNGLE (Metro-Goldwyn-Mayer, 1955). *Director*: Richard Brooks. *Producer*: Pandro S. Berman. *Screenplay*: Richard Brooks, based on the novel by Evan Hunter. *Photography*: Russell Harlan. *Art Direction*: Cedric Gibbons, Randall Duell. *Music*: Bill Haley and the Comets. *Editor*: Ferris Webster.

Cast: Sidney Poitier (Gregory W. Miller), Glenn Ford (Richard Dadier), Anne Francis (Anne Dadier), Louis Calhern (Jim Murdock), Margaret Hayes (Lois Judby Hammond), Hohy Hoyt (Mr. Warneke), Richard Kiley (Joshua Y. Edwards), Emile Meyer (Mr. Halloran), Warner Anderson (Dr. Bradley), Basil Ruysdael (Prof. A. R. Kraal), Vic Morrow (Artie West), Dan Terranova (Belazi), Rafael Campos (Pete V. Morales). Paul Mazursky (Emmanuel Stoker), Horace

McMahon (Detective), Jameel Farah (Santini) Danny Dennis (De Lica).

GOODBYE, MY LADY (Warner Brothers, 1956). *Director*: William A. Wellman. *Producer*: A Batjac Production. *Screenplay*: Sid Fleischman, from the novel by James Street. *Photography*: William H. Clothier. *Art Direction*: Donald A. Peters. *Music*: Laurindo Almeida, George Field. *Editor*: Fred MacDowell. *Production Manager*: Nate H. Edwards. *Unit Production Manager*: Gordon B. Forbes.

Cast: Sidney Poitier (Gates), Walter Brennan (Uncle Jesse), Phil Harris (Cash), Brandon de Wilde (Skeeter), William Hopper (Grover), Louise Beavers (Bonnie Dew), Vivian Vance (Wife), William Frawley (Husband).

EDGE OF THE CITY (Metro-Goldwyn-Mayer, 1957). *Director*: Martin Ritt. *Producer*: David Susskind. *Screenplay*: Robert Alan Aurthur, from his story and teleplay *A Man is Ten Feet Tall*. *Photography*: Joseph Brun. *Editor*: Sidney Meyers. *Art Direction*: Richard Sylbert. *Music*: Leonard Rosenman.

Cast: Sidney Poitier (Tommy Tyler), John Cassavetes (Axel Worth), Jack Warden (Charles Malid), Kathleen Maguire (Ellen Wilson), Ruby Dee (Lucy Tyler), Robert Simon (Mr. Nordmann), Ruth White (Mrs. Nordmann), William A. Lee (Davis), Val Avery (Brother), John Kellogg (Detective), David Clarke (Wallace), Estelle Hemsley (Lucy's Mother), Charles Jordan (Old Stevedore), Ralph Bell (Nightboss).

SOMETHING OF VALUE (Metro-Goldwyn-Mayer, 1957). *Director*: Richard Brooks. *Producer*: Pandro S. Berman. *Screenplay*: Richard Brooks, based on Robert C. Ruark's book. *Photography*: Russell Harlan. *Music*: Miklos Rozsa. *Editor*: Ferris Webster. *Art Direction*: William A. Horning, Edward Carfagno.

Cast: Sidney Poitier (Kimani), Rock Hudson (Peter McKenzie), Dana Wynter (Holly Keith), Wendy Hiller (Elizabeth Newton), Juano Hernandez (Njogu), William Marshall (Leader), Robert Beatty (Jeff Newton), Walter Fitzgerald (Henry McKenzie), Michael Pate (Joe Matson), Ivan Dixon (Lathela), Ken Renard (Karanja), Samadu Jackson (Witch Doctor), Frederick O'Neal (Adam Marenga), John J. Akar (Waithaka).

BAND OF ANGELS (Warner Brothers, 1957). *Director*: Raoul Walsh. *Screenplay*: John Twist, Ivan Goff, Ben Roberts, based on Robert Penn Warren's novel. *Photography*: Lucien Ballard. *Music*: Max Steiner. *Editor*: Folmar Blangsted. *Art Direction*: Franz Bachelin.

Cast: Sidney Poitier (Rau-ru), Clark Gable (Hamish Bond), Yvonne DeCarlo (Amantha Starr), Effrem Zimbalist (Ethan Sears), Patric Knowles (Charles de Marigny), Rex Reason (Seth Parton), Torin Thatcher (Capt. Canavan), Andrea King (Miss Idell), Ray Teal (Mr. Calloway), Russ Evans (Jimmee), Carolle Drake (Michele), Raymond Bailey (Stuart), Tommie Moore (Dollie), William Forrest (Aaron Starr), Noreen Corcoran (Young Manty).

MARK OF THE HAWK (Universal-International, 1958). *Director*: Michael Audley. *Producer*: Lloyd Young, W. Burston Marton. *Screenplay*: H. Kenn Carmichael and Lloyd Young, based on Young's original story. *Photography*: Erwin Hillier, Toge Fujihara. *Music*: Matyas Seiber. *Editor*: Edward

Jarvis. *Art Direction*: Terence Verity. *African Location Unit Director*: Gilbert Gunn.

Cast: Sidney Poitier (Obam), Eartha Kitt (Renee), Juano Hernandez (Amugu), John McIntire (Craig), Helen Horton (Barbara), Marne Maitland (Sundar Lal), Gerard Heinz (Governor General), Patrick Allen (Gregory), Earl Cameron (Prosecutor), Clifton Macklin (Kanda), Ewen Solon (Inspector), Lionel Mgakano (African Doctor), Andy Ho (Chinese Officer), John A. Tinn (Chinese Soldier).

THE DEFIANT ONES (United Artists, 1958). *Director*: Stanley Kramer. *Producer*: Stanley Kramer. *Screenplay*: Nathan E. Douglas and Harold Jacob Smith. *Photography*: Sam Leavitt. *Music*: Ernest Gold. *Editor*: Frederic Knudtson. *Art Direction*: Fernando Carrere. *Costume*: Joe King. *Special Effects*: Walter Elliott.

Cast: Sidney Poitier (Noah Cullen), Tony Curtis (John "Joker" Jackson), Theodore Bikel (Sheriff Max Muller), Charles McGray (Captain Frank Gibbons), Cara Williams (The Woman), Lon Chaney (Big Sam), King Donovan (Solly), Claude Akins (Mac), Lawrence Dobkin (Editor), Whit Bissell (Lou Gans), Carl Switzer (Angus), Kevin Coughlin (The Kid).

THE VIRGIN ISLAND (British Lion Release of a Countryman Film Production, 1958). *Director*: Pat Jackson. *Producer*: Leon Close, Grahame Thrope. *Screenplay*: Phillip Rush, based on the novel *Our Virgin Island* by Robb White. *Photography*: Freddie Francis. *Music*: Clifton Parker. *Editor*: Gordon Pilkington.

Cast: Sidney Poitier (Marcus), John Cassavetes (Evan), Virginia Maskell (Tina), Isabel Dean (Mrs. Lomax), Colin Gordon (The Commissioner), Howard Marion Crawford (Prescott), Edric Connor (Captain Jason), Ruby Dee (Ruth), Gladys Boot (Mrs. Carruthers), Julian Mayfield (Band Leader), Reginald Hearne (Doctor), Arnold Bell (Heath), Alonzo Bozan (Grant).

PORGY AND BESS (Columbia Pictures, 1959). *Director*: Otto Preminger. *Producer*: Samuel Goldwyn. *Screenplay*: Richard Nash, based on George Gershwin's operetta from the novel *Porgy* by Dubose Heyward. *Photography*: Leon Shamroy. *Music*: George Gershwin. *Editor*: Daniel Mandell. *Musical Director*: Andre Previn. *Choreography*: Hermes Pan.

Cast: Sidney Poitier (Porgy), Dorothy Dandridge (Bess), Sammy Davis, Jr. (Sportin' Life), Pearl Bailey (Maria), Brock Peters (Crown), Diahann Carroll (Clara), Leslie Scott (Jake), Ruth Attaway (Serena), Clarence Muse (Peter), Ivan Dixon (Jim), Everdinne Wilson (Annie), Joel Fluellen (Robbins), Earl Jackson (Mingo), Roy Glenn (Lawyer Frazier), Claude Akins (Detective), Maurice Manson (Coroner).

ALL THE YOUNG MEN (Columbia Pictures, 1960). *Director*: Hal Bartlett. *Producer*: Hal Bartlett. *Screenplay*: Hal Bartlett. *Photography*: Daniel Fapp. *Music*: George Dunning. *Editor*: Al Clark. *Art Direction*: George Dunning.

Cast: Sidney Poitier (Towler), Alan Ladd (Kincaid), James Darren (Cotton), Glenn Corbett (Wade), Mort Sahl (Crane), Anna St. Clair (Maya), Paul Richards (Bracken), Dick Davalos (Casey), Lee Kinsolving (Dean), Joe Gallison (Jackson), Paul Baxley (Lazitech), Charles Quinlivian (Lieutenant), Michael Davis (Cho), Mario Alcalde (Hunter), Maria Tsien (Korean Woman), Ingemar Johansson (Torgil).

RAISIN IN THE SUN (Columbia Pictures, 1961). *Director*: Daniel Petrie. *Producer*: David Susskind, Philip Rose. *Screenplay*: Lorraine Hansberry, based on her play. *Photography*: Charles Lawton. *Music*: Laurence Rosenthal. *Editor*: William A. Lyon, Paul Weatherwax. *Art Direction*: Carl Anderson.

Cast: Sidney Poitier (Walter Lee Younger), Claudia McNeil (Lena Younger), Ruby Dee (Ruth), Diana Sands (Beneatha), Ivan Dixon (Asagai), John Fiedler (Mark Lindner), Louis Gossett (George Murchison), Stephen Perry (Travis), Joel Fluellen (Bobo), Roy Glenn (Willie Harris), Ray Stubbs (Bartender), Rudolph Monroe (Taxi Driver), George De Normand (Employer).

PARIS BLUES (United Artists, 1961). *Director*: Martin Ritt. *Producer*: George Glass and Walter Seltzer. *Screenplay*: Jack Sher, Irene Kamp, and Walter Bernstein, from Lulla Adler's adaptation of the novel by Harold Flender. *Photography*: Christian Matras. *Music*: Duke Ellington. *Editor*: Roger Dwyre. *Art Direction*: Alexander Trauner.

Cast: Sidney Poitier (Eddie Cook), Joanne Woodward (Lillian Corning), Paul Newman (Ram Bowen), Louis Armstrong (Wild Man Moore), Diahann Carroll (Connie Lampson), Serge Reggiani (Michel Dugivne), Barbara Laage (Marie Seoul), Andre Luguet (Rene Bernard), Marie Versini (Nicole), Moustache (Ram's Drummer), Aaron Bridgers (Ram's Pianist), Roger Blin (The Gypsy Guitarist), Helene Dieudonne (The Pusher), Niko (Ricardo).

PRESSURE POINT (United Artists, 1962). *Director*: Hubert Cornfield. *Producer*: Stanley Kramer. *Screenplay*: Hubert Cornfield and S. Lee Pogostin, based on a narrative by Robert Lindner. *Photographer*: Ernest Haller. *Music*: Ernest Gold. *Editor*: Fred Knudtson. *Art Direction*: Rudy Sternad.

Cast: Sidney Poitier (Doctor), Bobby Darin (Patient), Peter Falk (Psychiatrist), Carl Benton Reid (Chief Medical Officer), Mary Munday (Bar Hostess), Barry Gordon (Boy), Howard Caine (Tavern Owner), Anne Barton (Mother), James Anderson (Father), Yvette Vickers (Drunken Woman).

LILIES OF THE FIELD (United Artists, 1963). *Director*: Ralph Nelson. *Producer*: Ralph Nelson. *Screenplay*: James Poe, based on the novel by William E. Barrett. *Photography*: Ernest Haller. *Music*: Jerry Goldsmith. *Editor*: John McCafferty.

Cast: Sidney Poitier (Homer Smith), Lilia Skala (Mother Maria), Lisa Mann (Sister Gertrude), Isa Crino (Sister Agnes), Francesca Jarvis (Sister Albertine), Pamela Branch (Sister Elizabeth), Sanley Adams (Juan), Dan Fracer (Father Murphy), Ralph Nelson (Mr. Ashton).

THE LONG SHIPS (Columbia, 1964). *Director*: Jack Cardiff. *Producer*: Irving Allen. *Screenplay*: Berkeley Mather and Beverly Cross, based on the novel by Franz Bengtsson. *Photography*: Christopher Challis. *Music*: Dusan Radles. *Editor*: Geoff Foot.

Cast: Sidney Poitier (Ali Mansuh), Richard Widmark (Rolfe), Russ Tamblyn (Orm), Rosanna Schiaffino (Aminah), Beba Loncar (Gerda), Oscar Holmolka (Krok), Edward Judd (Sven), Clifford Evans (King Harald), Jeanne Moody (Ylva), Colin Blakely (Rhykka), Gordon Jackson (Vahlin), David Lodge (Olla), Paul Stassino (Raschild), Lionel Jeffires (Ariz).

THE GREATEST STORY EVER TOLD (United Artists, 1965). *Director*: George Stevens. *Producer*: George Stevens. *Executive Producer*: Frank I. Davis. *Associate Producer*: George Stevens, Jr., Antonion Vellani. *Screenplay*: George Stevens, James Lee Barrett, script based on the books of the Old and New Testament, other ancient writings, the book *The Greatest Story Ever Told* by Fulton Oursler and other writings by Henry Deker with the creative consultation of Carl Sandburg. *Photography*: Loyal Griggs, William C. Mellor. *Music*: Alfred Newman. *Editors*: Harold F. Kress, Argyle Nelson, Jr., Frank O'Neill. *Art Direction*: Richard Day, William Creber. *Costumes*: Vittorio Nino Novarese, Marjorie Best. *Set Design*: David Hall. *Special Effects*: J. McMillan Johnson, Clarence Slifer, A. Arnold Gillespie, Robert A. Hoag.

Cast: Sidney Poitier (Simon of Cyrene), Max Von Sydow (Jesus), Dorothy McGuire (Mary), Robert Loggia (Joseph), Claude Rains (Herod the Great), Jose Ferrer (Herod Antipas), Marian Seldes (Herodias), John Abbott (Aben), Rodolfo Acosta (Harith, Captain of Lancers), Charlton Heston (John the Baptist), Michael Anderson (Little James), Robert Blake (Simon the Zealot), Burt Brinkerhoff (Andrew), John Considine (John), Jamie Farr (Thaddeus), David Hedison (Philip, Peter Mann (Nathaniel), David McCallum (Judas), Roddy McDowall (Matthew), Gary Raymond (Peter), Tom Reese (Thomas), David Sheiner (James the Elder), Michael Ansara (Herod Commander), Carroll Baker (Veronica), Ina Balin (Martha of Bethany), Pat Boone (Young Man at Tomb), Victor Buono (Sorak), Richard Conte (Barabbas), Philip Coolidge (Chuza), John Crawford (Alexander), Frank DeKova (Tormentor), Joanna Dunham (Mary Magdalene), Kim Hamilton (Simon of Cyrene's Wife), Van Heflin (Bar Amand), Martin Landau (Caiaphas), Angela Lansburry (Claudia), Vic Lundin (Pilate's Aid), Janet Margolin (Mary of Bethany), Sal Mineo (Uriah), Gil Perkins (Jacob), Nehemiah Persoff (Shemiah), Donald Pleasence (Dark Hermit), Telly Savalas (Pilate), Joseph Schildkraut (Nicodemus), Joe Sirola (Dumah), Abraham Solger (Joseph of Arimathea), Paul Stewart (Quester), Harold Stone (General Varus), John Wayne (Centurion), Shelley Winters (Woman of No Name).

THE BEDFORD INCIDENT (Columbia Pictures, 1965). *Director*: James B. Harris. *Producer*: James B. Harris. *Screenplay*: James Poe, based on the novel by Mark Rascovich. *Photography*: Gilbert Taylor. *Music*: Gerard Schurmann. *Editor*: John Jympson. *Art Direction*: Arthur Lawson.

Cast: Sidney Poitier (Ben Munceford), Richard Widmark (Capt. Eric Finlander), James MacArthur (Ensign Ralston), Martin Balsam (Dr. Chester Potter), Wally Cox (Seaman Merlin Queffle), Eric Portman (Commodore Schrepke), Michael Kane (Commander Allison), Gary Cockrell (Lt. Bascombe), Phil Brown (Chief Hospitalman McKinley), Brian Davies (Lt. Beckman), Edward Bishop (Lt. Hacker), George Roubichek (Lt. Berger), Michael Graham (Lt. Krindlemeyer), Bill Evans (Lt. Hazelwood), Donald Sutherland (Hospital Man), Warren Stanhope (Hospital Man), Colin Maitland (Seaman), Paul Tamarin (Seaman), Frank Lieberman (Seaman).

A PATCH OF BLUE (Metro-Goldwyn-Mayer, 1965). *Director*: Guy Green. *Producer*: Pandro S. Berman. *Screenplay*: Guy Green, from the novel *Be Ready with Bells and Drums* by Elizabeth Kata. *Photography*: Robert Burks.

Music: Jerry Goldsmith. *Editor*: Rita Roland. *Art Direction*: George W. Davis, Urie McCleary.

Cast: Sidney Poitier (Gordon Ralfe), Shelley Winters (Rose-Ann D'Arcey), Elizabeth Hartman (Selina D'Arcey), Wallace Ford (Ole Pa), Ivan Dixon (Mark Ralfe), Elisabeth Fraser (Sadie), John Qualen (Mr. Faber), Kelly Flynn (Yanek Faber), Debi Storm (Selina, Age 5), Renata Vanni (Mrs. Favaloro), Saverio LoMedico (Mr. Favaloro).

THE SLENDER THREAD (Paramount, 1966). *Director*: Sydney Pollack. *Producer*: Stephen Alexander. *Screenplay*: Stirling Silliphant, based on a magazine article by Shana Alexander. *Photography*: Loyal Griggs. *Music*: Quincy Jones. *Editor*: Thomas Stanford. *Art Direction*: Hal Pereira and Jack Poplin.

Cast: Sidney Poitier (Alan Newell), Anne Bancroft (Inga Dyson), Telly Savalas (Doctor Coburn), Steven Hill (Mark Dyson), Edward Asner (Detective Judd Ridley), Indus Arthur (Marion), Paul Newlan (Sergeant Harry Ward), Dabney Coleman (Charlie), H. M. Wynant (Doctor), Robert Hoy (Patrolman Steve Peters), Greg Jarvis (Chris Dyson), Jason Wingreen (Medical Technician), Marjorie Nelson (Mrs. Thomas), Steven Marlo (Arthur Foss), Thomas Hill (Liquor Salesman), Lane Bradford (Al McCardle), Janet Dudley (Edna), John Napier (Dr. Alden Van).

DUEL AT DIABLO (United Artists, 1966). *Director*: Ralph Nelson. *Producer*: Fred Engel, Ralph Nelson. *Screenplay*: Marvin Alpert, Michael Grilikhes, based on Alpert's novel *Apache Uprising*. *Photography*: Charles F. Wheeler. *Music*: Neal Hefti. *Editor*: Fredric Steinkamp. *Assistant Directors*: Emmett Emerson, Philip N. Cook.

Cast: Sidney Poitier (Toller), James Garner (Jesse Remsberg), Bibi Andersson (Ellen Grange), Dennis Weaver (Willard Grange), Bill Travers (Lt. Scotty McAllister), William Redfield (Sgt. Ferguson), John Hoyt (Chata), John Crawford (Clay Dean), John Hubbard (Major Novak), Kevin Coughlin (Norton), Jay Ripley (Tech), Jeff Cooper (Casey), Ralph Bahnsen (Nyles), Bobby Crawford (Swenson), Richard Lapp (Forbes), Armand Alzamora (Ramirez), Alf Elson (Colonel Foster), Dawn Little Sky (Chata's Wife), Eddie Little Sky (Alchise), Al Wyatt (First Miner), Bill Hart (Corporal Harrington), J. R. Randall (Crowley), John Daheim (Stableman), Phil Schumacher (Burly Soldier), Richard Farnsworth (First Wagon Driver), Joe Finnegan (Second Wagon Driver).

TO SIR WITH LOVE (Columbia Pictures, 1967). *Director*: James Clavell. *Producer*: James Clavell. *Executive Producer*: John R. Sloan. *Screenplay*: James Clavell, based on the autobiographical novel by E. R. Braithwaite. *Photography*: Paul Beeson. *Music*: Ron Grainer. *Songs*: "To Sir With Love" (Don Black, Marc London), "Off and Running" (Toni Wine, Carole Bayer), "Stealing My Love From Me" (Marc London), "It's Getting Harder All The Time" (Ben Raleigh, Charles Albertine). *Editor*: Peter Thornton. *Montage Sequence*: George White.

Cast: Sidney Poitier (Mark Thackeray), Christian Roberts (Denham), Judy Geeson (Pamela Dare), Suzy Kendall (Gillian), Faith Brook (Mrs. Evans), Christopher Chittell (Potter), Geoffrey Bayldon (Weston), Patricia Routledge (Clinty), Adrienne Posta (Moira Jackson), Edward Burnham

(Florian), Rita Webb (Mrs. Joseph), Fiona Duncan (Miss Phllips), Lulu [Marie Lawrie] (Barbara Pegg).

IN THE HEAT OF THE NIGHT (United Artists, 1967). *Director*: Norman Jewison. *Producer*: Walter Mirisch. *Screenplay*: Stirling Silliphant, based on the novel by John Ball. *Photography*: Haskell Wexler. *Music*: Quincy Jones. *Art Direction*: Paul Groesse. *Editor*: Hal Ashby.

Cast: Sidney Poitier (Virgil Tibbs), Rod Steiger (Bill Gillespie), Warren Oates (Sam Wood), Lee Grant (Mrs. Leslie Colbert), James Patterson (Purdy), Quentin Dean (Dolores Purdy), Larry Gates (Eric Endicott), Scott Wilson (Harvey Oberst), Jack Teter (Philip Colbert), Matt Clark (Packy Harrison), Anthony James (Ralph Henshaw), Kermit Murdock (H. E. Henderson), Khalil Bezaleel (Jess), Peter Whitney (George Courtney), William Watson (Harold Courtney), Timothy Scott (Shagbag Martin), Fred Stewart (Dr. Stuart), Arthur Malet (Ted Ulam), David Stinehart (Baggage Master), Buzz Barton (Conductor).

GUESS WHO'S COMING TO DINNER (Columbia Pictures, 1967). *Director*: Stanley Kramer. *Producer*: Stanley Kramer. *Screenplay*: William Rose. *Associate Producer*: George Glass. *Photography*: Sam Leavitt. *Music*: De Vol. *Editor*: Robert C. Jones. *Production Design*: Robert Clatworthy. *Song*: "Glory of Love" (Billy Hill): sung by Jacqueline Fontaine.

Cast: Sidney Poitier (John Prentice), Spencer Tracy (Matt Drayton), Katharine Hepburn (Christina Drayton), Katharine Houghton (Joey Drayton), Cecil Kellaway (Monsignor Ryan), Beah Richards (Mrs. Prentice), Roy E. Glenn, Sr. (Mr. Prentice), Isabell Sanford (Tillie), Virginia Christine (Hilary St. George), Alexandra Hay (Carhop), Barbara Randolph (Dorothy), D'Urville Martin (Frankie), Tom Heaton (Peter), Grace Gaynor (Judith), Skip Martin (Delivery Boy), John Hudkins (Cab Driver).

FOR LOVE OF IVY (Cinerama Releasing Corporation, 1968). *Director*: Daniel Mann. *Producer*: Edgar J. Scherick, Jay Weston. *Screenplay*: Robert Alan Aurthur, based on an original story by Sidney Poitier. *Photography*: Joseph Coffey. *Music*: Quincy Jones. *Editor*: Patricia Jaffe. *Production Design*: Peter Dohanos.

Cast: Sidney Poitier (Jack Parks), Abbey Lincoln (Ivy Moore), Beau Bridges (Tim Austin), Nan Mantin (Doris Austin), Lauri Peters (Gena Austin), Carroll O'Connor (Frank Austin), Leon Bibb (Billy Talbot), Hugh Hird (Jerry), Lon Satton (Harry), Stanley Greene (Eddie).

THE LOST MAN (Universal, 1969). *Director*: Robert Alan Aurthur. *Producer*: Edward Muhl, Melville Tucker. *Screenplay*: Robert Alan Aurthur, based on *Odd Man Out* by Frederick Green. *Photography*: Jerry Finnerman. *Music*: Quincy Jones. *Editor*: Edward Mann. *Art Direction*: Alexander Golitzen, George C. Webb. *Costumes*: Edith Head.

Cast: Sidney Poitier (Jason Higgs), Joanna Shimkus (Cathy Ellis), Al Freeman, Jr. (Dennis), Michael Tolan (Hamilton), Leon Bibb (Eddie), Richard Dysart (Barnes), David Steinberg (Photographer), Beverly Todd (Sally), Paul Winfield (Orville), Bernie Hamilton (Reggie), Richard Anthony Williams (Ronald), Virginia Capers (Theresa), Vonette McGee (Diane), Frank Marth (Warren), Maxine Stuart (Miss Harrison, George Tyle (Plainclothesman), Pauline Mayers (Grandma), Lee Weaver (Willie), Morris Erby (Miller), Doug Johnson (Teddy), Lincoln Kilpatrick (Minister).

THEY CALL ME MISTER TIBBS! (United Artists, 1970). *Director*: Gordon Douglas. *Producer*: Herbert Hirschman. *Screenplay*: Alan R. Trustman and James R. Webb, based on a story by Mr. Trustman based on characters created by John Ball. *Photography;* Gerald Finnerman. *Music*: Quincy Jones. *Editor*: Bud Molin. *Art Direction*: Addison F. Hehr. *Assistant Director*: Rusty Meek.

Cast: Sidney Poitier (Virgil Tibbs), Martin Landau (Reverend Logan Sharpe), Barbara McNair (Valeri Tibbs), Anthony Zerbe (Rice Weedon), Jeff Corey (Captain Marden), David Sheiner (Herbert Kenner), Juano Hernandez (Mealie), Norma Crane (Marge Garfield), Edward Asner (Woody Garfield), Ted Gehring (Sergeant Deutsch), Beverly Todd (Puff), Linda Towne (Joy Sturges), George Spell (Andrew), Wanda Spell (Ginny).

THE ORGANIZATION (United Artists, 1971). *Director*: Don Medford. *Producer*: Walter Mirisch. *Screenplay*: James R. Webb, based on characters created by John Ball. *Photography*: Joseph Biroc. *Music*: Gil Melle. *Editor*: Ferris Webster. *Art Direction*: George Chan.

Cast: Sidney Poitier (Virgil Tibbs), Barbara McNair (Valeri Tibbs), Gerald O'Loughlin (Jack Pecora), Sheree North (Mrs. Morgan), Fred Bier (Bob Alford), Allen Garfield (Benjy), Ron O'Neal (Joe Peralez), Lani Miyazaki (Annie Sekido), George Spell (Andy Tibbs), Wanda Spell (Ginny Tibbs).

BROTHER JOHN (Columbia Pictures, 1971). *Director*: James Goldstone. *Producer*: Joel Glickman. *Screenplay*: Ernest Kinoy. *Photography:* Gerald Perry Finnerman. *Music* Quincy Jones. *Editor*: Edward A. Biery. *Art Direction*: Al Brenner. *Set Decoration*: Audrey Blasdel. *Assistant Director*: Tom Schmidt.

Cast: Sidney Poitier (John Kane), Will Geer (Doc Thomas), Bradford Dillman (Lloyd Thomas), Beverly Todd (Louisa MacGill), Ramon Bieri (Orly Bail), Warren J. Kemmerling (George), Lincoln Kilpatrick (Charles Gray), P. Jay Sidney (Reverend MacGill), Richard Ward (Frank), Paul Winfield (Henry Birkhardt), Zara Cutty (Miss Nettie).

BUCK AND THE PREACHER (Columbia Pictures, 1972). *Director*: Sidney Poitier. *Producer*: Joel Glickman. *Screenplay:* Ernest Kinoy, based on a story by Kinoy and Drake Walker. *Photography*: Alex Phillips, Jr. *Music*: Benny Carter, featuring Sonny Terry and Brownie McGhee. *Editor*: Pembroke J. Herring. *Production Disigner*: Sydney Z. Litwack. *Costume Designer*: Guy Verhille.

Cast: Sidney Poitier (Buck), Harry Belafonte (Preacher), Ruby Dee (Ruth), Cameron Mitchell (Deshay), Denny Miller (Floyd), Nita Talbot (Madame Esther), John Kelly (Sheriff), Tony Brubaker (Headman), James McEachin (Kingston), Clarence Muse (Cudjo), Lynn Hamilton (Sarah). Doug Johnson (Sam), Errol John (Joshua), Ken Menard (Little Henry), Pamela Jones (Delilah), Drake Walker (Elder), Dennis Hines (Little Toby). Fred Waugh (Mizoo), Bill Shannon (Tom), Phil Adams (Frank), Walter Scot (Earl), John Howard (George), Enrique Lucero (Indian Chief), Julie Robinson (Sinsie), Jose Carlo Ruiz (Brave), Jerry Gatlin (Deputy), Ivan Scott (Express Agent), John Kennedy (Bank Teller).

A WARM DECEMBER (National General Pictures, 1973). *Director*: Sidney Poitier. *Producer*: Melville Tucker. *Screenplay*: Lawrence Roman. *Photography*: Paul Beeson.

Music: Coleridge-Taylor Perkinson. *Editor*: Pembroke J. Herring, Peter Pitt. *Art Direction*: Elliot Scott. *Assistant Director*: David Tomblin.

Cast: Sidney Poitier (Matt Younger), Esther Anderson (Catherine), Yvette Curtis (Stefanie), George Baker (Henry Barlow, Johnny Sekka (Myomo), Earl Cameron (George Oswandu), Hilary Crane (Marsha Barlow), John Beardmore ("Burberry"), Milos Kirek (General Kuznouski), Ann Smith (Carol Barlow), Stephanie Smith (Janie Barlow), Letta Mbula (Singer).

UPTOWN SATURDAY NIGHT (Warner Brothers, 1974). *Director*: Sidney Poitier. *Producer*: Melville Tucker. *Screenplay*: Richard Wesley. *Photography*: Fred J. Koenekamp. *Music*: Tom Scott. *Editor*: Pembroke J. Herring. *Production Design*: Alfred Sweeney.

Cast: Sidney Poitier (Steve Jackson), Bill Cosby (Wardell Franklin), Flip Wilson (The Reverend), Richard Pryor (Sharp Eye Washington), Rosalind Cash (Sarah Jackson), Roscoe Lee Browne (Congressman Lincoln), Paula Kelly (Leggy Peggy), Lee Chamberlin (Madame Zenobia), Johnny Sekka (Geechie's Henchman), Lincoln Kilpatrick (Slim's Henchman), Harold Nicholas (Little Seymour), Calvin Lockhart (Silky Slim), Ketty Lester (Irma Franklin), Harry Belafonte (Geechie Dan Beauford).

THE WILBY CONSPIRACY (United Artists, 1975). *Director*: Ralph Nelson. *Producer*: Martin Baum. *Screenplay*: Rod Amateau and Harold Nebenzal, based on a novel by Peter Driscoll. *Photography*: John Coquillon. *Music*: Stanley Myers. *Editor*: Ernest Walter.

Cast: Sidney Poitier (Shack Twala), Michael Caine (Jim Keogh), Nicol Williamson (Major Horn), Prunella Gee (Rina), Persis Khambatta (Persis Ray), Saeed Jaffrey (Mukerjee), Ryk de Gooyer (Van Heerden), Rutger Hauer (Baline Nierkirk), Joseph De Graf (Wilby), Brian Empson (Judge), Abdullah Sunado (Headman), Archie Duncan (Gordon), Helmut Dantine (Counsel).

LET'S DO IT AGAIN (Warner Brothers, 1975). *Director*: Sidney Poitier. *Producer*: Melville Tucker. *Screenplay*: Richard Wesley. *Photography*: Donald M. Morgan. *Music*: Curtis Mayfield. *Editor*: Pembroke J. Herring. *Production Design*: Alfred Sweeney.

Cast: Sidney Poitier (Clyde Williams), Bill Cosby (Billy Foster), Jimmie Walker (Bootney Farnsworth), Calvin Lockhart (Biggie Smalls), John Amos (Kansas City Mack), Denise Nicholas (Beth Foster), Lee Chamberlin (Dee Dee Williams), Mel Stewart (Ellison), Ossie Davis (Elder Johnson), Billy Eckstine (Zack), Julius Harris (Bubbletop Woodson), Paul E. Harris (Jody Tipps), Val Avery (Lt. Bottonley).

A PIECE OF THE ACTION (Warner Brothers, 1977). *Director*: Sidney Poitier. *Producer*: Melville Tucker. *Screenplay*: Charles Blackwell. *Photography*: Donald M. Morgan. *Music*: Curtis Mayfield. *Editor*: Pembroke J. Herring. *Production Design*: Alfred Sweeney.

Cast: Sidney Poitier (Manny Durrell), Bill Cosby (Dave Anderson), James Earl Jones (Joshua Burke), Denise Nicholas (Lila French), Hope Clarke (Sarah Thomas), Tracy Reed (Nikki McLean), Frances Foster (Bea Quitman), Titos Vandis (Bruno), Janet Dubois (Nellie Bond), Marc Lawrence (Lovie), Cyril Poitier (Mr. Theodore), Sherri Poitier (Cookie), Edward Love (Willie Maunger), Sheryl Lee Ralph (Barbara Hanley).

SELECTED BIBLIOGRAPHY

Baldwin, James. *The Devil Finds Work*. New York: Dial Press, 1976.

———. "Sidney Poitier." *Look*, 23 July 1968, pp.50-58.

Barthel, Joan. "He Doesn't Want to be Sexless Sidney." *New York Times*, 6 August 1967, sec. D, p. 9.

Bogle, Donald. *Toms, Coons, Mulattoes, Mammies, and Bucks*. New York: Bantam books, 1974.

Cripps, Thomas. *Slow Fade to Black: The Negro in American Film, 1900-1942*. New York: Oxford University Press, 1977.

Dudar, Helen et al. "The Sidney Poitier Story." *New York Post*, 30 March 1959-3 April 1959.

Ellison, Ralph. *Shadow and Act*. New York: Vintage Books, 1972.

Ewers, Carolyn. *Sidney Poitier: the Long Journey*. New York: Signet Books, 1969.

Feinstein, Herbert. "Three in Search of Cinema." *Columbia University Forum*, Summer 1965, p. 23.

Flatley, Guy. "Sidney Poitier as Black Militant." *New York Times*, 10 November 1968, sec. D, p. 15.

Hall, Dennis John. "Pride Without Prejudice: Sidney Poitier's Career." *Films and Filming* 20, no. 3 (December 1971): 40-44; and 20, no. 4 (January 1972): 41-44.

Hift, Fred. "Negro Actor's Impressions of South Africa." *New York Times*, 22 April 1951, sec. 2, p. 5, col. 5.

Hitchens, Gordon. "The Defiance in *The Defiant Ones*." *Film Culture*, no. 50-51 (Fall and Winter 1970), pp. 63-65.

Hoffman, William. *Sidney*. New York: Lyle Stuart, 1970.

Leab, Daniel J. *From Sambo to Superspade: The Black Experience in Motion Pictures*. Boston: Houghton Mifflin, 1978.

Leites, Nathan and Martha Wolfenstein. "Two Social Scientists View *No Way Out*." *Commentary* 10 (1950): 338-91.

Mapp, Edward. *Blacks in American Films: Today and Yesterday*. Metuchen, N. J.: The Scarecrow Press, 1972.

Marill, Alvin H. *The Films of Sidney Poitier*. Secaucus, N.J.: The Citadel Press, 1978.

Mason, Clifford. "Why Does White America Love Sidney Poitier So?" *New York Times*, 10 September 1967, sec. D, pp. 1, 21.

Morton, Frederic. "The Audacity of Sidney Poitier." *Holiday Magazine*, June 1962, pp. 64-78.

Murray, James P. *To Find an Image*. New York: Bobbs Merrill, 1973.

Newquist, Roy. *A Special Kind of Magic*. New York: Rand McNally, 1967.

Null, Gary. *Black Hollywood: The Negro in Motion Pictures*. Secaucus, N.J.: Citadel Press, 1977.

Patterson, Lindsay, ed. *Black Films and Filmmakers*. New York: Dodd, Mead, 1975.

Poirier, Normand. "Sidney Poitier's Long Journey." *Saturday Evening Post*, 24 June 1964, pp. 29-31.

Poitier, Sidney, "Dialogue on Film." *American Film*, September 1976, pp. 33-48.

———. "Entertainment, Politics, and the Movie Business." *Cineaste* 8, no. 3 (Winter 1977-78): 16-23.

———. "Thinking of Corruption." *Films and Filming* 7, no. 11 (August 1961): 7.

Wood, Michael. *America in the Movies*. New York: Delta Books, 1975.

INDEX